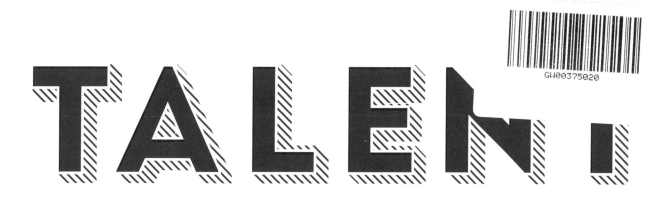

TALENT

1

WORKBOOK
WITH ONLINE PRACTICE

Weronika Salandyk

CAMBRIDGE
UNIVERSITY PRESS

CONTENTS

Graded practice

The Grammar and Vocabulary practice in the *Talent* Workbook has been graded according to difficulty.

This is indicated where you see the following icon:

VOCABULARY: Nationalities

1   Complete the sentences with the missing words.

    0   Adem is from Turkey. He's ....Turkish...... .

    1   They are from China. They're ....

    2   My teacher is .... She's from Germany.

    3   He is from Chile. He's ....

    4   Maria is from Spain. She's ....

The level of difficulty is shown by the number of bands that are shaded (from 1–4).

For example, an activity with this icon is more challenging than one with this icon .

A Origins

VOCABULARY: Nationalities

1 🔊 **Complete the sentences with the missing words.**

0 Adem is from Turkey. He's ....**Turkish**.......... .

1 They are from China. They're ....

2 My teacher is .... She's from Germany.

3 He is from Chile. He's ....

4 Maria is from Spain. She's ....

5 My friends are from Mexico. They're ....

6 Naomichi is .... He's from Japan.

7 Camille is .... She's from France.

8 Emma is from the UK. She's ....

GRAMMAR: *be* (all forms)

2 🔊 **Complete the sentences with the missing words.**

> 'm ▪ 're ▪ 're ▪ are ▪ 's ▪ 's ▪ 's

0 He ..'s........ German.

1 We .... at home.

2 It .... easy.

3 I .... from Morocco.

4 Amy and Tom .... happy.

5 You .... great!

6 Tracy .... from London.

3 🔊 **Correct the mistakes in these sentences.**

0 They is from the USA.
.........**They are from the USA.**.........

1 The bag are new.
....

2 The boys is at school.
....

3 We be late.
....

4 You is Spanish.
....

5 Our teacher am nice.
....

6 I are Italian.
....

4 🔊 **Complete the sentences with the negative form of *be*.**

0 This book ....**isn't**......... new.

1 They .... in Paris today.

2 It .... difficult.

3 We .... hungry.

4 Ellie .... from France.

5 I .... a teacher.

6 My friends .... at school.

7 You .... late.

8 My name .... Jake.

5 🔊 **Write questions using the verb *be*.**

0 your / name / Pedro?
.........**Is your name Pedro?**.........

1 you / British?
....

2 Noah / in / your / class?
....

3 we / ready?
....

4 it / cold / today?
....

5 your sisters / tall?
....

6 this film / interesting?
....

7 they / your / cousins?
....

8 I / a / good / friend?
....

6 🔊 **Complete the message with the correct form of the verb *be*.**

Hi Paul! 0 ....**Are**......... you at school now?
1 .... Mrs Green in the class?
It 2 .... 8 o'clock and I 3 ....
(*not*) at school. I 4 .... at home. My sister
5 .... at home too. We 6 ....
ill! Please, tell Mrs Green.

GRAMMAR: Subject pronouns and possessive adjectives

7 📶 Choose the correct option.

0 My brother is in the park. (He) / It isn't at home.
1 Max and I are in the same class.
   They / We are best friends.
2 James is my brother. She / He is 15.
3 This is my house. He / It is big.
4 Anna and Olga are from Poland.
   They / You are Polish.
5 My name's Katie. She / I am British.
6 Are you / he hungry, Jake?
7 This is our English teacher, Mrs Anders.
   She / We is very nice.
8 My mum and dad are at work. They / We are doctors.

8 📶 Write the possessive adjectives.

0 I   ....my........
1 you   ....
2 he   ....
3 she   ....
4 it   ....
5 we   ....
6 you   ....
7 they   ....

9 📶 Choose the correct option.

0 Tom is 16. .... brother is 14.
   A Her   (**B**) His   **C** Your
1 I'm Alice and this is .... friend Mike.
   A his   **B** her   **C** my
2 Lola and Mia are sisters. This is .... brother Alex.
   A her   **B** his   **C** their
3 Mr Parker is at home. .... car is here.
   A My   **B** His   **C** Its
4 Dylan, is this .... pencil?
   A his   **B** your   **C** her
5 Look at this house. .... door is pink.
   A Its   **B** Their   **C** His
6 We are in the park with .... dogs.
   A their   **B** your   **C** our
7 This is my best friend. .... name is Amelia.
   A Her   **B** My   **C** Your
8 Hey boys, are .... parents at home?
   A his   **B** their   **C** your

GRAMMAR: Possessive 's

10 📶 Complete the phrases with ' or 's.

0 Alice .'s... cat is called Sushi.
1 my brother .... phone
2 Emily .... bag
3 the children .... ball
4 the boys .... bikes
5 Liam .... sister
6 my friends .... books
7 my mum .... tablet
8 the students .... tests

GRAMMAR: Possessive pronouns

11 📶 Complete the sentences with the correct possessive pronouns.

0 This is Meg's book. It's ....hers........ .
1 This is my house. It's ....
2 This is Jack's desk. It's ....
3 This is my parents' car. It's ....
4 This is your pizza. It's ....
5 This is our school. It's ....
6 This is my sister's pen. It's ....

12 📶 Choose the correct option.

0 Sarah is in (her) / hers / she room.
1 Holly and Ben are from the USA.
   This is theirs / they / their address.
2 Chloe and I are friends. We / Ours / Our are 17.
3 This is my dad's / dads' / dad' watch.
4 This is Cathy's phone. The book
   is her / hers / she's too.
5 Are these sandwiches you / your / yours?
6 Ben is my / mine / Bens' brother.
7 Are these Nick's / Nicks' / Nick' parents?
8 My uncle is very rich. He / She / We has got
   a big house.

B We are family

VOCABULARY: Family

13 🔊 **Match the sentence halves.**

0 [e] My father's son is my
1 [ ] My aunt and uncle's son is my
2 [ ] My aunt's daughter is my dad's
3 [ ] My mum's dad is my
4 [ ] My aunt's son is my parents'
5 [ ] Sophie is her mum's
6 [ ] My father's sister is my

a niece.
b daughter.
c aunt.
d nephew.
e brother.
f cousin.
g grandfather.

14 🔊 **Write the missing words.**

	Male	Female
0	brother	sister
1	uncle	....
2	....	daughter
3	....	niece
4	husband	....
5	....	granddaughter
6	grandfather	....
7	....	cousin

GRAMMAR: have got (all forms)

15 🔊 **Write sentences with have got or has got.**

0   I / a new tablet
    I have got a new tablet.
1   My aunt and uncle / a dog
2   Matilda / two brothers
3   You / a blue pencil case
4   We / a big flat
5   Luke / a camera
6   My cousins / a garden
7   I / two cats
8   My dog / a lot of food

16 🔊 **Choose the correct option.**

0   I (haven't) / hasn't got a sister.
1   Mr and Mrs Parker haven't / hasn't got a cat.
2   Our teacher haven't / hasn't got a big family.
3   Jamie haven't / hasn't got a brother.
4   We haven't / hasn't got our books.
5   My book haven't / hasn't got lots of pictures.
6   Our mum haven't / hasn't got a cousin.
7   I haven't / hasn't got a new phone.
8   You haven't / hasn't got your school bag!

17 🔊 **Write the questions for these answers.**

0   ...... **Has your grandmother got a garden?** ......
    Yes, she has. My grandmother's garden is big.
1   ....
    Yes, we have. Our dog's name is Spiky.
2   ....
    No, I haven't. This is my old phone.
3   ....
    Yes, he has. Archie's brother is ten.
4   ....
    Yes, they have. Daniel and Ellie have got new bags.
5   ....
    Yes, she has. My aunt's bike is red.
6   ....
    Yes, we have. Mrs Williams is our new English teacher.

18 🔊 **Complete the telephone conversation between Sam and his mother with the correct form of have got.**

Mum   Hi Sam! I'm at work but it's time for school!
          0 **Have you got** (you) all your books?
Sam   Yes, I ¹.......................... .
Mum   ².......................... (your brother) his lunchbox?
Sam   Yes, he ³.......................... . Don't worry, Mum!
Mum   ⁴.......................... (you and your brother)
          sweaters? It's cold today.
Sam   No, we ⁵.......................... but I ⁶..........................
          a jacket and Harry ⁷.......................... a shirt.
          We are fine!
Mum   Great!
Sam   Mum, where is the money for the bus?
Mum   Oh, no! I ⁸.......................... it here! Sorry …

GRAMMAR: Indefinite article: *a / an*

19 Write *a* or *an*.

0 .....*a*...... blue car
1 .... English book
2 .... phone number
3 .... yellow bike
4 .... umbrella
5 .... American restaurant
6 .... sandwich
7 .... email address
8 .... orange flower
9 .... European language
10 .... happy dog

GRAMMAR: Plural nouns

20 Write the plurals in the correct column.

baby ▪ bench ▪ box ▪ bus ▪ child ▪
city ▪ country ▪ day ▪ family ▪ friend ▪
man ▪ match ▪ party ▪ person ▪ table ▪
tomato ▪ toy ▪ uncle ▪ woman

-s	-es	-ies	irregular
uncles			

GRAMMAR: *this / that / these / those*

21 Choose the correct option.

0 (*This is*) / *These are* my book.
1 *This is* / *These are* Tom's new shoes.
2 *This is* / *That is* Ethan's brother over there.
3 *These are* / *Those are* my friends here.
4 *That is* / *Those are* my keys.
5 *This is* / *These are* my room.
6 *These are* / *Those are* your parents over there.
7 *This is* / *That is* our teacher here.
8 *That is* / *These are* your bag.
9 *Is this* / *Are these* your children?
10 *Is this* / *Is that* Kate's bike over there?

22 Tick (✓) the correct sentences. Correct the mistakes.

0 ~~That~~ is my T-shirt here. **This**
These are my friends. ✓
1 These is my family.
2 Those are my aunt's children over there.
3 Come here and watch that video!
4 This is my brother over there.
5 Look! Are these your shoes?
6 This is the best cake.
7 These ball is mine.
8 That sandwiches over there are very good.

GRAMMAR: Question words

23 Choose the correct option.

0 '............. is your best friend?' 'Tanya.'
  (A) Who   B What   C Whose
1 '............. is your brother?' 'At school.'
  A Where   B Whose   C Who
2 '............. jacket is this?' 'Not mine.'
  A Who   B Which   C Whose
3 .... bread have you got? Brown or white?
  A Which   B Whose   C Where
4 '............. is that?' 'It's a rubber.'
  A When   B What   C Which
5 '............. is Luke's party?' 'On Sunday.'
  A Where   B When   C Whose
6 '............. are my shoes?' 'Under the table.'
  A Where   B Who   C Which

24 Complete the questions with *wh* words. Then match them to the answers.

0 [d] ....What....... is your favourite colour?
1 [ ] .... is your address?
2 [ ] .... are you now?
3 [ ] .... is your English teacher?
4 [ ] .... is your birthday?
5 [ ] .... pencil is this?
6 [ ] .... is your bike?

a On 12th May.
b At home.
c It's 64 Park Road, Brighton.
d Blue.
e Jessica's.
f Mr Stoller.
g The black one over there.

STARTER C High school

VOCABULARY: School subjects

25 🔊 Decide if the sentences are true (T) or false (F). Correct the false ones.

0 In English we learn about English grammar. ✓ ☐F
1 In geography we learn about computers. ☐T ☐F
2 In Spanish we learn to speak Spanish. ☐T ☐F
3 In history we learn about the past. ☐T ☐F
4 In ICT we play sports. ☐T ☐F
5 In science we learn about famous people. ☐T ☐F
6 In maths we learn about numbers. ☐T ☐F
7 In PE we play music. ☐T ☐F
8 In physics we learn about energy and force. ☐T ☐F

GRAMMAR: *there is / there are*

26 🔊 Tick (✓) the correct sentences.

0 ✓ There is a cafeteria.
  ☐ There are a cafeteria.
1 ☐ There is five boys.
  ☐ There are five boys.
2 ☐ There is a desk.
  ☐ There are a desk.
3 ☐ There is children.
  ☐ There are children.
4 ☐ There is two women.
  ☐ There are two women.
5 ☐ There is a bag.
  ☐ There are a bag.
6 ☐ There is families.
  ☐ There are families.

27 🔊 Write sentences with *there is* and *there are*.

0 three books
  There are three books.
1 two brothers
2 a box
3 a yellow bike
4 phones
5 cats and dogs
6 a camera
7 a library
8 museums

28 🔊 Choose the correct option.

0 There *isn't* / (*aren't*) five tablets.
1 There *isn't* / *aren't* a car.
2 There *isn't* / *aren't* a supermarket.
3 There *isn't* / *aren't* three pens.
4 There *isn't* / *aren't* ten bananas.
5 There *isn't* / *aren't* two students.
6 There *isn't* / *aren't* a map.
7 There *isn't* / *aren't* a teacher.
8 There *isn't* / *aren't* a school here.

29 🔊 Complete the questions with *Is there* or *Are there*.

0 ....**Is there**.... my key in the bag?
1 .... two windows in the living room?
2 .... a photo on the table?
3 .... three gyms at your school?
4 .... an English dictionary in your bag?
5 .... a cinema in your town?
6 .... a lot of pictures on the walls?
7 .... a cheese sandwich in the fridge?
8 .... ten boys in your class?

30 🔊 Use the following words to write five true sentences about your school.

- art room **There isn't an art room.**
- cafeteria
- classroom
- gym
- language lab
- library
- music studio
- science lab
- study room

GRAMMAR: *a / some / any*

31 🔊 Match the sentence halves.

0 ☐a There is   a a table.
1 ☐ There isn't   b any shoes.
2 ☐ There is a   c newspaper.
3 ☐ Is there   d an elephant.
4 ☐ Are there   e a park?
5 ☐ There aren't   f some books.
6 ☐ There are   g any trees?

32 Write one word in each gap.

Mum 0 ....Is.......... there a new language lab in your school?

Freya Yes, 1 .... is. It's great! There 2 .... twenty-five computers but there 3 .... twenty-five microphones. Two microphones aren't working so 4 .... are only twenty-three microphones now.

Mum A great language lab! Do you like it?

Freya Yes, I do but the room is dark. There aren't 5 .... windows but there are 6 .... lamps. I like classrooms with windows more.

Mum Is it loud in there?

Freya Not really. There are 7 .... walls between students. I can't hear my friends. There is also 8 .... special computer on our teacher's desk. She can listen to all of us.

VOCABULARY: Days, months, the time

33 Complete the crossword with the days of the week.

Across

0 Day 4 of the week
3 Day 6 of the week
4 Day 1 of the week
5 Day 5 of the week

Down

0 Day 2 of the week
1 Day 3 of the week
2 Day 7 of the week

34 Write the missing letters. Then put the months in the correct order.

11 N **OVE** MB **E** R	☐ FE _ _ _ _ RY
☐ J _ N _ _ R _	☐ M _ _
☐ A _ G _ ST	☐ J _ L _
☐ J _ N _	☐ _ _ RIL
☐ O _ _ _ BER	☐ DE _ _ _ BE _
☐ M _ RC _	☐ SE _ _ _ MB _ _

35 Look at the clocks and write the times.

0 ....ten....... ....past....... three

1 .... five

2 seven ....

3 sixteen 16:12

4 .... to ....

5 .... thirty 22:30

VOCABULARY: Prepositions of time

36 Write *at*, *in* or *on*.

0 ....on.......... Tuesday
1 .... 4 o'clock
2 2017
3 .... the weekend
4 .... the afternoon
5 .... May
6 .... Sunday
7 .... December
8 .... night
9 .... 9 am
10 .... Friday mornings

D Food

VOCABULARY: Food and drink

37 🔊 Circle the odd word out in each group.

0	pears	(rice)	grapes	peaches
1	spinach	peas	eggs	tomatoes
2	milk	olives	butter	cheese
3	potatoes	fish	beef	chicken
4	bread	yoghurt	muffins	biscuits
5	fruit juice	milk	tea	grapes
6	onion	strawberries	nectarines	pears

GRAMMAR: Countable and uncountable nouns

38 🔊 Write the nouns in the correct column.

bread · cheese · child · city · desk · family · beef · house · milk · money · potato · rice · tea · window

countable nouns	uncountable nouns
child,	bread,

39 🔊 Choose the correct option.

0 I've got two *cat* / (*cats*).
1 Do you like *banana* / *bananas*?
2 There is *butter* / *butters* on your list.
3 I've got three *friend* / *friends*.
4 I like *coffee* / *coffees*.
5 There are *tomato* / *tomatoes* in this salad.
6 I've got *pasta* / *pastas* for lunch.
7 We've got *water* / *waters* in the fridge.
8 These are my parents' *pen* / *pens*.
9 Does he like *fish* / *fishes*?
10 There are *olive* / *olives* in the bread.

GRAMMAR: *a / some / any* with countable and uncountable nouns

40 🔊 Choose the correct option.

0 There are .... apples.
   A an   (**B**) some   **C** any
1 Are there .... eggs?
   A an   **B** some   **C** any
2 There isn't .... water.
   A a   **B** some   **C** any
3 Is there .... tomato?
   A a   **B** some   **C** any
4 There is .... peach.
   A a   **B** some   **C** any
5 There is .... money.
   A a   **B** some   **C** any
6 There aren't .... people.
   A a   **B** some   **C** any
7 Is there .... yogurt?
   A a   **B** some   **C** any
8 There are .... strawberries.
   A a   **B** some   **C** any

41 🔊 Write sentences with *a*, *some* or *any* and *there is* or *there are*.

0 (+) banana   *There is a banana.*
   (?) rice   *Is there any rice?*
   (–) nectarines   *There aren't any nectarines.*
1 (?) tea
....
2 (–) muffin
....
3 (?) pears
....
4 (+) juice
....
5 (–) spinach
....
6 (?) peach
....
7 (+) beef
....
8 (–) olives
....

GRAMMAR: *much / many / lots of / a lot of*

42 Complete the questions with *much* or *many*.

0 How ......**many**........ biscuits are there?
1 How .... milk have you got?
2 How .... salt is there?
3 How .... bikes have you got?
4 How .... eggs are there?
5 How .... juice have you got?
6 How .... students are there?
7 How .... onions are there?
8 How .... money have you got?

43 Make sentences with *there is* or *there are* and *not much* or *not many*.

0 children   *There aren't many children.*
1 fruit juice
2 sugar
3 lessons
4 boxes
5 chicken
6 bread
7 grapes
8 homework

44 Tick (✓) the correct sentences. Correct the mistakes.

0 There's lots of cheese. ✓
  There aren't ~~much~~ pears. **many**
1 There's a lots of time.
2 How much friends have you got?
3 There are a lot of books.
4 There isn't many coffee.
5 How many rice have you got?
6 There are a lot of biscuits.
7 There aren't many people.
8 There's lots butter.

45 What food do you have at home? Write sentences using *not much*, *not many* and *lots of* or *a lot of*. Use the following words and your imagination.

- apples
- bananas
- biscuits
- bread
- cheese
- beef
- milk
- muffins
- pasta
- potatoes
- water
- yogurt

There isn't much cheese.

VOCABULARY: Numbers and dates

46 Write the cardinal numbers.

0 25   *twenty-five*
1 45   ....
2 72   ....
3 13   ....
4 100   ....
5 8   ....
6 99   ....
7 53   ....
8 15   ....

47 Complete the ordinal numbers.

0 10   TE <u>NTH</u>
1 1st   FI _ _ _
2 3rd   T _ _ RD
3 9th   NIN_ _
4 11th EL _ _ _ N _ _
5 12th TWE _ _ TH
6 13th TH _ _ TEEN _ _
7 30th TH _ _ T _ _ TH
8 52nd F_ _TY-S_ _ _ _ _
9 64th S _ _ TY - FO _ R _ _
10 85th E _ _ _TY-FI_ _ _

48 Correct the mistakes in the dates.

0 5st November   *5th November*
1 12nd February   ....
2 1th June   ....
3 23th April   ....
4 10rd October   ....
5 22th March   ....
6 11nd December   ....
7 15rd May   ....
8 31th January   ....

E Free time

VOCABULARY: Free-time activities

49 🔊 Match the words to make expressions.

0	b	watch	a	a book
1	☐	go	b	television
2	☐	read	c	the gym
3	☐	play	d	volleyball
4	☐	watch a	e	shopping
5	☐	meet	f	a bike ride
6	☐	go to	g	film
7	☐	play the	h	your friends
8	☐	go for	i	guitar

50 🔊 Write the missing word in each gap.

0 Ellie can't play ....the.......... piano.

1 I .... dance lessons on Mondays.

2 Can you go for a .... now?

3 Can you .... to your friend's house today?

4 We can't play video .... all day.

5 Can you go on .... media at school?

6 I .... magazines on Saturdays and Sundays.

7 I can't .... to the swimming pool today.

8 Josh has music .... on Friday evenings.

GRAMMAR: can for ability

51 🔊 Put the words in the correct order.

0 piano / I / the / play / can

    I can play the piano.

1 you / volleyball / can / play / ?

2 French / sister / my / speak / can't

3 teacher / our / make / can / pizza

4 songs / sing / we / any / can't / English

5 Ethan / drive / car / a / can / ?

6 swim / I / in / can't / water / cold

7 speak / you / three / can / languages / ?

8 jump / Bayram / high / can't / very

52 🔊 Cross out the extra word in each sentence.

0 Can he to play football?

1 Megan can't skiing ski.

2 We aren't can't speak Spanish.

3 The boys can swim swimming.

4 'Can Tom cook?' 'Yes, Tom he can.'

5 I can't not play tennis.

6 Do can they dance?

7 'Can you sing?' 'Yes, I can can't.'

8 My sister can rollerskate rollerskates.

53 🔊 Write a short answer to each question.

0 'Can Jennie swim?' 'Yes, ...she can.... '

1 'Can your friends speak French?' 'No, ... '

2 'Can Mike play basketball?' 'Yes, ... '

3 'Can a fish fly?' 'No, ... '

4 'Can you and your brother drive a motorcycle?' 'No, ... '

5 'Can you sing?' 'Yes, ... '

6 'Can your mum play the piano?' 'Yes, ... '

54 🔊 Complete the sentences and questions using can and the words in brackets.

0 ....Can you.......... (you / make) a sandwich?

1 (we / read) .... books in German.

2 'Can you make a cake?' 'No, (I) .... '

3 My little sister (not ride / a bicycle) ....

4 .... (He / count) to 10 in Chinese.

5 (they / run) .... 10 km?

6 This bird (this bird / not fly) ....

7 (Sarah / not play) .... chess.

8 (you / draw) .... an elephant?

GRAMMAR: *can* for requests, permission and possibility

55 🔊 **Choose the correct option.**

0 'Can [I] / *you* use your phone?' 'Yes, of course.'

1 'Can *I* / *you* give me some money?' 'No, I can't.'

2 'Can we go now?' 'Yes, we *can* / *can't*.'

3 We can *bring* / *brings* dictionaries to the class.

4 '*Have* / *Can* we drink some milk?' 'Yes, sure.'

5 'Can we *going* / *go* to the park?' 'Yes, you can.'

6 I can *used* / *use* my parents' tablet.

7 '*Do* / *Can* you buy me new shoes, please?'
'Sorry, I can't.'

8 Jacob can *meet* / *meets* us in the park at 5 o'clock.

56 🔊 **Write questions with *can*.**

0 You want to go shopping with your friends.
   Can I go shopping with my friends?

1 You want to eat a sandwich.
   ....

2 You and your brother want to watch a film.
   ....

3 You want to listen to music.
   ....

4 You want to go to your friend's house.
   ....

5 You and Abigail want to play the guitar.
   ....

6 You and your friends want to have a party.
   ....

GRAMMAR: The imperative

57 🔊 **What did they say? Rewrite the sentences using an imperative.**

0 You don't listen to me.
   Listen to me!
   You watch TV all the time.
   Don't watch TV all the time!

1 You don't do your homework.

2 You play football in your room.

3 You are late for school.

4 You don't make your bed.

5 You draw on the desk.

6 You read in class.

7 You eat too many biscuits.

8 You don't give me back my money.

58 🔊 **Complete the sentences with these verbs. If necessary, use *don't*.**

come ▪ drink ▪ eat ▪ have ▪ jump ▪
put ▪ sit ▪ talk ▪ use

0 ..*Don't jump*.. on the bed. It can break.

1 Be quiet! .... to your friends.

2 .... with your hands! Use a spoon.

3 .... fun at school!

4 .... down! You can't walk now.

5 .... your phone on the bus! People don't want to listen to you.

6 .... your jacket in the wardrobe. It can't lie on the chair.

7 .... here quickly! I want to show you something.

8 .... coffee in the classroom! Only water is OK.

GRAMMAR: Object pronouns

59 🔊 **Choose the correct option**

0 Help .... I can't do it.
   (A) me   **B** you   **C** my

1 Where is my pen? I can't see ....
   A its   **B** it   **C** them

2 Can you help .... ? We've got a problem.
   A us   **B** our   **C** you

3 Girls, can Oscar play video games with .... ?
   A him   **B** you   **C** me

4 This is Charlie. Sit with .... , please.
   A him   **B** his   **C** them

5 I know Mrs Shaw. I have dance lessons with .... on Mondays.
   A him   **B** them   **C** her

60 🔊 **Rewrite the sentences. Replace the underlined words with the correct pronoun.**

0 Can you see Amy? I want to talk to Amy. **her**

1 Are the boys in the park? Is Dad with the boys?

2 Where's my book? I want to read my book.

3 Oliver is a fantastic swimmer. Look at Oliver!

4 Jenny and I want to go shopping. Do you want to go with Jenny and me?

5 Mrs Wilson is at home. You can visit Mrs Wilson.

6 Don't help me with my homework. I can do my homework.

1 Behaviour

GRAMMAR PRACTICE

Present simple

Complete the rules.

In the present simple we add .... to the infinitive for *he*, *she* and *it*.

To make negatives we use .... and the infinitive without *to* for *I*, *you*, *we* and *they*.

We use .... and the infinitive without *to* for *he*, *she* and *it*.

To make questions we use .... and .... and the infinitive without *to*.

➡ See **GRAMMAR REFERENCE** page 117

1 🔊 **Choose the correct option.**

0 They (*have*) / *has* breakfast at 8 o'clock.

1 Your friends *play / plays* video games.

2 Amy *do / does* her homework in the morning.

3 I *read / reads* books in the evenings.

4 We *listen / listens* to music after school.

5 My sister *go / goes* to school.

6 Tim and Mia *text / texts* their friends every day.

7 You *wake / wakes* up early.

8 My parents *go / goes* shopping on Saturdays.

2 🔊 **Complete the sentences with the correct form of the words in the box.**

check ▪ get ▪ go ▪ meet ▪ play ▪ read ▪ watch

0 I ......**meet**........ my friends at school.

1 My cousins .... TV a lot.

2 You .... the piano a lot.

3 I .... dressed before breakfast.

4 My brother .... his phone all the time.

5 We .... for a bike ride on Fridays.

6 Jake .... a newspaper every morning.

3 🔊 **Circle the correct spelling of the third person singular verbs.**

0 (lives) / livs

1 mixs / mixes

2 tries / trys

3 worrys / worries

4 dances / dancies

5 misses / miss

6 washies / washes

7 dos / does

8 says / sayies

4 🔊 **Complete the table with the third person singular form of these verbs.**

bake ▪ buy ▪ brush ▪ carry ▪ cook ▪ copy ▪ enjoy ▪ fly ▪ go ▪ kiss ▪ marry ▪ play ▪ push ▪ study ▪ teach ▪ wake ▪ pass ▪ reply

-s	-es	-ies
bakes		

5 🔊 **Tick (✓) the correct sentences.**

0 I don't like spinach. ✓
   I doesn't like spinach.

1 Nathan doesn't go to school.
   Nathan don't goes to school.

2 My friends doesn't eat fish.
   My friends don't eat fish.

3 You doesn't read a lot.
   You don't read a lot.

4 We don't speaks Spanish.
   We don't speak Spanish.

5 My brother and I don't play tennis.
   My brother and I doesn't play tennis.

6 Our teacher doesn't talk a lot.
   Our teacher doesn't talks a lot.

6 🔊 **Rewrite the sentences in the negative form.**

0 I go for a bike ride at weekends.
   I don't go for a bike ride at weekends.

1 We finish school at 3 o'clock.

2 Mr Brown uses his computer.

3 Ellie asks a lot of questions.

4 We do homework on Sundays.

5 Cathy and Tom go to the gym every day.

6 Children play in the garden in the afternoons.

7 Mike runs fast.

8 My grandma lives in Bristol.

7 🔊 **Write questions using the prompts.**

0 you / go shopping / on Sunday mornings?
Do you go shopping on Sunday mornings?

1 your cat / drink / milk?

2 your dad / work / in a bank?

3 you / go on social media / a lot?

4 Amanda / meet her friends / at weekends?

5 your parents / clean your room?

6 your teachers / give you a lot of homework?

8 🔊 **Complete the questions with *do* or *does*. Then write short answers.**

0 '......*Do*...... they speak French?'
'Yes, ...*they do*...... .'

1 '........................ you read magazines?'
'No, ...'

2 '........................ your cousins like swimming?'
'Yes, ...'

3 '........................ they have dance lessons?'
'Yes, ...'

4 '........................ Emily live with her friends?'
'No, ...'

5 '........................ Anna's brother study history?'
'Yes, ...'

6 '........................ Jack and Pete play video games?'
'No, ...'

9 🔊 **Look at the family's diary and complete the sentences.**

	LUCY	CHLOE	JACK
Mon	5 pm swimming	5 pm swimming	
Tues		4 pm tennis	6:30 piano
Wed	4:30 Spanish		5:30 Spanish
Thur	7 pm dancing	7 pm dancing	
Frid	3:30 friends	4:00 library	5 pm football

0 Lucy and Chloe ......*go swimming*...... on Mondays.
Jack ......*doesn't go swimming*...... on Mondays.

1 Chloe .... on Tuesdays.

2 Lucy .... tennis on Tuesdays.

3 Lucy and Jack .... on Wednesdays.

4 Jack .... on Thursdays.

5 Chloe and Lucy .... on Thursdays.

6 Jack .... on Fridays.

7 Chloe .... on Fridays.

8 Lucy .... on Fridays.

10 🔊 **Correct the mistakes.**

0 We ~~doesn't~~ wear jeans to school. **don't**

1 Do your friend study Spanish?

2 Harry and Tim watches TV a lot.

3 Mum replys to her emails every day.

4 I don't lives in Cambridge.

5 You don't your homework.

6 Lily listen to music on her way to school.

7 You do help your sister?

8 Mark don't rides a bike.

11 🔊 **Complete the text about Hannah.**

This is Hannah Taylor. She ⁰......*goes*...... (*go*)
to Parkwood Secondary School. Hannah
¹........................ (*love*) dancing. Her dad is British but
her mum ²........................ (*not / come*) from the UK.
She's French, so at home they ³........................
(*speak*) English and French. Hannah also
⁴........................ (*study*) Italian. Every Tuesday and
Friday Hannah and her friends ⁵........................ (*have*)
dance classes. They ⁶........................ (*practise*)
different dance styles. Hannah ⁷........................
(*not / like*) folk dancing. What style ⁸........................
she .... (*like*) the most? Ballet.
At weekends Hannah and her family ⁹........................
(*go*) on trips so she ¹⁰........................ (*not / spend*)
a lot of time with her friends. Her best friend
sometimes ¹¹........................ (*visit*) her and they
¹²........................ (*play*) video games together.

READING SKILLS

12 [1.01] **Read the text and choose the best title. Then listen and check.**

1 Different hobbies, different friends
2 Best friends
3 Lessons from our brothers and sisters

13 Choose the photo that goes best with the text.

1

2

3

14 Read the text again and complete the sentences.

1 Freya is .... years old.
2 Freya and Megan are ....
3 Freya and Megan sometimes meet at ....
4 Psychologists believe that brothers and sisters shape our lives more than our ....
5 Parents teach children to be .... to other people and say 'thank you'.
6 Brothers and sisters show us how to work as ....
7 .... between brothers and sisters teach children to deal with conflicts.
8 We learn .... we are and .... we like from our brothers and sisters.
9 Your brother or sister is the person who you know for the .... time in your life.

15 Choose two possible explanations for each sentence.

0 I look like my mum.
   (A) We both have got brown hair and black eyes.
   (B) We both are tall.
   C We both like books.
1 I am like my brother.
   A We both are very hard-working.
   B I like spending time with him.
   C We both like basketball.
2 I take after my grandmother.
   A I am similar to her and I like the same things as she does.
   B We both have black hair.
   C My grandmother never cooks but I like cooking.
3 My brother looks like our dad.
   A They are both very intelligent.
   B They have got blue eyes.
   C They are thin.

16 Complete the sentences about yourself.

1 I look like ....
   because we ....
2 I take after my ....
   We both ....
3 I am like ....
   because we ....

Freya, 24, and Megan, 22, are sisters. They study at different universities and don't live with their parents any more. Freya and Megan sometimes talk on the phone or meet at their parents' house
5 but they don't keep in touch a lot. They've got different friends and different hobbies. But they both know they share more than childhood memories and a box of old photos. 'I am who I am because of my sister,' says Megan, and Freya
10 smiles. Is it true that brothers and sisters influence our lives more than parents?

Psychologists agree that as children and teenagers we learn a lot at home. Our parents teach us how to behave around people. They
15 show us how to follow the rules, how to eat at the table or how to be polite and say 'thank you' or 'good morning.'

Brothers and sisters, on the other hand, teach us to share, to work as a team or to take care of
20 each other. Surprisingly the greatest lesson we get from our brothers or sisters come from everyday quarrels. Freya and Megan remember their fights about clothes, toys, video games or television programmes. Psychologists agree that
25 these quarrels are great practice in dealing with conflict, negotiating and agreeing on a solution which is good for everyone. Brothers and sisters who fight a lot as kids find it easier to know what is right for them in difficult or stressful situations.
30 They also learn how to deal with negative emotions.

What's more, brothers and sisters encourage us to discover who we are and what we like. Megan is two years younger than Freya. This is a
35 small age difference and psychologists see that in such situations brothers and sisters often try to show that they are a different person. They want to wear different clothes and have different hobbies.

40 Despite all the conflicts and differences brothers and sisters often remain friends for life, even if not the closest ones. After all, your brother or your sister is probably the person who knows you for the longest in your whole life.

VOCABULARY

DAILY ROUTINES

17 Choose the correct option.

0   I wake (up) / out at 6 o'clock.
1   Dave usually gets / has up at 7:30.
2   I have / make a shower before breakfast.
3   My brother has / gets dressed in a hurry.
4   I use / go online every afternoon.
5   I leave the house / of the house at 8:20.
6   I make / do homework after school.
7   On Wednesdays I get home / to home at 4 o'clock.
8   I start school / the school at 9 o'clock.

18 Complete the texts with the words in the boxes.

start school ▪ leave the house ▪ get up ▪
have breakfast ▪ have a shower ▪ wake up

Toby

My mum 0 _wakes me_ up at 7:30 am.
It's hard for me to 1 .... so I spend
about 20 minutes in bed. Then, I go to
the bathroom and 2 ....
in a hurry. Sometimes I don't 3 ....
at home. I only drink a smoothie. I usually
4 .... at 8:30. I 5 ....
at 8:45 so I am often late for school. How can
I organise my mornings better?

do homework ▪ finish school ▪ get dressed ▪
get home ▪ go online

Jay

I like mornings. I do everything quickly.
Almost everything. It takes me a lot of time
to 6 .... because I never know what
to wear. My school day is long. I 7 ....
at 3:30 but I 8 .... at 5:30. Why so late?
Because I often stop at the café with my friends.
Then at home, I 9 .... and check my
friends' messages or read the news. Finally, I
10 .... at 8 o'clock but I'm very tired.
How can I find more time for homework?

19 What do you do every day? Use the verbs from exercise 18 and describe your day.

I wake up at 7:30. I check my phone first.

GRAMMAR PRACTICE

Adverbs of frequency

Choose the correct option.

We put adverbs of frequency (*always*, *never*, etc.) *between / before / after* the subject and the verb.

With the verb *be* we put the adverb of frequency *between / before / after* the verb.

We put expressions of frequency (*every day*, *twice a week*, etc.) *at the beginning / in the middle* and at the end of a sentence.

➡ See **GRAMMAR REFERENCE** page 118

20 🔊 Choose the correct option.

0 My parents (*often go*) / *go often* shopping.
1 I *usually am / am usually* tired after school.
2 Do *you always / always you* drink water?
3 *Every day Sarah / Sarah every day* calls her friends.
4 Sam *does his homework on Fridays / on Fridays does his homework*.
5 My mum *hardly ever / ever hardly* cooks fish.
6 We *never go / don't never go* for a bike ride.

21 🔊 Cross out the incorrect adverb or expression of frequency in each sentence.

0 I often go swimming ~~often~~.
1 Always she always smiles.
2 Every day my brother every day goes running.
3 I have music lessons twice a week weeks.
4 My parents usually are usually at work in the mornings.
5 On Sundays we on Sundays get up late.
6 We hardly ever watch TV hardly ever.

22 🔊 Write sentences talking about yourself. Use adverbs and expressions of frequency.

0 drink orange juice
.... I often drink orange juice. ....
1 go to school by bus
....
2 be busy
....
3 get presents
....
4 buy new clothes
....
5 clean my room
....

Verbs of preference + *-ing*

Complete the rule.

After a verb of preference (*like, hate*, etc.) we use the .... form of the verb.

➡ See **GRAMMAR REFERENCE** page 118

23 🔊 Complete the sentences with the correct form of the verb in brackets.

0 She likes ...*swimming*... . (*swim*)
1 My friends can't stand .... early. (*get up*)
2 Tim enjoys .... in the kitchen. (*help*)
3 We don't mind .... to classical music. (*listen*)
4 I'm into .... (*draw*)
5 I hate .... clothes. (*buy*)
6 My sister loves .... cakes. (*make*)

24 🔊 Complete the text with these words. There are two extra words.

> always ▪ do ▪ does ▪ doesn't ▪ don't ▪
> ever ▪ every ▪ into ▪ know ▪ mind ▪ play ▪
> spending ▪ twice a month

Q and A with Zach Brown

Q Why does everyone 0 .....*know*..... you at school?

A I 1 .... in a band, The Black Cat. We give concerts 2 .... I'm also 3 .... swimming.

Q You're busy! What 4 .... your typical day look like?

A I wake up at 5:30. I really don't 5 .... getting up early.
I 6 .... go to the gym in the morning. After school I go swimming. I get home at 6 o'clock.

Q 7 .... you do your homework then?

A No, I 8 ....
We have dinner together first. I hardly 9 .... miss it.
I enjoy 10 .... time with my family.

18   Unit 1

SPEAKING SKILLS

TALKING ABOUT FREQUENCY

25 Choose the correct option to complete the mini dialogues.

1 'How often do you have tests at school?'
'............ .'

A Usually   **B** Once a week   **C** Now

2 'When does Maggie go to the gym?'
'She goes to the gym ....'

A on Mondays   **B** usually   **C** often

3 'Our maths teacher is Mr Dawson.'
'Can you .... that, please?'

A say   **B** repeat   **C** understand

4 'What do you want to order as your entrée?'
'............ ? I don't understand.'

A Please   **B** Pardon   **C** I sorry

5 'It's £24.98.'
'Sorry, can you say that .... , please?'

A more   **B** once   **C** again

6 '............ do you go for a walk?'
'Twice a week.'

A When   **B** Where   **C** How often

26 Complete the conversation with these words.

> can ▪ how often ▪ please ▪ sorry ▪
> understand ▪ when

Ella	This is the photo of my family.
Daniel	You've got a big family! [1]........................ do you see everyone?
Ella	We all meet once a year on my grandad's birthday.
Daniel	[2]........................ , can you say that again, [3]........................ ?
Ella	We meet on my grandad's birthday.
Daniel	[4]........................ is it?
Ella	His birthday is on the same day as St Patrick's Day.
Daniel	Pardon? I don't [5]........................ .
Ella	It's on 17th March, St Patrick's Day.
Daniel	Oh, I see. Does your grandad live in Ireland?
Ella	No, he lives in Manchester.
Daniel	My cousins live there. Well, near Manchester. They live in Oldham.
Ella	[6]........................ you repeat that, please?
Daniel	Oldham. It's a town near Manchester.

LISTENING SKILLS

27 Look at these habits. Tick (✓) the ones that you think are good for you.

- ☐ eating fruit and vegetables
- ☐ drinking water
- ☐ playing video games all day
- ☐ exercising regularly
- ☐ watching TV for 3 hours every day
- ☐ eating fast food
- ☐ thinking positively

28 🎧 [1.02] Listen to the conversation. What is Lauren's main problem?

1 She doesn't have a lot of time.

2 She has a lot of bad habits.

3 She never does her homework.

29 🎧 [1.02] Listen again and decide if the sentences are true (T) or (F). Correct the false ones.

1 Lauren is worried about her science project.   ☐ T   ☐ F

2 Lauren and Jamie have got two more weeks to work on their science projects.   ☐ T   ☐ F

3 Jamie wants to start his project today.   ☐ T   ☐ F

4 Lauren always has breakfast at home.   ☐ T   ☐ F

5 Lauren wants to change her bad habits.   ☐ T   ☐ F

6 Lauren thinks it's hard to do homework three times a week.   ☐ T   ☐ F

7 It's a good idea to ask a friend to help you.   ☐ T   ☐ F

30 Replace the underlined word with a synonym.

0 <u>speak</u> quietly
  A look **B** talk **C** shout

1 an <u>awful</u> day
  A wonderful **B** good **C** terrible

2 the concert <u>finishes</u>
  A ends **B** begins **C** forgets

3 a <u>huge</u> house
  A large **B** tiny **C** wonderful

4 a long <u>trip</u>
  A ticket **B** receipt **C** journey

5 <u>get</u> a present
  A give **B** take **C** receive

6 <u>reply</u> soon
  A ask **B** answer **C** write

31 Read the text and answer the questions.

To: Jacob
From: Chloe
Emma wants to organise a surprise birthday party for Leo on Saturday. I can't come early to help her because I have a tennis lesson. Can you do it?

0 Who is writing the email?
  A Jacob **B** Chloe **C** Emma

1 Who is this email for?
  A Emma **B** Leo **C** Jacob

2 What does Chloe want?
  A Jacob's help **B** invite Leo to a party
  C play tennis with Jacob

32 Look at the messages. What do they say? Choose the correct options.

0

To: Dad
From: Jason
Can you come and pick me up at 6 o'clock today after school? I've got tennis club at 4:30 and there are no buses from school after 5:30.
Thanks,
Jason

  A Jason wants his dad to come to school by car at 5:30.
  B Jason doesn't want to go to school by bus today.
  C Jason wants his dad to wait for him in the car at 6:00.

1

Class 7a,
Please bring dictionaries from the library to our class on Tuesday. You can leave your books and notebooks at home on that day. I want you to read some magazines in English.
Mrs Carter

Mrs Carter wants students:
  A to stay at home on Tuesday.
  B to have a lesson in the library on Tuesday.
  C to read magazines in English on Tuesday.

2

Cathy
Do you want to go to the cinema with me on Friday evening? I've got two tickets to this new comedy.
Call me after 4 o'clock today and tell me if you can come.
Sarah

  A Sarah wants to go to the cinema with Cathy today at 4:00.
  B Cathy has got two cinema tickets.
  C Sarah invites Cathy to the cinema on Friday.

3

No piano lessons
on Monday. Mrs Wilson
is on a school trip
to the opera with Year 11.

The headteacher is writing a note to students to:

A   say that nobody has piano lessons
    with Mrs Wilson on Monday.

B   inform everyone that all Mrs Wilson's students
    are at the opera on Monday.

C   remind Year 11 students about their piano
    lessons with Mrs Wilson on Monday.

4

**Students – don't leave
empty bottles or other rubbish
in the cafeteria.
Make sure your table
is clean before you go.**

A   Students can't use bottles in the cafeteria.

B   Students can clean the tables before they start
    eating.

C   Students can't leave things in the cafeteria.

5

Bradley High School
Drama Club

Are you into dancing and singing?
We've got plans for a new musical.
Come on Friday at 6:30 pm
if you want to be one of our actors.

A   Bradley High School Drama Club wants
    to show a new musical on Friday at 6:30.

B   Bradley High School Drama Club needs
    new actors for a musical.

C   Bradley High School Drama Club meets
    every Friday at 6:30.

Reading – Gap fill

First, read the text quickly. Then reread the first
sentence that has a gap. It's important to read before
and after the gap. Think of a word, try it in the gap and
read the sentence to check. The words you need are
mostly grammar words (verbs, pronouns, articles) not
vocabulary (nouns, adjectives, etc.) Remember that
contractions, except *can't*, count as two words: *it's = it is*.

33   Write the missing word in each gap.

0   .... *Do* .... you like ice cream?

1   There .... two new students
    in Mr Bowman's class.

2   Has your brother .... a red bike?

3   Nathan, ... this your book?

4   Are there .... apples on the table?

5   When .... you do your homework?

6   I .... stand listening to loud music.

34   Correct the mistakes.

0   We haven't got ~~some~~ time. **any**

1   There are a black cat in my garden.

2   He don't play football every day.

3   When time is your bus?

4   How much schools are there in your town?

5   I hate go to the gym.

6   I don't watch the TV many often.

35   Write one word in each gap.

My friend [0] .... *does* .... not like her new school
very much. There aren't [1] .... pictures
or posters on the walls in the classroom
and the chairs are uncomfortable. The students in
her class have all [2] .... lessons in the
same classroom and they hardly [3] ....
go to the language lab. A lot of students do
[4] .... do any homework.
On the other hand, my new school is great!
The lessons are always interesting and the teachers
don't give [5] .... much homework.
[6] .... you like your new school?

GRAMMAR PRACTICE

Present continuous

Complete the rules.

To form the present continuous we use *am*, ...
or .... and the .... form of the verb.
We use the present continuous to talk about actions
happening *now / regularly* and *repeated / temporary*
actions which happen at around this time.

➡ See **GRAMMAR REFERENCE** page 119

1 Complete the sentences with the present
continuous of these verbs.

brush ▪ do ▪ get ▪ go ▪ have ▪
look ▪ read ▪ sing ▪ ~~watch~~

0 They ....**are watching**.... television at the moment.
1 We .... to the swimming pool today.
2 Holly and Sarah .... songs now.
3 You .... a science-fiction book.
4 My dad .... at his tablet at the moment.
5 They .... their teeth now.
6 I .... dressed now.
7 My brother .... his homework.
8 Ben .... a shower.

2 Choose the correct options to complete the text.

3 Complete the table with the *-ing* form of
these verbs.

~~catch~~ ▪ come ▪ dance ▪ eat ▪ help ▪
hit ▪ listen ▪ make ▪ put ▪ run ▪ ride ▪
stop ▪ swim ▪ try ▪ use

+ *-ing*	~~e~~ + *-ing*	double consonant + *-ing*
....catching....	....	....
....	....	....
....	....	....
....	....	....
....	....	....

4 Make the sentences negative.

0 I'm eating a sandwich.
   I'm not eating a sandwich.
1 We're playing football.
2 My friends are running in the park.
3 Emily is checking her phone now.
4 The sun is shining.
5 My dad is driving a car.
6 You're having lunch now.
7 They're waiting for the bus.
8 I'm taking a picture.

It's Sunday afternoon. We **0**............ at home because it **1**............ raining. My mum
2............ in the kitchen. My sister Jenny is **3**............ her. My dad and my younger
brother **4**............ at our photographs on the computer. They are **5**............
a new photo album. I'm **6**............ up my room. I **7**............ putting all my
clothes in the wardrobe. My friend Emma **8**............ coming soon.

0 (A) are staying   B staying   C is staying
1 A is   B are   C has
2 A cooking   B has cooking C is cooking
3 A help   B helping   C helps
4 A is looking   B looking   C are looking
5 A makes   B make   C making
6 A tidy   B tidies   C tidying
7 A are   B have   C am
8 A is   B are   C am

5 🔊 **Complete the sentences with the present continuous form of the verbs in brackets.**

0 Martha ...._isn't drinking_.......... tea. (not / drink)

1 I .... homework at the moment. (not / do)

2 We .... to school today. (not / go)

3 Jamie .... in his notebook. (not / write)

4 My teacher .... English now. (not / speak)

5 The cat .... (not / sleep)

6 My dad .... breakfast now. (not / make)

7 You .... me at all! (not / help)

8 Dan and Harry .... home now. (not / come)

6 🔊 **Choose the correct option.**

0 Where (are)/ is you going?

1 What are *you / he* doing at the moment?

2 *Is your dad / Your dad is* watching television now?

3 *Are / Is* Caitlin and Kieran having fun?

4 *What are / Are what* you eating?

5 Who is *Kate / they* texting?

6 Why *you are / are you* wearing your coat? It isn't cold!

7 Is it *snowing / snow* outside?

8 Why *you're / are you* sitting alone in your room?

7 🔊 **Write questions using the prompts. Then write short affirmative (+) or negative (–) answers.**

0 you / talk / to your friends? (+)
'**Are you talking to your friends?** 'Yes, I am.'

1 Caroline / open / the window? (–)
....

2 you / play / video games? (+)
....

3 your grandparents / relax / in the garden? (–)
....

4 Mr Taylor / repair / his bike? (–)
....

5 Sam and Max / play / tennis? (+)
....

6 your sister / clean / the kitchen? (+)
....

8 🔊 **Complete the message with the present continuous form of the verbs in brackets.**

George

What **0** ...._are_......... you ......_doing_....... (do) at the moment? I hope you **1** .... (not / do) your homework. It's Friday evening! Millie and I **2** .... (not / study) because there's a concert in the park this evening. Why don't you come with us? We **3** .... (get) ready to go. Right now, I **4** .... (wait) for Millie. Her mum **5** .... (drive) her to my house. Jack's already in the park because he **6** .... (buy) the tickets for all of us. Text me!

9 🔊 **Correct the mistakes.**

0 I ~~not am~~ playing a game.
I **am not** playing a game.

1 Are you studing at the moment?

2 We going to the cinema tonight.

3 My brother and I am walking to school now.

4 Jack doesn't listening to the teacher.

5 Why you are asking all these questions?

6 'Is Jessie having fun?' 'Yes, she has.'

7 We're stoping at this café.

8 I sitting on the sofa at the moment.

10 🔊 **Imagine it's Saturday night. Answer the questions.**

0 What's your best friend doing now?
She's listening to music. She's drawing some pictures.

1 What are your parents doing?
....

2 What are you doing?
....

3 What aren't you doing?
....

READING SKILLS

11 ◀[1.03] **Read and listen to the text. Then choose the best sentence to summarise the text.**

1   This text explains how classroom design can influence students' marks and skills.
2   This text gives advice on how students can feel good in a test.
3   This text shows that students enjoy studying when their classroom is colourful.

12 Read the text quickly. In which paragraph is the following information found?

1   windows ....
2   desks and chairs ....
3   sunlight ....
4   how much time British students spend at school ....
5   the percentage by which students' marks can change in a well-designed classroom ....
6   temperature ....
7   posters ....

13 Read the text again and decide if the sentences are true (T) or false (F). Correct the false ones.

1   Our emotions often depend on the time of the day. ☐T ☐F
2   A group of teachers and university professors are doing a study on classroom design. ☐T ☐F
3   Classroom design can help students acquire knowledge. ☐T ☐F
4   Physical comfort in the classroom means the right light and good air and sound quality. ☐T ☐F
5   Students complete tests well when the classroom is warm. ☐T ☐F
6   A lot of pictures on wall displays help students to study. ☐T ☐F
7   Students study when they don't see their own projects on the wall displays. ☐T ☐F
8   In a classroom where there are students' names on the chairs students get good marks. ☐T ☐F
9   At the moment schools don't want to change their classroom design. ☐T ☐F

The perfect

Architects believe that there is a link between how people feel and the place where they are. Buildings can change people's emotions and influence the way their brain works. One of the
5   best places to check this link for children and teenagers is school.

In the UK secondary school students spend about 714 hours a year in their classroom. Is it possible that classroom design can
10 influence students' skills and knowledge? Are students working well or badly because of their classroom? Can the same students' marks change when they take tests in different classrooms? A group of architects together
15 with university professors is trying to answer these questions.

Their studies show that classroom design can help students acquire knowledge. Students' results can change by 16% and their
20 knowledge and marks depend on the design of the classroom where they usually have lessons. The most important feature of classroom design is physical comfort. To feel physically good, students need the right light,
25 temperature, sound and air quality. Big windows with no direct sunlight help students to learn. Students also complete tests positively when their classroom has good ventilation and a pleasantly low temperature.

classroom

D A perfect classroom also needs the right 30 colours and wall displays. Bright colours and only a few posters are the best for studying. They help students do difficult exercises and concentrate. However, too many pictures and different colours can slow down the learning 35 process. Empty white walls have the same negative influence.

A well-designed classroom is a place which makes students feel that they belong there. Children and teenagers take part in the lessons 40 more actively when they see their own projects on the walls. Students' learning results are good when they see their names on the desks, chairs or lockers in the classroom.

E Some schools are now starting to change their 45 classroom design. They are doing this to help students acquire knowledge and skills. What about your school? Are the classrooms well-designed? If not, what are you doing at your school to help? 50

LEARNING

14 Choose the correct option.

0 A lot of students can't *know* / *use* the information from the coursebooks.

1 Asking questions is a good way to *practise* / *acquire* knowledge.

2 When students work *in* / *by* groups they solve the maths problems faster.

3 Where can I *access* / *look* the information I need?

4 In our schools we *take* / *get* exams twice a year.

5 I *acquire* / *learn* two languages – English and French.

6 Students often *receive* / *give* praise when they give the correct answer.

15 Match the definitions 0–8 to the words a–i.

0 [c] a time at school when a teacher teaches a subject

1 [ ] a school subject where students learn about geography, history, economics and politics

2 [ ] a meeting of all students and teachers at school

3 [ ] a person who controls the whole school

4 [ ] a list of times when lessons at school start

5 [ ] a letter or a number that shows how good a student's test or homework is

6 [ ] information about students' work at school which the teacher gives to parents

7 [ ] effects of what you have done earlier

8 [ ] a type of meeting where people talk about their experiences and learn something from each other

a assembly   f results
b headteacher   g social studies
c lesson   h timetable
d mark   i workshop
e report

16 Answer the questions.

1 Is there a class council in your school and what does it do?

2 What do teachers usually discuss at assemblies?

3 What don't you like about your timetable?

4 How often do you get marks and reports at school?

5 What do you do to access information about something?

6 What are the best ways to acquire knowledge?

GRAMMAR PRACTICE

Adverbs of manner

Complete the rule

Adverbs of manner describe how a person or a thing does an action. They usually end with ....

➡ See **GRAMMAR REFERENCE** page 119

17 **Change the adjectives into adverbs.**

0	careful	....*carefully*....
1	sad	....
2	nice	....
3	happy	....
4	bad	....
5	beautiful	....
6	fast	....
7	hard	....
8	quick	....

18 **Change the adjectives into adverbs. Then use them to complete the sentences.**

> calm ▪ early ▪ easy ▪ good ▪
> ~~late~~ ▪ loud ▪ quiet ▪ slow ▪ terrible

0 I usually wake up ....*late*........ and then I don't have enough time to get ready for school.

1 Tanya is never late. She comes .... to the bus stop.

2 My baby brother isn't a quiet baby. He cries ....

3 It's not difficult. I can do it ....

4 Max is a great artist. He draws ....

5 Don't make any noise! Please close the door ....

6 This is an awful game. Our team is playing .... today.

7 My little sister writes very .... She needs ten minutes to write one sentence!

8 Dad always speaks .... He doesn't shout at all.

Verbs of state and verbs of perception

Choose the correct option.

We don't use the present continuous with verbs which describe *state / action*, for example: *be, have, know, like*.

➡ See **GRAMMAR REFERENCE** page 119

19 **Complete the sentences with the present simple or the present continuous. In some cases the same tense can be used for both sentences.**

0 HAVE
  a I ....*am having*........ a shower now.
  b I ....*have*............ got two brothers.

1 THINK
  a I .... this is a great book.
  b I .... about the book that I'm reading now.

2 UNDERSTAND
  a I .... maths problems easily.
  b .... you .... what I'm trying to say?

3 LIKE
  a Emily .... pop music.
  b I .... this party!

4 KNOW
  a I always .... how to do my homework.
  b .... you .... where we're going?

Present simple v present continuous

Choose the correct option.

We use the present simple to talk about things which happen *now / regularly*. We use present continuous to talk about things which happen *at this moment or around now / every day*.

➡ See **GRAMMAR REFERENCE** page 119

20 **Complete the sentences with the present simple or the present continuous of the verbs in brackets.**

0 We always ....*spend*........ the summer with our cousins. (*spend*)

1 Every Sunday Tom .... to the swimming pool. (*go*)

2 Take the umbrella! It .... (*rain*)

3 .... your mum .... television every day? (*watch*)

4 Be quiet! The baby .... (*sleep*)

5 My brother often .... his phone. (*check*)

6 My friends .... video games at the moment. (*not / play*)

7 .... you .... this magazine now? (*read*)

8 I .... coffee. (*not / usually / drink*)

SPEAKING SKILLS

DESCRIBING A PICTURE

21 Look at the photo and decide if the sentences are true (T) or false (F). Correct the false ones.

1 It is a photo of three school friends. ☐T ☐F
2 The boy on the right has got a tablet. ☐T ☐F
3 The boy in the centre is wearing a blue T-shirt. ☐T ☐F
4 The girl on the right has got long dark hair. ☐T ☐F
5 There are some other students near them. ☐T ☐F
6 The boy in the centre hasn't got a school bag. ☐T ☐F

22 Choose the correct options to complete the conversation.

Holly Who's in this picture?
Mum It's you! You're walking to school on your first day.
Holly I don't remember that.
Mum ¹............ this is Maddison Perkins ²............ the left and you're ³............ the centre.
Holly Oh, yeah. Look! I ⁴............ a school bag with Bart Simpson. It's so cute! But who's that girl on the ⁵............ ?
Mum It's ⁶............ Caitlin.
Holly No, it isn't. Caitlin's got blonde hair. ⁷............ it's Lily Summers.
Mum ⁸............ our dog, Coco.
Holly She looks small here.
Mum She's probably 7 or 8 months old.

1 **A** I think **B** I've got **C** It's probably
2 **A** in **B** on **C** at
3 **A** at **B** on **C** in
4 **A** can't see **B** there's **C** 've got
5 **A** right **B** centre **C** near
6 **A** there's **B** think **C** probably
7 **A** Perhaps **B** I've got **C** It's probably
8 **A** I am seeing **B** I can see **C** I am looking

LISTENING SKILLS

23 Read the sentences and choose the most likely answers.

Harriet is 16 years old and lives in Glasgow.

1 Harriet lives *5 / 500* km away from school.
2 It takes Harriet 17 *minutes / hours* to get to school by bus.
3 Harriet pays *£2.45 / £24.50* for lunch at school.
4 Harriet starts school at 8:30 *am / pm*.
5 Harriet spends *six / sixteen* hours at school every day.
6 Harriet likes running. She runs 3 *metres / kilometres* every day.
7 Harriet likes hot chocolate. She pays *£2.60 / £0.60* for one cup of hot chocolate.

24 🔊 [1.04] Listen to the conversation. Who is the woman talking about?

1 She's giving information about a school trip.
2 She's telling students about their homework.
3 She's making plans for her family for next week.

25 🔊 [1.04] Listen again and complete the sentences.

1 The school trip is next ....
2 The students are going to At-Bristol .... Centre.
3 The trip is on ...., 12th ....
4 The bus is at ....
5 Students can bring a packed ...., notebooks and a ....
6 The workshop is called '......................... Detectives'.
7 The ticket to the museum costs £......................... .
8 The bus costs £......................... .
9 The museum website is www.at-......................... .org.uk.

ACADEMIC SKILLS

TRANSFERRING INFORMATION

26 Add a full stop (.), an exclamation mark (!) or a question mark (?) at the end of the sentences.

0 Do you like maths**?**

1 What time do you get up

2 This party is great

3 I usually have orange juice in the morning

4 Are you busy now

5 School starts at 8:30

6 I can't wait to see you

27 Rewrite the sentences using the correct punctuation.

0 It isnt late **It isn't late!**

1 Toms favourite food is ice cream eggs and chicken

2 Red blue and white are the colours of the British flag

3 Youre amazing

4 I dont believe you Mia

5 Where are you going

6 Ive got two brothers

7 There are no classes today and tomorrow Monday and Tuesday

8 Can you help me

29 Use the information in the fact file to write a short text about Newington Academy.

 fact file

Name Newington Academy

Location York, North of England

Type of school State secondary school

Rank 10th best high school in League tables of Yorkshire

Number of students 1,200

Age of students 11–18

School hours 8:45–3:30

School colours grey, red and blue

School since 1963

Number of teachers 203

Best extra-curricular activities (clubs)
Music bands (esp. jazz band), Drama society (end of term productions), Hockey, Football, Swimming, Book Club

28 Read the text about Thompson Secondary School and correct the information in the fact file.

THOMPSON SECONDARY SCHOOL

Thompson Secondary School is a grammar school in Liverpool in England. The school is almost 100 years old. There are about 880 students at Thompson Secondary School. All students are girls between the age of 11 and 18. There are 65 teachers at Thompson Secondary School.

The classes start at 8:50 and finish at 3:00. After school students can take part in a variety of extra-curricular activities. The most popular after-school clubs are Human Rights, Choir, Creative Writing, Netball, Rugby and Philosophy.

All students at school wear identical green and yellow uniforms. The uniform includes a green blazer, a green skirt, a yellow sweater or shirt, yellow socks or tights and black shoes.

 fact file

Name Thompson Secondary School

Location Manchester, England

Number of students 680

Boys / girls girls

Age of students 12–18

Type of school grammar school

School hours 8:50–3:00

School since 1920

Number of teachers 95

School uniform green blazer, green trousers, yellow sweater or shirt, green shoes, yellow socks or tights

Best extra-curricular activities (clubs)
Human Rights, Choir, Creative Reading, Netball, Volleyball, Philosophy

30 Read the audio script. The underlined sentence matches the image with a tick. Cross out the sentences that refer to the other images.

0 What doesn't Liz do in the morning?

A   B ✓   C

Teacher	Liz, you are late again!
Liz	I'm sorry, Mrs Thompson. I don't know what's wrong with me. I always wake up at 6 o'clock. I really feel that I've got a lot of time in the morning. ~~I finish my homework,~~ then ~~I have a shower~~ and get ready for school. When I go downstairs it's suddenly 8:15 and I don't have time for breakfast. I run to the bus stop and I often miss the bus, just like today. I'm so sorry.

1 What time is the football match?

A   B   C

Mike	Where are you going, Ryan?
Ryan	To football practice. It starts at 2:30.
Mike	Isn't your practice at 4:30?
Ryan	It usually is but today practice is early. We're playing a match later against Oakland Secondary School. I'm very excited. Do you want to come and see it?
Mike	Of course. What time?
Ryan	5:30.
Mike	See you there!

31 [1.05] Choose the correct options (A, B or C).

0 What does the girl eat for breakfast?

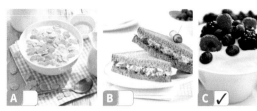

A   B   C ✓

1 What time does the concert start?

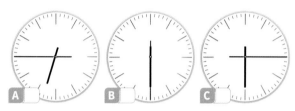

A   B   C

2 Where does the boy usually go after school on Wednesdays?

A   B   C

3 Where is the boy now?

A   B   C

4 What is the woman doing now?

A   B   C

5 What do they need to buy?

A   B   C

REVISE AND ROUND UP

1 🔊 **Write sentences and questions using the present simple.**

0 Emma and Tom / play tennis / every weekend?
Do Emma and Tom play tennis every weekend?

1 my mum / not / go shopping / at weekends

....

2 you / eat / a lot of potatoes?

....

3 we / visit / our family / every summer

....

4 Sophie / study / Spanish / at school?

....

5 I / not / use / a tablet

....

6 my grandmother / live / in Germany

....

7 Mr Gibson / drive / a car / to work?

....

8 we / tidy up / the living room / every day

....

2 🔊 **Complete the sentences with the correct spelling of the verbs in brackets.**

0 My dad ......*teaches*...... music. (*teach*)

1 Alan .... the dishes at weekends. (*wash*)

2 Max looks before he .... the street. (*cross*)

3 Our cat often .... mice. (*catch*)

4 Tim .... school early on Tuesdays. (*finish*)

5 Emre .... history at the university. (*study*)

6 My aunt .... new clothes all the time. (*buy*)

7 My dog .... me when I'm away. (*miss*)

8 She .... to Paris twice a year. (*fly*)

3 🔊 **Write six sentences about your daily routine. Use adverbs and expressions of frequency.**

~~always~~ ▪ hardly ever ▪
every Monday ▪ never ▪ often ▪ once a week ▪
on Sundays ▪ sometimes ▪ twice a month ▪ usually

0 *I always have breakfast before school.*

1 ....

2 ....

3 ....

4 ....

5 ....

6 ....

4 🔊 **Complete the sentences about yourself. Use these expressions.**

cook ▪ dance ▪ eat pasta ▪ go by bus ▪ fly ▪
listen to music ▪ play video games ▪
read books ▪ swim ▪ ~~study English~~ ▪
walk in the rain ▪ watch science-fiction films

0 I like ....*studying English*............ .

1 I'm into ....

2 I love ....

3 I enjoy ....

4 I can't stand ....

5 I hate ....

6 I don't mind ....

5 🔊 **Complete the sentences with the present continuous.**

0 I .....*'m baking*..... (*bake*) a cake.

1 We .... (*sit*) on the sofa.

2 .... you .... (*wear*) a new sweater?

3 Mike .... (*not / talk*) to his friends now.

4 What .... they .... (*look*) for?

5 I .... (*not / have*) breakfast at the moment.

6 .... Amy .... (*write*) an email?

7 He .... (*repair*) his bike now.

8 My friends .... (*not / order*) burgers today.

6 🔊 **Write the -ing form of the verbs.**

0 plan ......*planning*......

1	travel	....	5	take ....
2	lose	....	6	smile ....
3	hope	....	7	sleep ....
4	walk	....	8	chat ....

7 🔊 **Tick (✓) The correct sentences. Correct the ones which are wrong.**

0 I am ~~liking~~ bananas. **like**
I have got two brothers. ✓

1 I am understanding this now.

2 I'm thinking about my summer holiday.

3 I'm loving this place!

4 Do you want to have ice cream now?

5 You're being a great friend.

6 I have my lunch now.

8 📶 Choose the correct option.

0 .... you like singing? Join our band!
Who are we?
We all **1** .... to St James Secondary School.
Josh and Marco **2** .... the guitar, Emily **3** ....
the drums but we **4** .... for a singer at the
moment.
When **5** .... we practise?
We **6** .... twice a week. Today we **7** .... our
third concert. Josh's sister **8** .... with us tonight
but this is her last concert.
Are you interested?
Please email me at FaithJones@mymail.com.

0	**A** Do	**B** Does	**C** Are
1	**A** goes	**B** going	**C** go
2	**A** plays	**B** is playing	**C** play
3	**A** plays	**B** don't play	**C** play
4	**A** look	**B** are looking	**C** looking
5	**A** do	**B** don't	**C** does
6	**A** meets	**B** are meeting	**C** meet
7	**A** are playing	**B** is playing	**C** play
8	**A** sings	**B** is singing	**C** doesn't sing

9 📶 Correct the mistakes.

0 Look! Someone ~~opens~~ the door to your car.
is opening

1 I drink hardly ever coffee in the morning.

2 My dad don't go to work by car.

3 Harry and Leo is going to the gym.

4 I'm not do any homework today.

5 What you are watching now?

6 How often is Suna meet her friends?

7 Lucas has sometimes lunch in a fast food restaurant.

8 Can you help me? I carry a heavy bag.

CONCEPT CHECK

Read the sentences and answer the questions.

1 *I play football.*

(Answer Yes / No)

0 Is this an action in the present? **Yes**

1 Is it happening at the moment of speaking?

2 Does it happen regularly?

3 Can you put *now* at the end of this sentence?

4 Can you put *every day* at the end of this sentence?

2 *He usually goes to school by bus.*

(Answer Yes / No)

0 Do you know when he goes to school by bus? **No**

1 Do you know how often he goes to school by bus?

2 Can you replace *usually* with *never*?

3 Can you replace *usually* with *today*?

3 *They're drinking fruit juice.*

(Answer Yes / No)

0 Is this an action in the past? **No**

1 Is it happening at the moment of speaking?

2 Does it happen regularly?

3 Can you put *at the moment* at the end of this sentence?

4 Can you put *often* in the middle of this sentence?

4 *She likes apples.*

(Answer Yes / No)

0 Is this an action? **No**

1 Is this a state of mind?

2 She has apples to eat. Is she happy?

5 *Students complete tests well in perfect classrooms.*

0 Who is doing the actions? **The students**

1 Which is the verb in the sentence?

2 What type of word describes how someone does an action?

3 What is the position of this word?

4 How do the students do the action?

➡️ See **GRAMMAR REFERENCE** pages 117-120

3 Technology

GRAMMAR PRACTICE

Past simple: *be*

Complete the rule and choose the correct option.

The past simple form of the verb *be* is .... for *I*, *he*, *she*, *it* and .... for *you*, *we* and *they*. We use the past simple to talk about states in the *future* / *past*.

➡ See **GRAMMAR REFERENCE** page 120

1 🔊 **Choose the correct option.**

0 My friends *was* / (*were*) in Rome last summer.
1 Laura *was* / *were* at the museum yesterday.
2 I *was* / *were* hungry after school.
3 My grandparents *was* / *were* in the park on Sunday.
4 It *was* / *were* cold yesterday.
5 There *was* / *were* ten people in the cinema.
6 My first bike *was* / *were* purple.
7 We *was* / *were* excited about our trip.
8 In 2006 you *was* / *were* five years old.

2 🔊 **Rewrite the sentences using the past simple.**

0 She is nervous about the test.
   .... **She was nervous about the test.** ....
1 My parents are at home.
   ....
2 I'm very tired.
   ....
3 There are ten desks in the classroom.
   ....
4 These shoes are very expensive.
   ....
5 Cats are important in ancient Egypt.
   ....
6 You are angry with me.
   ....
7 The shop assistant is helpful.
   ....
8 We are on holiday in Turkey.
   ....
9 They are happy.
   ....
10 I am online.
   ....

3 🔊 **Complete the sentences with *wasn't* or *weren't*.**

0 My mum ..... **wasn't** ..... good at sports at school.
1 The café .... crowded.
2 My dad .... at work on Friday.
3 I .... at school all week.
4 Josh and Dave .... at the party last night.
5 You .... into dancing when you were younger.
6 It .... a nice email.
7 They .... busy yesterday morning.
8 Emma .... at the concert with Tom and Max.

4 🔊 **Write sentences with *wasn't* or *weren't*.**

0 Our teacher / late
   Our teacher wasn't late.
1 I / a good friend
2 My coffee / hot
3 It / sunny / on Monday
4 My sister / in London / last week
5 Students / happy / with their test results
6 The film / very interesting
7 You / here / yesterday
8 We / in France / in 2015
9 The email / very long
10 He / at home

5 🔊 **Complete the sentences with *wasn't* or *weren't*. Use these words or your own ideas.**

at home ▪ school ▪ cinema ▪ gym ▪
big ▪ busy ▪ crowded ▪ difficult ▪ easy ▪
happy ▪ sleepy ▪ small ▪ tired

0 Yesterday I **wasn't at the cinema** .
1 I .... after the last party.
2 My first school ....
3 I .... in the morning.
4 Yesterday it .... day.
5 My friends and I .... last summer.
6 My last English test ....
7 My parents and I .... last weekend.
8 I .... this morning.

GRAMMAR PRACTICE

6 🔊 Complete the questions using the words in brackets and *was* or *were*. Then match the questions 0–6 to the answers a–g.

0 [b] ...Was it... cold? (*it*)
1 [ ] .... late for the bus? (*George*)
2 [ ] .... sad yesterday? (*you*)
3 [ ] .... at her friend's house on Sunday? (*Sophie*)
4 [ ] .... good students at primary school? (*you and your brother*)
5 [ ] .... ill last week? (*your friends*)
6 [ ] .... sunny in the morning? (*it*)

a No, she wasn't.　　e Yes, I was.
b Yes, it was.　　f No, he wasn't.
c Yes, they were.　　g Yes, we were.
d No, it wasn't.

7 🔊 Make questions using the prompts. Then write short affirmative (+) or negative (–) answers.

0 you / tired yesterday after school (–)
'Were you tired yesterday after school?'
'No, I wasn't.'

1 your parents / in the garden on Sunday morning (+)

2 Oliver / worried about his first day at a new school (–)

3 you and your sister / surprised at the news (+)

4 Madison's old trousers / blue (–)

5 the cake / sweet (–)

6 you / in New Zealand two years ago (+)

8 🔊 Make sentences and questions using the prompts.

0 garden / the / there / a lot / were / in / of / flowers
There were a lot of flowers in the garden.

1 your / was / a / grandmother / doctor / ?

2 book / wasn't / good / the

3 sister / was / baby / beautiful / a / my

4 were / Paris / last / in / we / week

5 my / weren't / these / my / favourite / jeans

6 party / the / the / was / music / loud / at / ?

7 weren't / the / the / box / in / video games

8 were / 10 / class / the / boys / there / in

9 🔊 Write a few sentences about last week using *was*, *wasn't*, *were* and *weren't*.

Last week

Monday
I was at school on Monday. It was a sunny day.

Tuesday

Wednesday

Thursday

Friday

Saturday

Sunday

READING SKILLS

10 🔊 [1.06] **Read and listen to the text. Cross out the sentence that does not summarise it.**

1 It's easy for all inventors to get rich.
2 Not every inventor will be successful.
3 A good idea is only the beginning of the inventor's work.

11 **Read the text again and choose the correct options.**

1 What, according to the text, do people dream of when they want to be inventors?
   A Creating something new and earning money.
   B Becoming famous.
   C Selling their product to the biggest companies in the world.
   D Moving back in time and working with Thomas Edison.

2 An inventor needs to have a great idea and some:
   A money.
   B luck.
   C success.
   D history.

3 What kind of plan can make an inventor successful?
   A How to introduce their product to the public.
   B How to make more inventions.
   C How to organise their work.
   D How to spend the money they earn.

4 Thomas Edison was the first person to:
   A work on the invention of the electric light bulb.
   B be successful in selling his light bulb.
   C keep his promise by selling cheap candles.
   D work with other people on the same project.

5 What problem did James Dyson have?
   A His product was very difficult to produce.
   B He had no idea how to sell his product outside the UK.
   C British shops refused to sell his product.
   D People in the UK were afraid to use such a modern invention.

6 Why is Steve Wozniak and Steve Jobs' success story unusual?
   A They were just a team of two people who worked at home.
   B They quickly joined a big company and worked in a team with other people.
   C They had no place to work.
   D They were the first ones to open a company in a garage.

INVENTORS AND THEIR *slow road* TO SUCCESS

12 **Read the text again and write answers to the questions.**

1 Who are examples of successful inventors from the past?
2 What makes an invention successful?
3 Why is Thomas Edison famous for inventing a light bulb although he wasn't the first person to work on it?
4 What did James Dyson invent?
5 What did James Dyson achieve In Japan?
6 What happened to James Dyson's product after ten years?
7 How, according to the text, can you become a successful inventor today?

Do you dream of making a career for yourself as an inventor? Do you have an idea and feel you can create something really unique and hope to make a lot of money by selling your product? Do you want
5 to be like Thomas Edison with his electric light bulb or Alexander Graham Bell with his telephone? They both had a brilliant idea that changed the world and made them rich. Is it really that easy to become an inventor?

10 As history shows us, the invention can start with a clever idea but even an original idea for a product doesn't always turn its creator into a successful inventor. What the inventor also needs is luck and a plan of how to produce and sell the product.
15 For example, Thomas Edison wasn't the first person to work on an electric light bulb. There were many others who tried to do the same thing. Edison's idea, however, was the first one to become a commercial success. Why? He promised that using his light
20 bulbs could be cheaper than using candles. He kept his word and opened a company which produced electricity. This was a real revolution.

A lot of modern inventions are a better version of what someone designed a few years earlier.
25 People are quite likely to buy a new model of a mobile phone but what about a better coffee maker or a vacuum cleaner? James Dyson had this problem when he invented the first bagless vacuum cleaner in 1983. Nobody in the UK wanted
30 to produce or sell his product. Companies were worried that Dyson's invention could have a negative effect on the sales of vacuum cleaner bags. Dyson did manage to sell his product in Japan where he won the 1991 International Design Fair Prize.
35 But it took him ten years of hard work to finally appear on the British market.

Although Steve Wozniak and Steve Jobs built their first computer in Jobs' garage, most of today's modern inventions come from a collaboration
40 among a team of people in big companies. So if you dream of becoming an inventor, hopefully you can join their team one day.

MULTIMEDIA

13 Match the technology devices to sentences. Use each device only once. There is one extra.

> cable ▪ charger ▪ console ▪
> desktop computer ▪ earphones ▪ e-reader ▪
> external hard disk ▪ game controller ▪
> hard disk ▪ laptop ▪ mouse ▪ memory stick ▪
> scanner ▪ speakers ▪ printer ▪ tablet

You use it to:

0 write documents or check emails
tablet, laptop, desktop computer

1 listen to music on your computer or phone

2 store and move data outside your computer

3 play games

4 make copies of documents

5 read books

6 charge the battery in your phone

7 store data on your computer

8 connect your desktop computer to a power source

14 Choose the correct options to complete the text. Then answer the questions.

1 Would you like to have an app like this? Why / Why not?

2 How can you improve this app?

 WORD DRAG
4,7 ☆
INSTALL
10,000,000 download

It's a new app for studying English words.
This is how it works.

* 0*Install* / (*Search*) for words you want to learn in a dictionary.

* 1*Attach* / *Select* the words you like by 2*clicking* / *pasting* on them twice. This helps you 3*create* / *check* your word list.

* 4*Upload* / *Log* photos to your word list.

* 5*Drag* / *Press* the hardest word to the top of the list.

* 6*Swipe* / *Cancel* left to hear the word. 7*Touch* / *Swipe* right to see the picture.

* 8*Post* / *Delete* the words you already know or you don't want to revise.

* Check your word list twice a day and see how your English gets better!

GRAMMAR PRACTICE

See **GRAMMAR REFERENCE** page 120

Past simple affirmative: Irregular verbs

Choose the correct option.

A lot of verbs in English have an irregular past simple form. Look at it and learn it from the *second / third* column of the irregular verbs table on page 113.

15 **Write the verbs in the past simple.**

0	do	........*did*........
1	go	....
2	find	....
3	learn	....
4	say	....
5	come	....
6	think	....
7	know	....
8	begin	....
9	tell	....
10	fly	....

16 **Imagine that you had a really bad day yesterday. Write eight sentences about what happened using these verbs.**

- break
- forget
- leave
- take
- buy
- go
- lose
- throw
- come
- have
- make
- wake up
- do
- hurt
- send
- write

0 .... I lost my phone. ....
1 ....
2 ....
3 ....
4 ....
5 ....
6 ....
7 ....
8 ....

Past simple affirmative: Regular verbs

Complete the rule.

We add .... to make the past simple of regular verbs.

See **GRAMMAR REFERENCE** page 000

17 **Complete the table with the past simple of the verbs.**

arrive • carry • cry • dance • drop • enjoy • help • like • live • paint • plan • prefer • reply • stay • stop • study • travel • try • use • visit

-ed	-d	y̶ + -ied	double consonant + -ed
...helped...	....	....	....
....	....	....	....
....	....	....	....
....	....	....	....
....	....	....	....

18 **Write what each person did yesterday.**

0 Drew / study for a test
Drew studied for a test.

1 Lucy's parents / wash the car
2 Mr Smith / cook fish for lunch
3 They / plan a trip to Barcelona
4 Jenny and Isabella / chase the cat in the garden
5 Someone / rob the bank
6 I / mop the floors
7 Mia / return the books to the library
8 Paul / empty the dishwasher

19 **Complete the text with the correct form of the verbs in brackets.**

Topic: Looking after a baby brother!

Julie, Today at 4:30 pm

Yesterday my parents [0] .....*went*..... (*go*) shopping and I [1] .... (*look*) after my baby brother. This [2] .... (*be*) the first time my baby brother Ben and I [3] .... (*be*) alone at home. Well, it [4] .... (*not / be*) easy. My mum [5] .... (*leave*) at 10:30 and Ben [6] .... (*start*) crying at 10:31. I [7] .... (*give*) him some milk and I [8] .... (*sing*) him a song but he [9] .... (*keep*) crying. I [10] .... (*tell*) him a funny story. Nothing [11] .... (*help*). He [12] .... (*smile*) again when my parents finally [13] .... (*come*) home. I think he [14] .... (*miss*) them. I wonder what I can do the next time Mum leaves Ben with me. Any advice?

SPEAKING SKILLS

DESCRIBING PAST EVENTS

20 Complete the conversation with these questions.

> Who was there? ▪
> Where were you on Sunday evening? ▪
> What about you? ▪ Was it good?

Noah ¹ ....
Connor I went bowling.
Noah Lucky you! ² ....
Connor Yes, we had a lot of fun.
Noah No way! ³ ....
Connor Just me and my cousins. They go bowling at weekends so they asked me to join them.
⁴ ....
Noah I stayed at home and watched a football match on TV.

21 Choose the correct options to complete the dialogues. Then decide if the answers show surprise (S), interest (I) or envy (E).

1. **A** I won £20 in a lottery!
   B *Lucky / Luck* you! ....
2. **A** I read ten books last month.
   B That's *interesting / interested*. ....
3. **A** This is a beautiful city!
   B *Oh / It's*, yes. ....
4. **A** Zoe and I started going to the gym.
   B I want to *have / do* that too! ....
5. **A** I ate ten pieces of pizza yesterday.
   B *Really / Real*? ....
6. **A** Amy broke the school swimming record last week.
   B No *possible / way*! ....
7. **A** I won the photo competition!
   B *Wow / Strong*! ....

22 Look at the photos and say what Susan did last weekend.

LISTENING SKILLS

23 Look at the picture and the title of the listening activity exercise 24. What do you think it will be about?

24 [1.07] Listen and choose the correct options.

A TECH-LESS SCHOOL IN A HIGH-TECH PLACE

1. This is a *radio / TV* programme.
2. It's an interview with a boy who *went / would like to go* to school in the Silicon Valley.
3. The school is very *modern / traditional*.
4. Henry thinks it's *okay / not okay* to use modern technologies in the classroom.

25 [1.07] Listen again and decide if the sentences are true (T) or (F). Correct the false ones.

1. The programme is on Radio 17. T F
2. Henry returned to London two months ago. T F
3. Henry spent two years at Waldorf School in the Silicon Valley in California. T F
4. Henry's school wasn't like other schools. T F
5. There were a lot of laptops and computers in the school. T F
6. In California Henry studied how to draw, sing and do woodwork. T F
7. Henry's school in California was for students who want to be artists in the future. T F
8. People in Henry's school thought that technology kills creative thinking. T F
9. Henry prefers the school in California. T F

26 Tick (✓) the sentences you agree with.

- [ ] Technology helps students to find out information more quickly.
- [ ] The best way to understand how something works is to watch a YouTube clip about it.
- [ ] Too much technology slows down thinking.
- [ ] When students use technology in the classroom they improve their social skills.
- [ ] Technology is more distracting than helpful.
- [ ] The internet teaches you to think creatively.

EXAM SKILLS

Reading – Multiple matching

Before you decide that one of the texts matches
a person's profile, compare both texts again.
Make sure that the text matches the profile exactly.
You won't find the same words in the texts as
in the profiles. Instead look for synonyms (words
with similar meanings).

27 Matilda and Freddie want to buy a dictionary. Read
the descriptions about the dictionaries they found.
Follow the steps below to answer the question.

1 Underline the expectations of each person.
There are three expectations for each person.

2 Underline the characteristic features
of the dictionary.

3 Compare the expectations and the features.
Complete the table.

4 Who would like this dictionary more?

Matilda wants a dictionary which has got
grammar explanations and examples of sentences
with new words. She's interested in the present-day
language which young people in the UK use.

Freddie is looking for a small dictionary
which includes slang and modern words.
He wants to see how to use new words in sentences,
not only read their definitions.

The Modern Dictionary of English
is a dictionary for people who want to learn
slang and contemporary words you hear on
the streets in Britain today. Each word has got
a definition, a short note about its grammar
rules and some authentic sentences. This makes
the *Modern Dictionary* the most comprehensive
and the biggest dictionary on the market.

Matilda's expectations	Freddie's expectations	Features of the dictionary
0 *grammar explanations*	3	6 ....
1	4	7 ....
		8 ....
2	5	9 ....
		10 ....

28 These people want to go to a theme park. On the
next page you will find a description of seven
different parks. Choose the park (A–G) best
suited to each person (1–4).

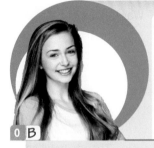

0 B Ella is scared of high roller
coasters and other extreme
rides but she likes crowds,
music, arcade games and boat
rides. She is looking for a place
where she can buy delicious
milkshakes and ice cream.

1 Luke enjoys extreme
amusement park attractions.
He is looking for fast roller
coasters and high drop towers.
He likes loud music and does
not mind waiting in queues.
Luke wants to choose a place
where he can buy lunch if he
gets hungry.

2 Amelia wants to visit the park
with her seven-year-old sister.
She is looking for a less
crowded place with no queues.
Amelia is interested in family
attractions such as bumper cars
and small roller coasters.
She also likes parks with
themed attractions, like magic
or vampires.

3 Harper is planning to visit a
family theme park. She enjoys
arcade games, water slides
and kid-friendly roller coasters.
Harper dreams of visiting a
really popular park with lots
of visitors.

4 Joshua loves extreme water
slides and high roller coasters.
He prefers a park with not too
many people because he hates
waiting in a queue. He is also
keen on arcade games.

A **Thrill Paradise** is one of the most popular theme parks in Europe. It is full of huge fast roller coasters, tall shots and drop towers and extreme bumper cars. If you like colourful neon lights, lots of music and scary rides, you definitely have to visit Thrill Paradise. The park has a great choice of restaurants offering fast food and healthy snacks.

B **Fun Town** is an old-fashioned theme park. There is only one small roller coaster and there aren't any dangerous rides. But Fun Town is always full of people. They love the lively music from the 70s and 80s and old arcade games. People often come here to enjoy the boat rides on the lake or get the best ice-cream and milkshakes in the UK. When you feel hungry enjoy a meal in a pizza restaurant or choose an ice-cream dessert.

C **Big Island** Are you looking for some fun in a small theme park? Big Island is your best option. It isn't too crowded but there are lots of arcade games and a few great rides for those who aren't too scared. The most popular are *Swish*, an extremely fast roller coaster, and *Splash*, the only water coaster in the UK which slowly goes up and then within seconds drops you into a landing pool.

D **Ahoy, pirates!** is a place which takes you to the world of pirates. Children love the family rides such as *Pirate Roller Coaster*, *Crazy Ship Swing* or *Bumping Boats* (they work like regular bumper cars but look like small pirate boats). The park is huge and there are lots of rides so you never wait in queues.

E **Adventure spot** is a popular theme park which offers a variety of extreme rides and superfast roller coasters. This year the park opened its newest attraction *The Beast of Speed*, the longest and fastest roller coaster in the UK. The park has got a big picnic area but there aren't any restaurants so bring your own packed lunch if you want to stay for the whole day.

F **Magic World** is a great park for families with younger children but there are some attractions for teenagers too. Apart from small roller coasters, arcade games and carousels there are a few bigger rides and a water park. Last year the magazine *Adventure News* chose Magic World as the number one park in the UK with the most visitors a year.

G **Water Craze** is a family-friendly water park. There are two swimming pools and lots of water slides which are suitable for younger kids. Bigger kids enjoy spending time in a wave pool and in a fast-flowing river. Come early in the morning if you want to avoid the crowds in the summer.

4 Appearance

GRAMMAR PRACTICE

Past simple negative and questions

Complete the rules.

To make negative sentences in the past simple we use
.... and the infinitive without *to*.

In questions we use .... and the infinitive
without *to*.

➡ See **GRAMMAR REFERENCE** page 121

1 🔊 **Cross out the extra word in each sentence.**

0 I didn't understand ~~understood~~ the teacher.

1 We didn't aren't fly to Paris last week.

2 The teacher didn't explain explained the exercise.

3 Isabel wasn't didn't forget her umbrella.

4 I did didn't get any emails yesterday.

5 You didn't came come to the party.

6 Didn't it didn't take a long time.

7 They do didn't do their homework.

8 The man drive didn't drive fast.

2 🔊 **Make the sentences negative.**

0 We watched a great film.
...........*We didn't watch a great film.*...........

1 Jack ate my sandwich.
....

2 Our team won the match.
....

3 Dad asked me a lot of questions.
....

4 He left the house early in the morning.
....

5 She told us about the trip.
....

6 I bought a pair of jeans and a T-shirt.
....

7 We arrived late at the party.
....

8 The cat jumped from a tree.
....

3 🔊 **Think about the things you did last month.
What did not you do? Write eight sentences using
the negative form of the past simple.**

0 *I didn't finish reading a book.*

4 🔊 **Choose the correct option.**

0 Did you *had* / have milk for breakfast?

1 What time *did they* / *they did* get up?

2 How much *did these leggings cost* / *did cost these
leggings*?

3 Did you *sent* / *send* me an email yesterday?

4 Where *did you* / *you did* stay on your holiday?

5 Did Ella and Mark *go* / *went* skiing in January?

6 Did Mum *cook* / *cooked* pasta last week?

5 🔊 **Complete the questions and short answers in
the past simple. Use the correct form of the
verbs in brackets.**

0 '*Did you visit*... (*you / visit*) your grandparents
last weekend?' 'Yes, ...*we did*...... .'

1 '.......................... (*Ethan / wear*) a shirt and jeans
on Friday?'
'No, ...'

2 '.......................... (*you / hurt*) your foot during
the football practice?'
'Yes, ...'

3 '.......................... (*your dad / build*) this treehouse
when you were little?'
'Yes, ...'

4 '.......................... (*Jake / give*) Mrs Willis the flowers?'
'No, ...'

5 '.......................... (*they / close*) all the windows
at night?'
'No, ...'

6 🔊 **Write a question about the underlined words.**

0 We swam <u>in the ocean</u> last summer.
...........*Where did you swim last summer?*...........

1 My little sister drew <u>a picture of our family</u>.
....

2 We played chess <u>after lunch</u>.
....

3 Tim read <u>two</u> books last month.
....

4 I helped <u>my brother</u> with the project.
....

5 Jenny invited all her friends <u>to a café</u>.
....

6 My friends had lunch in the park <u>on Sunday</u>.
....

7 🔊 Complete the questions with these words. Then write short answers.

Noah / lock ▪ ~~you / eat~~ ▪ Clara / play ▪
your dad / wear ▪ Toby / go ▪ you / have ▪
Lucas and Sam / take ▪ your mum / give ▪ you / listen

0 'Did you eat all the muffins yesterday?'
'Yes, I did .'

1 '........................ their English exam yesterday?'
'Yes, ...'

2 '........................ the guitar last night?'
'No, ...'

3 '........................ you a shopping list?'
'Yes, ...'

4 '........................ to music last night?'
'No, ...'

5 '........................ dinner at 7 o'clock?'
'Yes, ...'

6 '........................ the door before he left the house?'
'Yes, ...'

7 '........................ a uniform when he was at primary school?'
'Yes, ...'

8 '........................ to school at 7:45 in the morning?'
'No, ...'

8 🔊 Rewrite the sentences using the past simple.

0 Arthur doesn't read any magazines.
Last summer Arthur didn't read any magazines .

1 Do you wear this jacket in winter?
.... last winter?

2 I don't take part in any art competitions.
Last year ....

3 Where do you buy these T-shirts?
....

4 Martha doesn't know about our summer plans.
....

5 We don't study history this semester.
.... last semester.

6 Do Lexi and Anna take a lot of photos?
.... on their holiday?

7 What time do you go to school?
.... on Monday?

8 Does Beth feel better today?
.... yesterday?

9 🔊 Complete the message using the correct form of these verbs.

go ▪ have ▪ not / buy ▪ ~~not / call~~ ▪
not / take ▪ not / want ▪ take

Hi Theo!
I'm sorry I [0] didn't call you yesterday.
My parents decided to go shopping. They
[1]........................ to hear about our plans. I wanted to
text you from the car but I [2]........................ my
phone with me. Sorry! So tell me – how was
everything yesterday? [3]........................ you
.... to the concert with Sarah?
[4]........................ you .... fun?
[5]........................ you .... some photos
with the band after the concert? Guess what?
I spent three hours in the shopping centre and
I [6]........................ anything! Not even a pair of jeans!

Talk to you later,
Julia

10 🔊 A friend of yours asks you what you did last weekend. Complete the conversation using the past simple.

Your friend What did you do at the weekend?
You I ....
....

Your friend Did ....?
You ....
Then, I ....
....
but I didn't ....
....

Your friend What ....?
You I ....
....

Your friend ....?
You No, I ....
I ....
....

Your friend ....
....?
You ....
....

READING SKILLS

11 ◢ [1.08] **Read the text and choose the correct heading for each paragraph. Then listen and check.**

1 ☐ To die for a colour
2 ☐ Colours in society
3 ☐ The first dyes
4 ☐ For girls and boys

12 Choose the correct meaning of the words highlighted in the text.

1 unsuccessful
   A not ending well
   B bring great results
2 discovery
   A an act of finding out something
   B to make experiments
3 amount
   A colour
   B quantity, number of things
4 accuse
   A explain why something happened
   B say that someone did something wrong
5 indicated
   A understood
   B showed
6 picking out
   A choosing
   B looking good
7 turned upside down
   A remained the same
   B changed completely

13 Complete the sentences with information from the text.

1 We know that people dyed fabrics in .... BCE.
2 In the past people made dyes from .... materials like plants or animals.
3 William Henry Perkin invented synthetic ....
4 People used .... to make Tyrian purple.
5 Some emperors didn't let people wear .... clothes.
6 In the times of Queen Elizabeth I .... people wore light-coloured clothes.
7 In 1918 blue was the colour for .... because people thought it was more delicate.

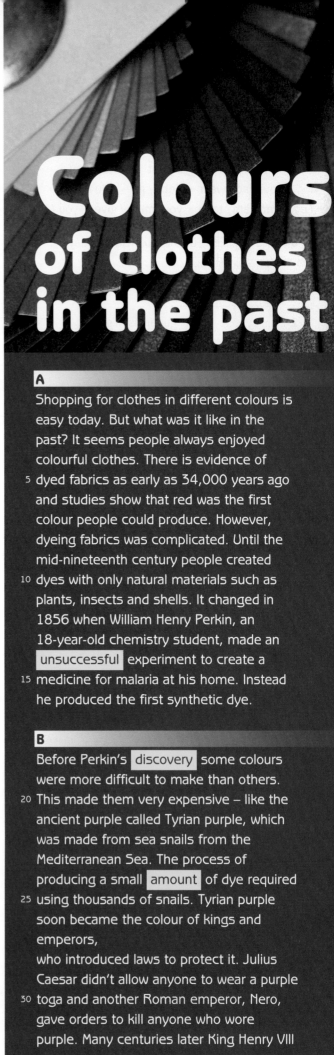

Colours of clothes in the past

A

Shopping for clothes in different colours is easy today. But what was it like in the past? It seems people always enjoyed colourful clothes. There is evidence of
5 dyed fabrics as early as 34,000 years ago and studies show that red was the first colour people could produce. However, dyeing fabrics was complicated. Until the mid-nineteenth century people created
10 dyes with only natural materials such as plants, insects and shells. It changed in 1856 when William Henry Perkin, an 18-year-old chemistry student, made an unsuccessful experiment to create a
15 medicine for malaria at his home. Instead he produced the first synthetic dye.

B

Before Perkin's discovery some colours were more difficult to make than others.
20 This made them very expensive – like the ancient purple called Tyrian purple, which was made from sea snails from the Mediterranean Sea. The process of producing a small amount of dye required
25 using thousands of snails. Tyrian purple soon became the colour of kings and emperors, who introduced laws to protect it. Julius Caesar didn't allow anyone to wear a purple
30 toga and another Roman emperor, Nero, gave orders to kill anyone who wore purple. Many centuries later King Henry VIII

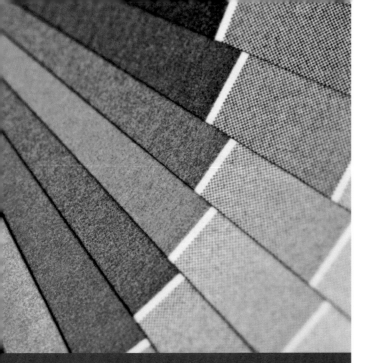

accused the Earl of Surrey, Henry
Howard, of treason. King Henry VIII
35 sentenced Henry Howard to death
and one of the arguments against him
was the fact that someone saw him
wearing purple.

C

40 Colours of clothes indicated social
position. In the times of Queen Elizabeth I
purple was still the colour of kings and
queens, while gold, silver or dark blue
were the colours of nobility. Poor people
45 usually wore lighter colours because they
were easier to make.

D

Picking out pink for girls and blue for boys
50 is quite new. For centuries white was the
colour that parents chose for their babies.
Pastel colours for children, along with pink
and blue, started to become popular in the
mid-nineteenth century. In 1918 the
55 magazine *Earnshaw's Infants' Department*
recommended blue for girls because it was
more delicate. Pink, on the other hand, was
for boys because it was stronger. In the
1940s this trend turned upside down
60 and pink became the colour for girls and
blue the colour for boys.

VOCABULARY

CLOTHES

14 Circle the odd word out in each group.

0	leggings	jeans	(T-shirt)	combats
1	jewellery	jumper	hoodie	shirt
2	trainers	lace-up shoes	tights	sandals
3	pocket	collar	button	plain
4	patterned	handbag	striped	checked
5	dress	cardigan	sweatshirt	jumper
6	sunglasses	belt	coat	tie
7	scarf	gloves	cap	shorts
8	boots	joggers	heels	trainers

15 Read the sentences and replace the incorrect words with the words from the box.

belt ▪ button ▪ checked ▪ handbag ▪ pockets ▪
scarf ▪ tights ▪ trainers ▪ T-shirt

0 On hot summer days I usually wear shorts and
gloves. **a T-shirt**
1 A plain jumper has got a lot of squares on it.
2 My mum left her tie at home. Inside there was her
phone and the money.
3 When I play basketball I always wear heels.
They are the best shoes for sports.
4 I lost one collar from my favourite jacket.
I can't find it anywhere.
5 Women usually wear joggers with a dress.
They keep their legs warm and look nice.
6 You should wear a sweatshirt around your neck on
cold days.
7 My jeans are too loose around the waist.
I need a glove.
8 My new combats have got a lot of sandals.
I don't need to carry anything in my hands anymore.

**16 Describe in detail what you are wearing.
Use words from exercises 14 and 15.**

0 It's your birthday party
**I'm wearing heels, black tights and a striped
dress. I'm also wearing some jewellery.**
1 It's the last day of school before the summer
holiday.
2 It's a snowy day in winter. You're going for a walk.
3 You're visiting your grandparents. You're having
dinner at their house.
4 You are in the gym.
5 It's April. You're meeting your friends in a café.

GRAMMAR PRACTICE

See **GRAMMAR REFERENCE** page 121

Why ...? / Because ...

Complete the rules and choose the correct options.

When we want to ask about a reason we start
a question with .... We begin the answer to
this question with .... We also use *because*
in the middle of a sentence to give a *reason / question*.

17 **Rewrite the sentences and questions using the words in brackets.**

0 Did you go back to the shop? (*why*)
......**Why did you go back to the shop?**......

1 I screamed I saw a big spider. (*because*)
....

2 'Why aren't you drinking your coffee?'
'I don't like it.' (*because*)
....

3 Liam went to bed early he was sleepy. (*because*)
....

4 'Why you walk to school today?'
'Because my bike broke down.' (*did*)
....

5 'Is she crying?' 'She's sad because she quarreled
with her best friend.' (*why*)
....

18 **Combine the sentences using *because*.**

0 I had a sandwich. I was hungry.
.....**I had a sandwich because I was hungry.**.....

1 Tim was late to school. Tim missed his bus.
....

2 Ellie had a headache. Ellie didn't go to school.
....

3 They didn't watch the film. They were tired.
....

4 Harry was happy. Harry got good marks at school.
....

5 We are watching a funny film. We are laughing.
....

6 It's cold today. I'm wearing a coat and a scarf.
....

7 My old phone broke. I need to buy a new phone.
....

8 I didn't have anything to wear. I forgot to do
the laundry.
....

19 **Answer the questions 1–5 using *because*. Then write three questions 6–8 using *why* and answer with *because*.**

0 Why did Oliver forget to buy milk?
Because he didn't write it on his shopping list.

1 Why did Henry come back at 10 o'clock on
Saturday?

2 Why didn't you check your emails in the morning?

3 Why did Leo and Katie stay at home at the weekend?

4 Why did your parents buy a new tablet?

5 Why did you call me three times yesterday?

6 ....
....

7 ....
....

8 ....
....

Expressions of past time

Choose the correct option.

In the past simple we use expressions of *finished /
unfinished* time, for example *yesterday evening*, *last
year*, *two months ago*, *in 2016*.

See **GRAMMAR REFERENCE** page 121

20 **Choose the correct option.**

0 five days (ago) / *last*

1 *last / yesterday* month

2 *in the yesterday / yesterday* afternoon

3 three years *ago / back*

4 *in / on* 2015

5 *ago / last* week

6 *in / yesterday* morning

7 *in / on* the nineteenth century

8 twenty minutes *last / ago*

21 **Correct the mistakes.**

0 ~~I don't~~ wear shorts last month. **I didn't**

1 Did people travelled a lot in the eighteenth century?

2 We went shopping last evening.

3 I told you about the party ago three days.

4 Tyler doesn't go swimming last week.

5 How long ago did you bought this handbag?

6 Did travel you to Ankara in 2016?

SPEAKING SKILLS

ASKING FOR AND GIVING OPINIONS

22 Complete the sentences with these words.

> about ▪ do ▪ does ▪ one ▪ prefer ▪
> quite ▪ sure ▪ think ▪ you

1 What do you .... of these combats?
2 Do .... like this cardigan?
3 I prefer this ....
4 .... you think this is nice?
5 I'm not ....
6 It's .... nice.
7 Do you .... a plain or checked jacket?
8 .... this suit me?
9 I like this! What .... you?

23 Rewrite the sentences. Try to be kinder using these expressions.

- It looks / seems a bit …
- It's quite …
- Do you think you need a …?
- I'm afraid it …
- You could try …
- Isn't it a bit …?
- I'm not sure about …
- I don't think …

0 This scarf is too long.
  This scarf seems a bit too long.
  ....

1 I don't like this jumper.
  ....
  ....

2 Try a smaller size.
  ....
  ....

3 It doesn't suit you.
  ....
  ....

4 This shirt is tight.
  ....
  ....

5 You don't look good in those sunglasses.
  ....
  ....

6 This tie is the wrong colour.
  ....
  ....

LISTENING SKILLS

24 What are your favourite clothes?

25 ◢ [1.09] Listen to the conversation and choose the correct photo.

1 How much did Zach pay for his trainers?

A ☐   B ☐   C ☐

2 What kind of dress does Anna want to buy?

A ☐   B ☐   C ☐

3 Where did Timmy wear his jacket last?

A ☐   B ☐   C ☐

4 Where is Grace's cardigan from?

A ☐   B ☐   C ☐

5 What are Isaac's favourite clothes?

A ☐   B ☐   C ☐

26 ◢ [1.09] Listen again and match the people to the sentences.

1 ☐ Zach   4 ☐ Grace
2 ☐ Anna   5 ☐ Isaac
3 ☐ Timmy's dad

a wants to ask a family member to do something for him / her
b has seen something he / she likes online
c is making plans for tomorrow
d knows about a shop with great prices
e is thinking of wearing something different to school

ACADEMIC SKILLS

DESCRIBING TRENDS

27 Circle the opposite meaning of the word in bold.

0 The number of children in the classroom went **up** over the last century.

(A) down **B** strong **C** high

1 They're doing everything to improve the **strong** economy in the country.

A high **B** weak **C** great

2 The prices **increased** dramatically last month.

A decreased **B** grew **C** went up

3 I've got **high** expectations for this language course.

A positive **B** big **C** low

4 The situation changed **slowly**.

A suddenly **B** slightly **C** gently

5 The sales didn't **rise** sharply at the beginning of the year.

A increase **B** fall **C** jump up

6 The wages in the factory went up **sharply** in the summer.

A quickly **B** gradually **C** fast

28 The graph below represents the opinions of consumers about online purchases they made from 2005–2015. Look at the chart and correct the bold numbers in the text.

29 The graph below shows what influenced young people when buying clothes from 1990 to 2015. Describe the graph. Use the sentences in exercise 27 and the text in exercise 28 as a model.

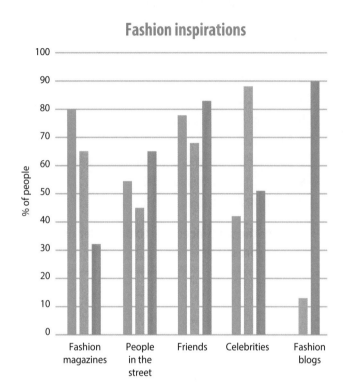

Fashion inspirations

■ 1990 ■ 2005 ■ 2015

THE SHOPPING EXPERIENCE

The bar chart compares how people felt about online shopping from [0] ~~2000~~ *2005* to 2015. In general, the chart indicates that the experience of shopping for clothes online improved over the period shown.

In detail, in 2005 only [1] **35%** .... of shoppers believed that finding clothes online was easy. However, the convenience of finding the desired item of clothing online increased to [2] **85%** .... in 2010 and then it went up sharply reaching 85% in [3] **2005** .... The figures for finding the right size remained fairly stable in the years 2005 and 2015. It rose slowly but these weren't significant changes. [4] **54%** .... of shoppers had no problem in finding the right size in 2005 and this number increased gradually to [5] **89%** .... in 2015. Over the same period of time, finding good prices for clothes online rose sharply from [6] **4%** .... in 2005 to 89% in [7] **2005** .... Similarly, offers of free delivery went up dramatically from 5% in 2005 to [8] **25%** .... in 2015.

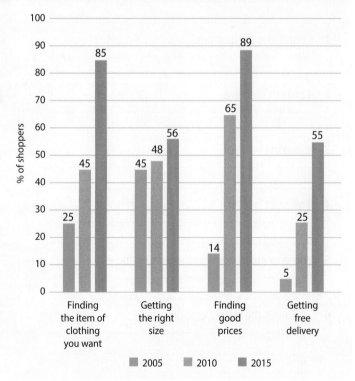

■ 2005 ■ 2010 ■ 2015

Listening – Multiple choice

In multiple choice listening activities, you will hear a longer text which can be a monologue or an interview. Before you start listening, read the questions and all three possible answers. Think about the context of the listening. During the listening, concentrate on the details, usually all the options are mentioned, so listen carefully to what the speakers say about each one.

30 ◤ **[1.10]** **Listen to a girl named Lucy who talks about her blog. What does she write about?**

1 her school life **2** fashion **3** books she reads

31 ◤ **[1.10]** **Listen to Lucy again and choose the correct option.**

0 Lucy decided to start blogging:
(A) two years ago.
B every day.
C before her friends started blogging.

1 In her diary Lucy:
A wrote about her school life.
B shared her opinions about fashion.
C wrote about her hobbies.

2 Lucy's friends from school:
A had blogs before Lucy had hers.
B started blogging at the same time as Lucy.
C started blogging after they read Lucy's blog.

3 Lucy chose the topic of her blog after talking to:
A her friends.
B her English teacher.
C her mum.

4 At the beginning the only people / person who knew about Lucy's blog was / were:
A Lucy.
B her friends.
C her mum.

5 Lucy's English teacher:
A helps her to choose books.
B says what she thinks about Lucy's book reviews.
C doesn't know about the blog.

32  **[1.11]** **You are going to listen to an interview with Oscar, a boy who won a photography competition. For each question, choose the correct option A, B or C.**

0 Oscar's photo won first place in which category?
A School.
B People.
(C) Sports.

1 Oscar thinks he won first place because:
A the rain and clouds make the photo look amazing.
B the photo shows a disappointed player at the moment when he didn't score a goal.
C the photo shows how the school team scored a goal.

2 Oscar:
A can't say which photo was his favourite.
B liked the photo of a boy playing rugby the most.
C thinks the picture of marathon runners is his favourite.

3 Oscar's dad kept all the photos which Oscar took when he was:
A five years old.
B seven years old.
C nine years old.

4 Why didn't Oscar attend photography classes?
A He wanted to learn on his own.
B His parents didn't have money for a course.
C There were no classes for him.

5 What are Oscar's plans for the future?
A He doesn't want to take photos in the future.
B He wants to take part in another photo competition.
C He wants to think about other possibilities.

6 What does Oscar say about winning the competition?
A It helps him take more photos.
B It helps him in everything he does.
C It helps him in other competitions.

REVISE AND ROUND UP

1 🔊 **Write sentences or questions using the past simple form of the verb *be*.**

0 they / tired / yesterday evening
   ....**They were tired yesterday evening.**...........

1 Ruby and Mille / not / in the park / yesterday
   ....

2 I / excited / about the weekend
   ....

3 you / pleased / with the exam results?
   ....

4 they / on holiday / last month
   ....

5 William / in the cinema / on Monday?
   ....

6 our teacher / not / in a good mood
   ....

2 🔊 **Write the verbs in the past simple.**

0 swim   ....**swam**........

1 break   ....   **6** eat   ....
2 read   ....   **7** win   ....
3 teach   ....   **8** make   ....
4 drink   ....   **9** stand   ....
5 think   ....   **10** fall   ....

3 🔊 **Complete the sentences with the past simple form of the verbs in brackets.**

0 Jayce ......**arrived**...... (*arrive*) late at the bus stop.
1 Stephanie .... (*study*) a lot before the test.
2 He .... (*reply*) to my email immediately.
3 The teacher .... (*like*) my essay.
4 Albert .... (*drop*) a glass with orange juice.
5 I .... (*try*) to take a lot of photos.
6 We .... (*enjoy*) our holiday in Venice.

4 🔊 **Complete the sentences. Write about things you didn't do.**

0 Yesterday ......**I didn't wear jeans to school**...... .
1 Last week ....
2 In 2011 ....
3 One hour ago ....
4 At the weekend ....
5 On Tuesday ....
6 Last winter ....

5 🔊 **Change these sentences into questions. Then write a short answer.**

0 I had a great day. (+)
   'Did you have a great day?' 'Yes, I did.'
1 They played video games on Sunday. (+)
2 Jessica came back at 10 o'clock. (–)
3 My neighbours bought a new car. (–)
4 That man stole my wallet. (+)
5 The dog caught the ball. (+)
6 I paid £10 for my leggings. (–)

6 🔊 **Complete the sentences about you.**

0 .....**I forgot to call my best friend**..... yesterday.
1 .... 2015.
2 .... last week.
3 .... yesterday afternoon.
4 .... the past.
5 .... last summer.
6 .... two hours ago.
7 .... last year.
8 .... ten years ago.

7 🔊 **Rewrite the sentences using the words in bold.**

0 She got up early on Sunday morning. She had a flight to Paris at 9 o'clock.   **why** ▪ **because**
   'Why did she get up early on Sunday morning?'
   'Because she had a flight to Paris at 9 o'clock.'
1 My parents couldn't help me. They weren't at home.   **because**
   ....
2 Olivia bought some cheese and tomatoes. Olivia wants to make pizza.   **why** ▪ **because**
   ....
   ....
3 Dylan didn't go to his friend's house on Sunday. Dylan's friend didn't invite him.   **because**
   ....
4 I did all my homework. I didn't want to get a bad mark.   **because**
   ....
5 They got lost. They didn't have a map   **why** ▪ **because**
   ....
   ....

8 🔊 Choose the correct options to complete the text.

Last year I **0**............ my own style. **1**............ about it? Not even for one minute! Clothes **2**............ my thing. I **3**............ whatever T-shirt or hoodie I **4**............ in my wardrobe.

But my best friend Ava **5**............ happy about it. In fact she **6**............ worried about me. For my 16th birthday Ava **7**............ me an unusual present – a session with a fashion stylist, Jacob. He **8**............ shopping with me and **9**............ me what to wear. **10**............ helpful? Definitely! My friends say I look great now and this is exactly how I feel. Thank you, Ava and Jacob!

0	**(A)** didn't have	**B** don't have	**C** weren't have
1	**A** Was I think	**B** Did I thought	**C** Did I think
2	**A** weren't	**B** didn't be	**C** wasn't
3	**A** weared	**B** wore	**C** did wear
4	**A** found	**B** finded	**C** find
5	**A** weren't	**B** wasn't	**C** didn't be
6	**A** was	**B** were	**C** did
7	**A** did give	**B** gived	**C** gave
8	**A** went	**B** wented	**C** goed
9	**A** telled	**B** told	**C** didn't told
10	**A** Did it be	**B** Did it was	**C** Was it

9 🔊 Correct the mistakes.

0 I ~~taked~~ my dog for a walk yesterday.
.......**I took my dog for a walk yesterday.**.......

1 Was your teacher talk to you yesterday?
....

2 We weren't at home afternoon yesterday.
....

3 Ethan didn't at school last week.
....

4 Why did you bought another striped T-shirt?
....

5 Cynthia did watch a great film on TV yesterday.
....

6 I tidyed up my room twenty minutes ago.
....

7 I was late for school why I missed the bus.
....

8 Where bought people clothes in the 1970s?
....

CONCEPT CHECK

Read the sentences and answer the questions.

1 *I was busy last Sunday.*

(Answer Yes / No / Your own words)

0 Is this an action in the present, future or in the past? **Past**

1 Do you know when it happened?

2 Can you replace *last Sunday* with *now*?

3 Can you replace *busy* with *in the cinema*?

4 Can you add *not* to this sentence? If so, where?

5 Can you replace *I* with *we*?

2 *We went to London on Monday.*

(Answer Yes / No / Your own words)

0 Is this an action in the present, future or in the past? **Past**

1 Do you know when it happened?

2 Can you replace *on Monday* with *at the moment*?

3 Can you add *not* to this sentence? If so, where?

4 Can you replace *we* with *she*?

3 *I bought a pair of jeans yesterday.*

(Answer Yes / No / Your own words)

0 Does the word *yesterday* show an action in the present, future or in the past? **Past**

1 Can you put *last* in front of *yesterday*?

2 Do you know when it happened?

3 Can you replace *yesterday* with *two days ago* or *last month*?

4 *'Why did she stay at home?' 'Because she had a lot of homework.'*

(Answer Yes / No / Your own words)

0 Do you use *why* to ask about the reason or the opinion? **Reason**

1 Can you use questions with *why* only in the past?

2 Do you use *because* in answers or in questions?

3 Does the sentence with *because* explain what happened?

See **GRAMMAR REFERENCE** pages 120-121

5 Work

GRAMMAR PRACTICE

be going to for predictions and intentions

Choose the correct options.

We use *be going to* to talk about *past / future* plans or to talk about intentions and make predictions when we *have / don't have* present evidence.

→ See **GRAMMAR REFERENCE** page 121

1 **Complete the sentences with *be going to* and the verbs in brackets.**

0 My friends **are going to have** (*have*) a barbecue on Sunday.

1 Be careful! You .... (*spill*) the juice.

2 I .... (*work out*) regularly this year.

3 Chloe .... (*cook*) for her family tonight.

4 We've got a lot of work. It .... (*be*) a long day.

5 My neighbours .... (*move out*) next month.

6 We .... (*do*) a challenge for a charity on our web channel.

7 Jason .... (*drink*) a healthy smoothie every day next week.

8 Our town .... (*build*) a new skatepark next year.

2 **Use *be going to* and the words in brackets to write negative sentences.**

0 Olivia hasn't got any flour. (*she / bake a cake*)
She isn't going to bake a cake.

1 It's too windy today. (*you / play badminton*)

2 We want to stay at home tonight. (*we / go / to the party*)

3 You don't need a hat and gloves today. (*it / snow*)

4 Dylan's got a job at the ice-cream shop in the summer. (*he / work / at the café*)

5 I failed two tests last month. (*I / finish / the Spanish course / in June*)

6 Liz doesn't like maths. (*she / be / an accountant*)

7 I haven't got any money. (*I / buy / any clothes / this month*)

8 My parents are busy. (*they / come / to the meeting*)

3 **Add a missing word to each question.**

0 What **are** you going to do at the weekend?

1 When is he going take some time off?

2 Is Ethan to tidy up his bedroom?

3 Are you going to your homework at the weekend?

4 'Are they going to take part in the competition?' 'Yes, they.'

5 Is going to be a warm day today?

6 How long you going to stay at your aunt's in Cambridge?

4 **Why is *be going to* used in these sentences and questions? Choose A or B.**

0 We're going to visit New York this summer.
A prediction   (B) intention

1 The road is very icy. Alice is going to fall down.
A prediction   B intention

2 I'm not going to eat any fast food this month.
A prediction   B intention

3 The wind is very strong. I'm going to lose my hat.
A prediction   B intention

4 He doesn't look when he crosses the street. The car is going to hit him.
A prediction   B intention

5 Are you going to go bowling on Friday?
A prediction   B intention

6 Look at the electricity bill. We aren't going to save any money this month.
A prediction   B intention

5 **Use the prompts to write sentences describing what each person is going to do.**

0 We're hungry. *order / a pizza*
We're going to order a pizza.

1 Tina's tired. *have / a relaxing bath*

2 Henry's dad works in a restaurant but Henry *not / be a waiter*

3 We go jogging every day. *take part / in a marathon / in the autumn*

4 I love taking photos. *be a photographer / when I grow up*

5 They love Asia. *visit China / next year*

6 The school is collecting books and gift cards for the lottery. *you / bring?*

6 📶 Write three things you are going to do or not going to do for each situation.

0 It's a sunny day.
  I'm *going to* walk to school. I'm *not going to* take an umbrella. I'm *going to* wear sunglasses.

1 You and your friend are going to have a party at your house this weekend.

2 Your laptop broke down last night.

3 Your mum is taking you shopping on Friday.

4 Your best friend is turning sixteen next week.

7 📶 Complete the predictions using *be going to* and these verbs.

be fit ▪ be sunburnt ▪ get angry ▪ get a ticket ▪ get wet ▪ miss the bus ▪ not finish a school project

0 I spilt coffee on the sofa in the morning.
  Mum .... **is going to get angry** ....

1 I spent the morning on the beach but I forgot to use sunscreen.
  I ....

2 Ben didn't hear the alarm clock and woke up twenty minutes late.
  He ....

3 Dad left his newspaper in the garden. It started to rain ten minutes ago.
  The newspaper ....

4 Erin always does her homework online. There's no internet connection today.
  She ....

5 My uncle is driving too fast. The police are following his car.
  He ....

6 We go to the gym every day.
  We ....

8 📶 Write what you think is going to happen.

0 Sally hasn't got a swimsuit and she's going on holiday next week.
  Sally is going to buy a swimsuit.

1 There are dark clouds in the sky.

2 Mike spent the whole weekend studying. He thinks the test was easy.

3 I'm not feeling well.

4 My mum's car broke down. She can't use it to go to work this week.

5 This is my first skiing lesson.

6 It's cold outside. I can't wear a T-shirt.

9 📶 Rewrite the sentences using *be going to*.

0 We plan to spend a weekend in the mountains.
  We're going to spend a weekend in the mountains.

1 Alex wants to make a tomato salad tonight.
  ....

2 Don't worry, Mum. We can call you when we get there.
  ....

3 I forgot to finish my science project yesterday. I know that I can get a bad mark.
  ....

4 He doesn't plan to play football tonight.
  ....

5 Look at all these cars in the car park! This means there are a lot of people in the shops.
  ....

6 It's my plan to go to bed before midnight every day this school year.
  ....

10 📶 Complete the conversation between the girls. Use *be going to* and the verbs in brackets.

Lauren I hate packing! I always take the wrong clothes with me.

Aisha I can help you. **⁰ We're going to prepare** (*we / prepare*) clothes for each day of your stay in London.

Lauren That sounds great.

Aisha What ¹ .... (*you / do*) on the first day?

Lauren ² .... (*we / visit*) a few museums.

Aisha ³ .... (*you / spend*) a lot of time outside?

Lauren No, ⁴ .... (*we / not / be*)! The bus ⁵ .... (*take*) us everywhere.

Aisha Perfect! ⁶ .... (*you / not / need*) any warm clothes then. Why don't you take a light jacket, jeans and a shirt?

Lauren Good idea.

Aisha What about shoes?

Lauren ⁷ .... (*I / wear*) my blue trainers.

Aisha No, ⁸ .... (*you / not / wear*) those! They're old and ugly. How about your new black shoes?

Lauren OK! Day one is ready. What about the next day?

READING SKILLS

11 ⏵ [1.12] **Read and listen to the text and choose the sentence that summarises it best.**

1 The article shows what kind of people companies are going to employ in the future.
2 The article presents skills which people aren't going to need at work.
3 The article explains what to do at a future job interview.

12 Read the text again and decide who each sentence is about: Oliver, Amanda or Mark.

1 .... works in an IT company.
2 .... met and talked to people who wanted to work for his / her company.
3 .... believes that the most important thing is when a person wants to work and enjoys it.
4 .... doesn't think that the best education guarantees the best jobs.
5 .... is going to employ a person who other people are going to like and trust.
6 .... is looking for a person who other employees are going to follow when he / she introduces changes in the company.
7 .... is going to have a new employee who understands other people's problems and can communicate with them easily.

13 Read the text again and complete the gaps.

Where do they work?

Oliver ¹...

Amanda ²...

Mark ³...

What does their company do?

Oliver ⁴...

Amanda ⁵...

Mark ⁶...

What kind of employee are they looking for?

Oliver ⁷...

Amanda ⁸...

Mark ⁹...

FUTURE JOB SKILLS

Are you going to have a great career and earn a big salary? Read about who the employers in companies around the world are going to hire this year.

Oliver, Silicon Valley, California – I run a
5 company which develops new apps. This year we're going to employ people who are creative and able to think critically. There are so many new digital products and we need people who can think in a fresh new way and choose which projects are going to succeed.
10 In fact, I don't really care if my future employee has got a university degree or not but I hope to find a person with passion and lots of motivation.

Amanda, London – I work for an online fitness magazine. We are a small team of 15 people but this
15 month we're going to have two new people joining us. They are a perfect addition to our company. Why? They love sport and are very professional. They have excellent communication skills and can connect with our customers. We need these people to run our social
20 media websites so they need to be trustworthy, friendly, understanding and creative.

Mark, Munich – My company produces parts for cars. The engineers who work for us have got the necessary qualifications and usually have years of
25 experience. However, now we're looking for people who can be great team leaders. Our company is going to go through some changes this year. We want it to be more modern and efficient. Not everyone in our company thinks this is a good idea, so we need a great
30 team leader who other employees are going to listen to and respect. I spent weeks at interviews with potential candidates. It wasn't easy to find a person who is flexible, open to new ideas and able to solve conflicts between people.

35 Oliver, Amanda and Mark are just a few of many employers who think soft skills (skills that allow you to interact with other people easily) are as important as or even more important than professional qualifications. So when you think about a well-paid job in the future
40 make sure you develop these skills as well.

VOCABULARY

JOBS AND WORK

14 Correct the incorrect job names.

0 A lawyer works with animals at the farm. **farmer**
1 A plumber repairs cars.
2 A shop assistant designs computer programmes.
3 An engineer helps sick people.
4 A hairdresser checks and counts the money in a company.
5 A waiter works on a construction site.
6 A police officer serves food in a restaurant.
7 A cook catches criminals.
8 A fashion designer answers the phone and arranges meetings in an office.

15 Choose the correct option. Then decide if it is a positive (P) or a negative (N) experience.

0 ....P...... Maria (got) / *gave* a pay rise.
1 .... Jack arrived late at work every day so after two months he lost his *work* / *job*.
2 .... Tanya *earned* / *got* a job in a big company last week.
3 .... Our neighbours' son is *employer* / *unemployed* at the moment.
4 .... In April I earned my first *salary* / *shifts*.
5 .... Cathy worked hard and got a *sack* / *promotion*.
6 .... Sarah is an experienced *degree* / *employee* and she's got a *well* / *good*-paid job.
7 .... Tim surfed the internet all day at work. When his boss found out he got *overtime* / *the sack*.

16 What is your ideal career and what are the main skills you need for it? Describe them using the expressions from exercise 15 and your own ideas.

....
....
....
....
....
....
....
....
....
....
....

GRAMMAR PRACTICE

Expressions of future time

Complete the rule.

When we talk about the future we often use expressions of future time. They usually go at the .... or at the .... of sentences.

➡ See **GRAMMAR REFERENCE** page 121

17 **Choose the correct option.**

0 *Future* / (*Next*) month my parents are going to take some time off.

1 *At* / *In* the next few weeks we're going to read Shakespeare's plays.

2 My dad is going to come back home *in* / *by* twenty minutes.

3 He isn't going to get the sack *this* / *in this* year.

4 I'm going to be a top manager *by* / *on* 2030.

5 We aren't going to take a test the day *after* / *past* tomorrow.

6 I'm going to work as a software designer *in the future* / *in future*.

7 Our company is going to change a lot in the next *a few* / *few* years.

8 We're going to have lunch later *on* / *after*.

18 🔊 **Use these time expressions to write about what you're going to do in the future.**

> ~~next week~~ ▪ tomorrow ▪ tomorrow evening ▪
> the day after tomorrow ▪ in the next few days ▪
> in an hour ▪ next year

0 ....I'm going to go shopping next week..........

1 ....

2 ....

3 ....

4 ....

5 ....

6 ....

Present tenses for the future

Choose the correct option.

We sometimes use present tenses to talk about the future. We use present *simple* / *continuous* to talk about future official events and timetables. We use present *simple* / *continuous* to talk about planned future arrangements.

➡ See **GRAMMAR REFERENCE** page 122

19 🔊 **Complete the sentences using the present simple and the verbs in brackets.**

0 The film ....**starts**........ (*start*) at 6:30 at the Odeon Cinema.

1 What time .... (*the meeting* / *begin*)?

2 Grandma's plane .... (*arrive*) tomorrow evening.

3 What day .... (*the festival* / *start*)?

4 The next train to London .... (*leave*) at 6:10 from platform 5.

5 The workshop .... (*take place*) on Wednesday afternoon.

6 When .... (*the summer holiday* / *end*)?

20 🔊 **Look at Mark's diary. Write a few sentences about his plans using the present continuous.**

Mark is going to the dentist on Monday.

Monday, 10th June dentist	**Friday,** 14th June barbecue at Jill and James' house
Tuesday, 11th June dinner in the Green Plate restaurant	**Saturday,** 15th June Sue and Tom – get married, 11 am
Wednesday, 12th June job interview, Barclays Bank, 9 am	**Sunday,** 16th June trip to Southampton
Thursday, 13th June 6 pm – Amy and Rachel, Sun Café	**Notes** next week, 23:06 – flight to Stockholm July – a weekend in the mountains

21 🔊 **Choose the correct option.**

0 The show .... at 6 pm.
   A start   **B** starts   **C** is starting

1 We .... a lunch break at school at 12:30 pm.
   A have   **B** having   **C** are having

2 My aunt and uncle .... to visit us tonight.
   A come   **B** are coming   **C** is coming

3 Frank .... to Liverpool on Tuesday.
   A driving   **B** drives   **C** is driving

4 What day .... the art exhibition .... ?
   A will … opening   **B** do … open   **C** does … open

5 .... you .... with Daniel in the next few days?
   A Do … meet   **B** Are … meeting   **C** Is … meeting

SPEAKING SKILLS

TALKING ABOUT INTENTIONS

22 Choose the correct option.

1 **A** Sarah's not coming tonight!
   B You*'re* / *'ve* joking!

2 **A** Jessie got her first job last week.
   B *No / Not* way! That's *joking / incredible*.

3 **A** I'm going to read all Agatha Christie's books this week!
   B *Really / Real*? I don't *joke / believe* you.

4 **A** I'm not going to eat any chocolate this week.
   B *Because / If* you say so …

5 **A** I met Beyoncé at the airport yesterday.
   B Yeah, *true / right*!

6 **A** Jimmy is taking us to the amusement park tomorrow.
   B Wow! That's *amazing / amazed*!

7 **A** I'm going to get a new laptop for my birthday.
   B Oh, *yeah / so*?

23 Complete the conversation with these words.

> are you ▪ going to ▪ going to work ▪ I'm ▪ joking ▪
> really ▪ to ▪ way ▪ yeah

Aiden Guess what? I'm ¹......................... at the Art Museum.

Natasha ²......................... ? That's incredible.

Aiden I know! ³......................... going to work there every Tuesday and Thursday after school.

Natasha Oh, ⁴......................... ? What ⁵......................... going to do there?

Aiden I'm going to work in the Modern Art Hall. I'm ⁶......................... guide the visitors and answer their questions.

Natasha No ⁷......................... ! You're ⁸......................... ! This is your dream job. How much are you going to earn?

Aiden Well, it's a volunteer job but I think that I can show them how good at art I am and later they're going ⁹......................... employ me part-time.

Natasha Let's hope so! Good luck.

LISTENING SKILLS

24 Which part-time job you would most like to do? Order the jobs from 1 (the best) to 8 (the worst).

- ☐ shop assistant
- ☐ waiter
- ☐ actor
- ☐ helping at the library
- ☐ helping at the animal shelter
- ☐ babysitter
- ☐ sports camp instructor
- ☐ fashion model

25 [1.13] Listen to the conversation and answer the questions.

1 Who is Ellie calling?
2 Where is Ellie?
3 Why is Ellie calling Tom?
4 How does Tom feel about the idea?
5 Who is going to fill in the form for Tom?
6 When is the deadline for filling in the form?
7 When is Tom going to ask his parents?

26 [1.13] Listen again and complete the text.

Would you like to work as a model for ¹......................... shops?

Fill in the application and wait for our phone call. We're going to invite 100 people to a photo shoot with ²......................... Caine in London on 9th ³......................... at 6 pm. Top 25 models to come on a shop tour around the UK. Visit our shops in London, ⁴......................... , Manchester and many other places!

WE'RE WAITING FOR YOU!

Name: _Tom_ ⁵......................... Male ☑ Female ☐
Date of birth: ⁶......................... Height: ⁷.........................
Eye colour: ⁸......................... Hair colour: _brown_
Contact: _07700 900173_ ⁹☐ email ☐ call ☐ text

EXAM SKILLS

EXAM STRATEGY

Reading – Gapped text

Read the text first, then look at the sentences.
Remember there are eight sentences but only five gaps, so you won't need three of the sentences.
Look for a sentence that contains similar information to the paragraph. Read the sentences before and after the first gap and choose the sentence that best fits.
Then read again to check it sounds right.

27 **Choose the sentence (A or B) which means the same as the first sentence.**

  0 Most people visit London in the summer.
  A There aren't many tourists in London in the summer.
  (B) There are more tourists in London in the summer than in the winter.

  1 There's going to be an increase in people looking for jobs in the services sector.
  A More people are going to apply for jobs in services.
  B The services sector is going to need more employees.

  2 People enjoy music festivals in the open air.
  A People are into listening to music during outdoor festivals.
  B People can't stand outdoor music festivals.

28 **Complete the gaps 1–5 with sentences a–h.**

  a As a result, not only big cities like Atlanta joined the movement.
  b However, some people don't enjoy it.
  c What is my favourite part?
  d It's strange to see the city without cars in the streets.
  e There's not a single car in sight.
  f Atlanta Streets Alive is a popular event.
  g Open Streets started in Bogotá, Colombia.
  h The first Open Streets event in Atlanta took place on 23rd May 2010 and attracted 3,000 people.

EXPLORE THE CAR-FREE STREETS
by *Tamara Crandall*

10th June, 2018. It's a sunny day in Atlanta, Georgia. My parents, my brother and I are riding our bikes along Peachtree Street in downtown Atlanta, my hometown. Next to us there are
5 hundreds of other cyclists, some people are roller-skating, some are walking, and others are skateboarding. [1]............. This is my favourite city event. It's called Atlanta Streets Alive.

Atlanta Streets Alive is a part of a bigger project
10 called Open Streets which aims at giving people car-free access to streets which they can use to ride bikes, walk, run or play games. It promotes a healthy lifestyle but it also builds local communities, showing people how to spend
15 their time outdoors. [2]............ Today, only eight years later, around 370,000 people come to enjoy the traffic-free streets of Atlanta.

Currently more than one hundred American cities are involved in the Open Streets
20 movement. However, every year there are new cities and towns in the USA and around the world which decide to join the project.

[3]............ In 1974 Jaime Ortiz Mariño organised the first Ciclovía, which means bikeway in
25 Spanish. Despite the increasing popularity

of Open Streets in the United States, Bogotá remains the leader of the movement. These days the Colombian capital closes its streets regularly every Sunday from 7 am to 2 pm
30 when over 1.5 million people gather to have fun in its streets.

An important aspect of the Open Streets project is its promoting a healthy lifestyle in local communities. ⁴............. Cornwall, New York,
35 with a population of 12,307, and Simcoe, Ontario, with a population of 14,422, are the smallest towns which decided to organise Open Streets. At the moment about 28% of cities with Open Streets movements have a population
40 of less than 100,000.

What can you expect to see when you come to Atlanta Streets Alive or other Open Streets events? Apart from meeting other bikers, skateboarders, roller-skaters and walkers you can
45 usually take part in free yoga, dance or fitness classes. You can ask someone to repair your bike at a bike repair shop. You can lie down on a pop-up lawn, drink an iced tea and read a book. ⁵............. It's really hard to say but
50 probably the gigantic board games and large playgrounds both for children and adults.

29 **Read the exam questions and complete the notes with your own ideas.**

1 Your English teacher has asked you to write a story. The title for your story is: *A long journey*.

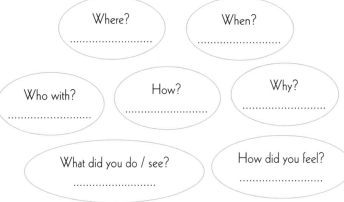

Where? .... When? ....
Who with? .... How? .... Why? ....
What did you do / see? .... How did you feel? ....

2 Your English teacher has asked you to write a story. The story must begin with this sentence:
I opened the box and couldn't believe what was in it.

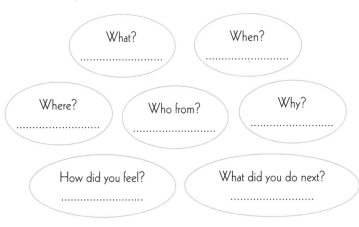

What? .... When? ....
Where? .... Who from? .... Why? ....
How did you feel? .... What did you do next? ....

30 **Choose one of the ideas from exercise 29 and write the story.**

- Use linkers to join sentences.
- Write a short conclusion.
- Write about 100 words.

6 Health

GRAMMAR PRACTICE

will / won't

Choose the correct options.

We use *will* and *won't* to talk about the *past* / *future*.
We use *will* and *won't* to talk about *planned* / *spontaneous* decisions made at the time of speaking, offers, *promises* / *intentions* and predictions based on what we *think* / *see*.
We use *will* with the *-ing* / *infinitive* form of the verb for positive sentences and *negatives* / *questions*. We use *won't* with the *-ing* / *infinitive* form of the verb for *negatives* / *questions*.

➡ See **GRAMMAR REFERENCE** page 122

1 **Write sentences using *will*.**

0   I / explain / it / to you
    I will *explain it to you*.
1   My parents / arrive / soon
2   I / call / you / tomorrow
3   He / wait / for us
4   We / ask / Jack / about it / later
5   Emily / show / you / the pictures
6   My cousin / lend / us / some money
7   I'm sure / you / enjoy / our trip to Paris
8   This medicine / help / you / with your throat infection

2 **Complete the sentences with *won't* and the verbs in brackets.**

0   They ..**won't have**... (*have*) dinner at the restaurant tonight.
1   Your secret is safe with me. I .... (*tell*) anyone.
2   The Zika epidemic .... (*spread*) all over the world.
3   I'm sorry but Hannah .... (*remember*). She forgets everything at the moment.
4   The supermarket closes at 6 pm today. We .... (*have*) time to do the grocery shopping.
5   Don't worry! I .... (*forget*) to turn off the lights at night.
6   The doctor .... (*prescribe*) you these pills. They are too strong.

3 **Cross out the extra word in each sentence.**

0   What time d̶o̶ will he come back home?
1   Will carry you carry these boxes for me?
2   What will they will have for breakfast?
3   When Megan will Megan open her presents?
4   How old will your dad be is next year?
5   Will email Mrs Smith email our parents?
6   You will you pass me the butter, please?

4 **Write affirmative (+) or negative (–) short answers.**

0   Will Tom bring your book? (+) **Yes, he will.**
1   Will you lend me £5? (+)
2   Will your mum pick you up? (–)
3   Will you help me? (+)
4   Will your brother take us to the concert? (+)

5 **Complete the sentences with *will* / *won't* and these verbs.**

answer ▪ a̶s̶k̶ ▪ brush ▪ make ▪ not / like ▪ pay ▪ win

0   'Has George got any extra tickets for the football match?' 'I don't know. I **'ll ask**............. him.'
1   I .... my teeth and then I'll be ready!
2   'Mum, I'm so hungry!' 'Dad .... you a sandwich in a minute.'
3   Your phone is ringing. .... you .... it?
4   I'm sure Becky .... the poetry competition. Her poems are very good.
5   He .... the exhibition. He prefers modern art.
6   Put your wallet away. I .... for the coffee.

6 **Write sentences and questions using the prompts and *will*.**

0   Go to bed. it / make / you / feel better
    It will make you feel better.
1   Let's go! we / call / Mark / later
2   where / you / go / after school?
3   I / not think / they / sell / their car
4   I / sure / she / pass / her exams
5   you / look / great / in these jeans
6   you / make / me / a cup of tea?

will / be going to for predictions

Complete the rules.

To make predictions about the future we use *be going to* and *will*. We use .... for a prediction based on a present fact. We use .... for a prediction based on an opinion.

➡ See **GRAMMAR REFERENCE** page 122

7 🔊 **Choose the correct option.**

0 So many years of research and there is no cure for cancer.
   A I think scientists are going to find one soon.
   (B) I think scientists will find one soon.

1 'Tom sings beautifully.'
   A 'Yes, he does. I'm sure he's going to be famous one day.'
   B 'Yes, he does. I'm sure he'll be famous one day.'

2 'Look at our team today! This is their best match ever.'
   A 'Yes, they're playing well. The score is 8–1, they're going to win!'
   B 'Yes, they're playing well. The score is 8–1, they will win!'

3 Look at his face, he's completely white.
   A He's going to be sick.
   B He will be sick.

4 'This is the funniest TV show ever.'
   A 'I agree! I think Luke will like it too.'
   B 'I agree! I think Luke is going to like it too.'

8 🔊 **Complete the sentences with the correct form of *be going to* or *will / won't*.**

0 I'm sure we ....**will**......... be friends forever.

1 'I can't find my credit card.' 'Don't worry. I .... call the bank.'

2 My sister .... have a baby next week.

3 You are still eating breakfast and the bus leaves in a minute. You .... catch it.

4 I .... open the windows. It's hot in here.

5 This was the last time. It .... happen again, I promise!

6 'Oh no! I can't be late for school again.' 'It's OK. Josh .... give you a lift.'

7 You're driving too fast! We .... have an accident.

8 'Do you want a glass of orange or apple juice?' 'I .... have orange juice, please.'

9 🔊 **Complete the text messages *be going to* or *will* and the verbs in brackets.**

0 Can you bring me my book to school tomorrow?

   Of course! I promise I **won't forget** (*not / forget*).

1 I lost my phone yesterday. I need to tell my dad.

   Oh no! He .... (*not / be*) happy.

2 There's so much snow!

   Yes! They .... (*close*) the school!

3 There's no milk at home.

   OK, I .... (*buy*) a carton on my way back from school.

4 We're on our way to the airport! See you in two weeks!

   Enjoy Majorca! I'm sure you .... (*have*) great time!

5 I've got important news but I need to tell you in person. Are you free?

   Yes, I .... (*be*) at your house in 20 minutes.

6 Another beautiful day! But still no rain! The flowers in the garden .... (*die*). Can you water them?

   Sure!

10 🔊 **Complete the predictions using *be going to* or *will*.**

0 In 2040 people ......**will travel to the moon**...... .

1 Look at the sky! It ....

2 I think in ten years there .... in our school.

3 She looks tired. She ....

4 I suppose that in the next episode the main character ....

5 Good luck on your first day at the new school. I'm sure you ....

6 Watch out! This boy can't ride a bike. He ....

7 I expect my parents ....

8 In 2030 nobody ....

READING SKILLS

11 ◢ [1.14] **Look at the title of the text and the photos. What do you think the text will be about? Tick (✓) the sentences you agree with. Then read and listen to check if you were right.**

This text will be about …

- ☐ the problems that doctors have in their work.
- ☐ how doctors' work will change in the future.
- ☐ modern technologies which will help doctors and patients.
- ☐ how future students of medicine will study at university.
- ☐ the dangers that modern technologies can cause to our health.
- ☐ the research that the scientists are doing to improve patients' treatment.

12 Read the text again and match the photos A–C with paragraphs 1–3.

13 Read the text again and decide if the sentences are true (T) or false (F). Correct the false ones.

1 The predictions in the article come from current research. ☐T ☐F

2 There are hospitals which are using Watson Health. ☐T ☐F

3 Watson Health recognises the patient's symptoms from a picture. ☐T ☐F

4 Watson Health looks for information about the patient's illness in different medical documents. ☐T ☐F

5 It takes Watson Health a lot of time to check all the information sources. ☐T ☐F

6 Wearable sensors will know how we feel 24 hours a day. ☐T ☐F

7 Although the patient needs immediate help sensors can't call a doctor. ☐T ☐F

8 Pills with sensors will show doctors when patients take their medicine. ☐T ☐F

9 Sensors in the patient's teeth will show how well he / she sleeps at night. ☐T ☐F

14 Choose the correct option.

0 A (doctor) / prescription can help you when you're ill.

1 The doctor cured / prescribed me a medicine.

2 Penicillin / Bacteria can cause many operations / diseases, for example pneumonia or tuberculosis.

3 People should prevent the spread of illness / infections with vaccinations / treatments and good hygiene.

4 There is still no cure / prescribe for the Ebola virus.

THE FUTURE OF MEDICINE

What will change in medicine in the future? Here are a few predictions based on the research that scientists are doing at the moment.

1 ARTIFICIAL INTELLIGENCE AND THE DIAGNOSIS
In the future computers will help doctors diagnose their patient's illness and make decisions about treatments. One of these computers is IBM Watson Health. So how does this supercomputer work?
5 First, the doctor types in the patient's symptoms. Then, Watson Health checks the patient's medical and family history and analyses data from different sources such as treatment guidelines, doctors' notes, research materials, clinical studies
10 or articles in medical magazines. Watson Health can do this very fast: it reads 200 million pages of text in three seconds! Finally, it gives advice about the best treatment. Today only a few hospitals around the world use Watson Health
15 but soon artificial intelligence will help all doctors in their daily work.

2 REAL-TIME DATA
In the future patients won't need to inform the doctor about their symptoms. Wearable sensors, like biometric tattoos, will monitor our
20 health day and night. They will analyse our heart rate, blood or neurological symptoms. Doctors will receive the information from the sensors in real time. In case of an emergency, like a heart attack, the sensor will immediately send an alert
25 and call the ambulance. It's possible there will be cases when doctors will know before the patient that there is something wrong with them.

3 MORE SENSORS
Tiny sensors which scientists can attach to objects are receiving a lot of attention
30 at the moment. Some companies are working on attaching sensors to pills. In this way the doctor will always know if and when the patient takes their medicine. Other scientists are trying to attach sensors
35 to the patient's teeth. These sensors will recognise jaw movements and classify them as eating, drinking, smoking or coughing. This data will give doctors information about the patient's eating habits, smoking or stress levels.

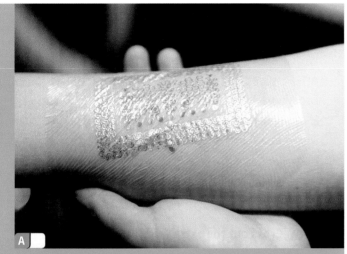

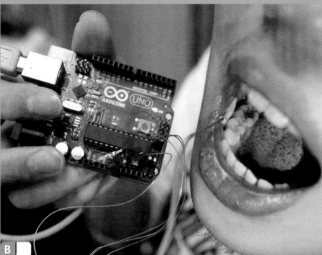

The future looks bright for medicine but there is one question still to ask: Will we, the patients, be happy that doctors will know what we do 24 hours a day?

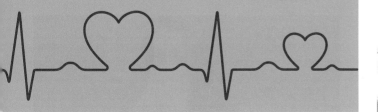

VOCABULARY

THE BODY

15 Complete the gaps with these words. There are two extra.

> arm • chest • elbow • feet • fingers • foot • ~~hand~~ • hip • knee • leg • neck • shoulder

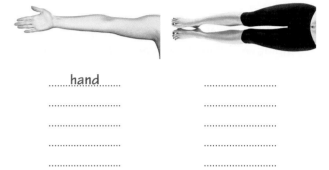

.......hand....... ....

....

....

....

....

16 Choose the correct option.

0 Amy is holding flowers in her ....
  A back   **B** feet   (**C**) hand

1 Dave lay down on his .... and looked at the sky.
  A foot   **B** back   **C** teeth

2 Erin's heart is beating fast in her ....
  A chest   **B** neck   **C** elbow

3 I ate something bad and now my .... hurts.
  A stomach   **B** shoulder   **C** head

4 Fashion models can't look down when they walk. They hold their .... up high.
  A fingers   **B** knees   **C** heads

17 Look at the advert for a new brand of vitamin. Choose the correct options. Then order the benefits from what you consider most important (1) to the least important (7).

WonderPills will:

☐ improve your (*heart*)/ *brain* rate.

☐ make your *blood* / *skin* look better.

☐ make your *immune* / *bones* stronger.

☐ help build your *skin* / *muscles*.

☐ improve your *bone* / *blood* circulation.

☐ boost your *brain* / *immune* system.

☐ make your *skin* / *brain* work faster.

GRAMMAR PRACTICE

Infinitive of purpose

Choose the correct options.

We use the *infinitive / -ing form* to explain the purpose of a thing or an action. We ask about the purpose using the question *Why? / What?*

➡️ See **GRAMMAR REFERENCE** page 122

18 **Complete the sentences using the to-infinitive of these verbs and a *wh* question word.**

> buy ▪ check ▪ find ▪ get ▪ invite ▪
> make ▪ protect ▪ send ▪ watch

0   Josh went shopping ......**to buy**....... some milk.
1   We are waiting for a taxi ....
    to the airport.
2   '.......................... are you going to the post office?'
    '.......................... a birthday card to my friend
    in Canada.'
3   I used a dictionary .... the meaning
    of some words.
4   Mum turned on the TV .... the news.
5   '.......................... is she checking the map on her
    phone?' '.......................... the way to the railway
    station.'
6   I called Alice .... her to my party.
7   '.......................... is Jessica taking vitamins?'
    '.......................... her hair and skin look better.'
8   They're wearing helmets ....
    their heads.

19 **Write sentences using the words in CAPITALS and an infinitive of purpose.**

0   COMPUTER
    ___I use a computer to check my emails.___
1   MEDICINE
    ....
2   CAR
    ....
3   PEN
    ....
4   DOCTOR
    ....
5   LIBRARY
    ....
6   SUNGLASSES
    ....

First conditional

Choose the correct options.

We use the first conditional to predict the result of a possible *past / future* action. We make the first conditional with two sentences which are linked with *if / because*. After *if / because* we use *will / the present simple* and in the other sentence we use *will / the present simple*.

➡️ See **GRAMMAR REFERENCE** page 122

20 **Cross out the extra word in each sentence.**

0   You'll have fun if you ~~ll~~ stay at the party a bit longer.
1   What will don't you do if there is no school
    tomorrow?
2   If it will rains, I won't go on a bike trip.
3   My knee will hurt again if I will start running.
4   We are will be tired if we don't go to bed now.
5   If Jason waits for his friends, if he will be late
    for school.
6   If will you tell me about the homework if I call you
    in the afternoon?
7   Matilda and Tom will get a promotion if they
    will finish all their projects on time.
8   If they don't come, I don't won't go.

21 **Choose the correct options.**

Mum   Your eyes are red. **0** (Are you going to) /
              Will you cry?
Melissa   No, **1** *I'm not / I don't*. It's my allergy.
Mum   Did you take your allergy pill this morning?
Melissa   No, I forgot! **2** *I'm going to / I'll* take it now.
Mum   If you **3** *will start / start* taking these pills
              regularly, they **4** *will help / help* you.
Melissa   I know but I just keep forgetting about them.
Mum   Why don't you set up an alarm on your
              phone? It can ring **5** *to remind / of reminding*
              you about your pills.
Melissa   Great idea, **6** *I'll / I'm going to* do it now.
Mum   If you **7** *don't / won't* get better in a week,
              we **8** *call / will call* Dr McCarthy.
Melissa   Thanks, Mum. I already feel better!

SPEAKING SKILLS

TALKING ABOUT FEELINGS

22 **Complete the dialogues with these words. For each one there are two extra words.**

> hurts ▪ matter ▪ soon ▪ very ▪ wrong

1 **A** What's the .... with you?
 B My back .... a bit.
 A It'll get better ....

> days ▪ great ▪ hurts ▪ OK ▪ shame ▪ wrong ▪ worry

2 **A** What's .... with you?
 B I don't feel .... but I'll be ....
 A Don't .... We all have bad
  ....

> awful ▪ feel ▪ hard ▪ poor ▪ really ▪ with ▪ what's

3 **A** I .... terrible.
 B .... the matter .... you?
 A My arm .... hurts.
 B .... you!

> be ▪ better ▪ don't ▪ down ▪ I ▪ luck ▪ you

4 **A** You look sad. What's wrong with .... ?
 B I didn't score any goals today. I'm really
  ....
 A Bad .... but .... worry.
  Maybe next time …
 B I know. I'll .... fine.

> bit ▪ fine ▪ isn't ▪ more ▪ pity ▪ so

5 **A** My neck hurts a .... I'll lie down
  for a moment.
 B That's a .... I've got two tickets
  to a concert tonight.
 A Really? I don't feel .... bad any
  .... I'll go with you if you want!

23 **Respond to the sentences. Express your feelings and show empathy.**

0 My finger hurts a bit. **Poor you!**
1 I fell over and didn't finish the race.
2 I missed the train.
3 I don't feel very well today.
4 I can't go to the party tonight.
5 I didn't sleep at all last night. I was worried about
 the test.
6 You look tired. What's the matter with you?

LISTENING SKILLS

24 **Look at the photo and answer the questions.**

1 What is the name of the sports competition
 that requires the use of this equipment?
2 What three sports are a part of this competition?
3 Which part of this competition do you like?
4 Which part of this competition don't you like?

25 [1.15] **Listen again and choose the correct option.**

1 James wants to prepare for a *marathon* / *triathlon*.
2 At the moment James runs *twice* / *four* times
 a week.
3 Right now James runs for around *5* / *6* km each time.
4 James normally goes for a bike ride *once* / *twice*
 a week.
5 James usually rides his bike for *15* / *25* km.
6 James's favourite sport is *running* / *swimming*.
7 A year ago James went to the pool *three* / *five*
 times a week.
8 In the past James stayed in the water for *15* / *50*
 minutes.
9 James had a *shoulder* / *leg* injury.

26 [1.15] **Listen again and complete the table.**

Name: *James Stevens*

Triathlon training plan
Week 1-2

	Frequency	Distance Week 1	Distance Week 2
Running	.... a week	.... km	.... km
Cycling	.... a week	.... km	.... km
Swimming	.... a week	.... m	.... m
Recovery	.... a week	-	-

ACADEMIC SKILLS

DESCRIBING CHARTS AND TABLES

27 Look at the graph and choose the correct options.

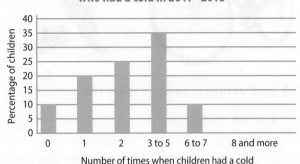

Percentage of children at Thomas Primary School who had a cold in 2017–2018

(y-axis: Percentage of children; x-axis: Number of times when children had a cold — 0, 1, 2, 3 to 5, 6 to 7, 8 and more)

0 The .... shows information about the frequency of colds at Thomas Primary School.
(A) graph   **B** percentage   **C** axis

1 The .... refers to the 2017–2018 school year.
A data   **B** axis   **C** quarter

2 The .... axis presents the number of times children had a cold.
A vertical   **B** horizontal   **C** top

3 The .... axis presents the percentage of children who had a cold.
A graph   **B** horizontal   **C** vertical

4 The .... of children who had a cold more than five times a year is lower than the percentage of children who had a cold once a year.
A axis   **B** data   **C** percentage

5 .... in ten children didn't have a cold in 2017–2018.
A One   **B** Ten   **C** Five

6 .... of children had a cold once in 2017–2018.
A 10%   **B** 20%   **C** 25%

7 A .... of children had a cold twice in 2017–2018.
A half   **B** fifth   **C** quarter

8 .... children had between 6 and 7 colds a year.
A One of ten   **B** One from ten   **C** One out of ten

28 Match the percentages to the expressions with the same meaning.

0 [d] 10%   **a** 40 out of 100
1 [ ] 33%   **b** a half
2 [ ] 70%   **c** a quarter
3 [ ] 50%   **d** 1 in 10
4 [ ] 25%   **e** a third
5 [ ] 40%   **f** 8 out of 10
6 [ ] 80%   **g** 70 out of 100

29 The graph below shows the injuries that the Field Dragons team had in 2017. Look at the graph and complete the text with the missing information.

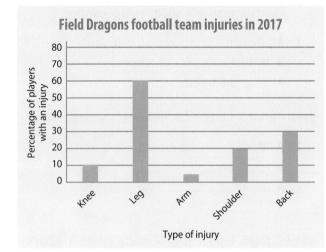

Field Dragons football team injuries in 2017

(y-axis: Percentage of players with an injury; x-axis: Type of injury — Knee, Leg, Arm, Shoulder, Back)

The graph shows the types of injuries which the Field Dragons football players had in **0** ..... _2017_ ..... . The most common injury was a **1** .... injury. Six out of **2** .... players suffered from this type of injury in 2017. The second most common injury was a back injury. **3** ....% of players complained that their back got hurt during the 2017 football season. A fifth of the Field Dragons players had **4** .... injuries. The least frequent problems were knee and arm injuries. **5** .... in ten players suffered from knee injuries and only **6** ....% of players complained about different types of arm injuries.

30 The graph below shows the favourite vitamins and supplements of *Run the World* readers. Describe the graph. Use the sentences from exercises 27 and 28 and the text from exercise 29 as a model.

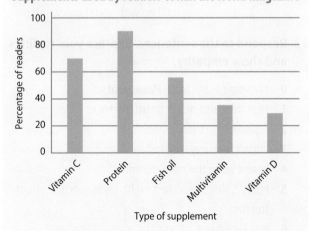

Supplements used by readers of *Run the World* magazine

(y-axis: Percentage of readers; x-axis: Type of supplement — Vitamin C, Protein, Fish oil, Multivitamin, Vitamin D)

Listening – Sentence completion

You will hear one person talking about a topic and you have to listen and complete some notes. Before you start listening, read the notes and think what words are missing. Are these nouns, verbs or adjectives? These are usually one or two words, numbers or names. Try to think about the context and predict the missing words. Is this going to be a type of film, a name of a job or a price? After you finish listening read the notes again and check the spelling of the words.

31 **Read the sentences and choose the most likely answers.**

0 The book of the week: ....
  A chapter
  (B) *Exam Success*
  C William Shakespeare

1 The author of the book: ....
  A England
  B Paul Tucker
  C famous

2 The original language of the book: ....
  A English
  B Spain
  C Europe

3 Type of book: ....
  A helpful
  B useful
  C self-help

4 Date of publishing: ....
  A Monday
  B today
  C 2014

5 The main topic: ....
  A tips for studying
  B 268
  C seven chapters

6 Reasons why people like the book: ....
  A good advice
  B often
  C hip-hop

32 **Correct the spellings.**

0	taecher	....teacher....
1	adress	....
2	Febuary	....
3	intresting	....
4	potatoe	....
5	tommorrow	....
6	Wendesday	....
7	waether	....
8	clotes	....
9	begining	....
10	librerry	....
11	mauntins	....
12	neibour	....

33 [1.16] **You are going to listen to a presentation about a new course for children. Complete the gaps with the missing information.**

Notes about Public Speaking for Teenagers

The classes start in [0] ....October..... .

During the class you'll learn to talk in front of a [1] .... group of people.

Some people feel that it's [2] .... to learn to overcome the fear of speaking in public.

Speaking comfortably in public is a [3] .... which is useful for everyone.

The class is especially good for those who have no or little [4] .... of speaking in public.

Day of the class: [5] ....

The maximum number of people in the class: [6] ....

REVISE AND ROUND UP

1 🔊 **Complete the sentences. Use** *be going to* **to express an intention.**

0 At the weekend <u>I'm going to watch a lot of TV</u> .

1 In the next few months ....

2 On Sunday ....

3 In the future ....

4 When I finish school ....

5 In the summer ....

6 Next year ....

7 This evening ....

8 Tomorrow ....

2 🔊 **Choose the correct options to complete the email.**

Hi Martha,

How are you? I'm great! This is the first day of my summer holiday and I've got a lot of plans.
⁰ .... evening my dad is taking me to the cinema. We're leaving ¹ .... an hour so I need to write this email quickly.
Tomorrow ² .... my friends and I are going shopping. We're having a barbecue ³ .... the evening so we need to buy a few things.
⁴ .... tomorrow I'm going to my first yoga class in the park. I'm very excited about it. ⁵ .... I'm meeting Sue. We're going to learn how to decorate our trainers. I hope I'll have a pair of unique trainers ⁶ .... the end of the summer.
⁷ .... I'm going to visit my aunt Lucy in Cornwall. It's going to be a wonderful summer and I know I'll be busy ⁸ .... but let's stay in touch.
Take care,
Tamara

0 **A** Today   **B** These   **C** This ⓒ
1 **A** on   **B** in   **C** at
2 **A** the morning **B** morning   **C** at the morning
3 **A** tomorrow   **B** on the   **C** in
4 **A** After   **B** The day after **C** Day after
5 **A** On later   **B** Later on   **C** On
6 **A** to   **B** with   **C** by
7 **A** Next week **B** Next few week **C** Later week
8 **A** in the next few weeks
   B on the next weeks
   C in the next a few weeks

3 🔊 **Write sentences using the present simple for future.**

0 The museum / open / at 11:30 am / tomorrow
   The museum opens at 11:30 am tomorrow.

1 My piano classes / begin / in June

2 The plane to Madrid / not / leave / at noon

3 What time / you / have / a lunch break / at school?

4 The race / finish / at 5:30

5 The English lesson / start / in ten minutes

6 When / the conference / take place?

7 Our train / arrive / at 3:15 / at London Waterloo

8 What time / the café / close / next Friday?

4 🔊 **Rewrite the sentences using the present continuous for future.**

0 Julie has got an appointment at the hairdresser on Friday.
   Julie is going to the hairdresser on Friday.

1 I made a plan to meet my friends at the beach on Sunday.

2 We've got tickets to the opera for Tuesday.

3 Owen and Max decided to play basketball after school tomorrow.

4 My plan is to go to the cinema at the weekend.

5 David has got an appointment to see his dentist on Monday.

5 🔊 **Complete the dialogues using** *will.*

0 **A** What do you think will happen in 2060?
   B <u>I think people will have robots at home</u>

1 **A** This is a secret! Nobody can know about it.
   B I promise ....

2 **A** I can't find my pen. .... ?
   B Of course. Here you are.

3 **A** What do you think about space travel?
   B I don't think that in ten years' time people
   ....

4 **A** Let's have a picnic!
   B That's a great idea! I ....

5 **A** Which sweater do you want? The blue one is £30 and the red one is £40.
   B I think ....

6 **A** Tom is a great basketball player.
   B I agree. I think ....

7 **A** The show starts at 8 o'clock.
   B I'm sorry but ....

8 **A** I can't reach the books on the top shelf.
   B Don't worry. I ....

6 🔊 Complete the sentences in the first conditional using the verbs in brackets.

0 His stomach ....**will hurt**..... (*hurt*)
if he ......**eats**......... (*eat*) all those sweets.

1 If it .... (*be*) hot tomorrow,
we .... (*go*) to the swimming pool.

2 If you .... (*see*) Patrick, ...
(*you / tell*) him about the party?

3 Maggie .... (*not / get*) a pay rise
if she .... (*not / listen*) to her boss.

4 The baby .... (*cry*) if you ....
(*take*) his toys.

5 .... (*you / tell*) me your secret
if I .... (*promise*) to keep it?

6 If we .... (*walk*) slowly to the bus stop,
we .... (*not / catch*) the bus.

7 If they .... (*spend*) the summer
in England, their English .... (*improve*).

8 Sarah .... (*go*) for a hike with her cousin
if it .... (*not / rain*).

7 🔊 Complete the sentences using the *to-*infinitive of these verbs.

get ▪ cut ▪ earn ▪ ~~study~~ ▪ check ▪
tell ▪ buy ▪ answer ▪ take

0 They will to stay at home ...**to study**... for the test.
1 My mum sometimes works over the time
.... more money.
2 Mike texted his friends .... them the
good news.
3 We went to the bookshop .... some
magazines.
4 "Why did you leave the room?" "......................... a
phone call."
5 I took the knife .... the cake.
6 "Why do you go online?" "......................... my emails."
7 He brought a camera .... some pictures.
8 We drank tea with honey .... warm after
the walk.

Read the sentences and answer the questions.

1 *I'm going to study medicine.*

(Answer Yes / No / Your own words)

0 Does this sentence refer to the present,
future or past? **Future**
1 Is it a plan or a quick decision?
2 Has this person made any arrangements to do it
or is it only an intention?
3 Can you add *not* to this sentence? If so, where?

2 *I will help you tidy up the living room.*

(Answer Yes / No / Your own words)

0 Is this an action in the present, future
or in the past? **Future**
1 Is it a quick decision or a type of plan that
someone had for a long time?
2 Can you add *not* to this sentence? If so, where?
3 Can you replace *I* with *She*?

3 *I often call my friends to talk about school.*

(Answer Yes / No / Your own words)

0 What is the form of the verb after *friends*?
Infinitive
1 Will the form of the verb *talk* change when we
start this sentence *He often calls his friends to …*?
2 What question word can you use to fill the gap
in this question?
'......................... *do you call your friends?*'
'*To talk about school.*'
3 Can you change this sentence into the past
or future? Which part of the sentence will change?

4 *If I finish my homework early, I will meet you
in the café.*

(Answer Yes / No / Your own words)

0 Does this sentence refer to the present, future or
past? **Future**
1 How do you translate *if* into your language?
2 Do we use this sentence to predict the results
of possible future or past actions?
3 Can you use *will* after *if*?
4 Can you change the order of the sentences
and start with *I will meet …*?

➡ See **GRAMMAR REFERENCE**
pages 121-122

7 Happiness

GRAMMAR PRACTICE

Comparative and superlative adjectives

Complete the rules.
To make the comparative form of adjectives we add
.... to short adjectives or ....
before long adjectives.
To make the superlative form of adjectives we add
the + ... to short adjectives or *the* +
.... before long adjectives.
Some adjectives have irregular comparative and
superlative forms, for example *good* (*better*, *the best*)
and *bad* (*worse*, *the worst*).

See **GRAMMAR REFERENCE** page 123

1 **Choose the correct form of the comparative adjectives.**

0	**happy**	(happier) / more happy
1	**hot**	hoter / hotter
2	**hard-working**	harder-working / more hard-working
3	**noisy**	noisyer / noisier
4	**intelligent**	intelligenter / more intelligent
5	**wet**	wetter / more wet
6	**dangerous**	dangerouser / more dangerous
7	**clean**	cleaner / more clean
8	**difficult**	difficulter / more difficult
9	**far**	farer / further
10	**tall**	taller / more tall

2 **Write sentences using the comparative.**

0 Alec / old / Charlotte
   Alec is older than Charlotte.
1 Playing video games / good / playing board games
2 Football / popular / handball
3 Our classroom / dark / the cafeteria
4 A knife / useful / in the mountains / a fork
5 My arms / strong / my legs
6 This book / serious / the one I read last week
7 Messi / famous / Arda Turan
8 Your explanation / logical / mine
9 A restaurant / expensive / a pub
10 Salad / healthy / French fries

3 **Complete the dialogue using the comparative form of the adjectives in brackets.**

Chris   How do you like your new flat?
Erin   It's great! It is **0** .....**more spacious**..... (*spacious*)
       than our old flat but the old one was
       1 .... (*convenient*).
Chris   Oh really?
Erin   Getting to school is **2** ....
       (*complicated*) now. I need to take two buses.
       But the area around the flat is
       3 .... (*nice*)
       and **4** .... (*green*) than
       the place where we lived before.
       There's a park right next to our block of flats.
Chris   How do you like your new room?
Erin   It's amazing! It's a bit **5** ....
       (*big*) than my old room. It's also
       6 .... (*bright*) because it's got
       two huge windows. You need to come and see
       it! How about tomorrow?
Chris   Great, see you then.

4 **Write the superlative form of the adjectives.**

0	big	............**the biggest**............
1	beautiful	....
2	sad	....
3	quick	....
4	ambitious	....
5	simple	....
6	bad	....
7	kind	....
8	good	....
9	pretty	....

5 **Choose the correct option.**

0 The Pacific Ocean is the .... ocean in the world.
   (A) deepest   **B** most deep   **C** most deepest
1 My brother is the .... person in our family.
   He's got school and two jobs.
   A busyest   **B** busiest   **C** most busy
2 Gizem is the .... girl in our class.
   A thinnest   **B** thinest   **C** most thin
3 This is the .... building in our town.
   A modernest   **B** most modern   **C** more modern
4 Listen to the .... news!
   A lateest   **B** most late   **C** latest

6 **Choose the correct option.**

0 Abby is *more honest* / (*the most honest*) girl I know.

1 Is Sam *more talkative* / *the most talkative* than Jake?

2 The bed is *softer* / *the softest* than the sofa.

3 Science-fiction books are on *lower* / *the lowest* shelf.

4 My uncle is a *better* / *best* footballer than my dad.

5 Jenny is the *smarter* / *smartest* student in the class.

6 When I came back home very late my mum was *angrier* / *the angriest* than my dad.

7 Watermelons are one of *juicier* / *the juiciest* fruit.

8 Today's film was *more frightening* / *the most frightening* than the one we watched last week.

7 **Use the information below to complete the sentences about the watches.**

Price
£45

Weight
50 g

Diameter
35 mm

A

Price
£80

Weight
140 g

Diameter
45 mm

B

Price
£35

Weight
11 g

Size of the dial
20x30 mm

C

0 A *is cheaper than* B. (*cheap*)

1 B .... of all the watches. (*expensive*)

2 C .... A. (*light*)

3 C .... of all the watches. (*small*)

4 C .... A. (*cheap*)

5 B .... of all the watches. (*heavy*)

6 B .... A. (*big*)

8 **Complete the sentences with the comparative or superlative form of these adjectives.**

close ▪ large ▪ ~~long~~ ▪ rare ▪ cheap ▪ thick ▪ wide

0 Your hair is ......**longer**....... than mine. Why don't you go to the hairdresser?

1 Elephants have got .... ears than hippos.

2 This is .... book in the library. It's got 987 pages.

3 The river is .... here than over there but you can use the bridge to walk across it.

4 Abigail is my .... friend. We tell each other everything.

5 This was .... ticket. It only cost £10.

6 These purple orchids are .... wild flowers in the UK. They don't grow in many places.

9 **Rewrite the sentences. Use the comparative or superlative form of the adjectives in CAPITALS.**

0 This magazine is good, but that newspaper is boring.
INTERESTING *The magazine is more interesting than the newspaper* .

1 Ally is 15 years old and Jason is 17 years old.
YOUNG ....

2 The weather in August was nice but the weather in September was very unpleasant.
BAD ....

3 Comedies with Jim Carrey are funny but I laugh the most when I watch films with Ben Stiller.
FUNNY ....

4 I had no problems with the English test but the French homework was very difficult.
EASY ....

5 The brown box weighs 10 kg, the white box weighs 6 kg and the black box weighs 8 kg.
HEAVY ....

6 When our class organises a race Tom always comes first. He's a very fast runner.
FAST ....

10 **Make sentences using comparative or superlative adjectives.**

0 a dog / a horse *A dog is smaller than a horse.*

1 a house / a flat

2 a computer / a laptop / a mobile phone

3 grapes / peaches

4 a bike / a car / a plane

READING SKILLS

11 [1.17] **Read and listen to the text and choose the best definition of 'happiness set point'.**

1 It's a level of happiness which changes when people get old.
2 It's a level of happiness which influences 50% of people's feelings.
3 It's a level of happiness which remains the same in people's life.

12 **Read the text again and answer the questions.**

1 What school do Owen and Carter go to?
2 What job does Carter want to do in the future?
3 What does Owen like?
4 How are Owen and Carter different?
5 When did Owen and Carter learn about a *happiness set point*?
6 According to a *happiness set point* theory how do extreme life events change our level of happiness?
7 What did the twin study prove?
8 How much of our happiness depends on external factors?
9 What percentage of our happiness depends on us and what we do?
10 Can Carter influence his own well-being?

13 **Read the text again and correct the mistake in each sentence.**

1 Carter is good at playing football.
2 Owen wants to be a software designer in the future.
3 Carter is cheerful.
4 Sometimes Carter complains because Owen is positive about everything.
5 Carter and Owen attended a psychology workshop at the library.
6 The level of the people's happiness doesn't change at all during their life.
7 A study shows that people who won the lottery or had a healthy spine returned to their usual level of happiness after some time.
8 Genes influence 40% of our happiness.
9 Psychologists believe that people like Carter can't improve their well-being.
10 Carter will feel happy if he starts working.

THE LIMIT OF HAPPINESS

Carter goes to Midway Secondary School in Leeds.
Carter loves skateboarding and is good at computers.
He's going to be a software designer in the future.
Carter's got a lot of friends at school but he often
5 complains. His friends think he's pessimistic.
Owen is Carter's friend. They are in the same class.
Owen enjoys playing football. He's ambitious and studies
a lot. He wants to be a doctor. Owen, unlike Carter,
is always happy. Owen and Carter get on well.

10 But sometimes Carter doesn't understand why Owen is
so positive about everything. Owen, on the other hand,
can't convince Carter to be more cheerful.

Two weeks ago Owen and Carter had a psychology
workshop about happiness at school. This workshop helped
15 them understand why some people, like Carter, are less
happy whereas other people, like Owen, are more
optimistic. It turns out that the level of people's happiness
doesn't change much during their whole life. This is called
a *happiness set point*.

20 This theory shows that happiness doesn't depend
on external factors. In one study psychologists compared
the level of happiness of people who won the lottery and
people who had a serious spine injury. People who won the
lottery were at first extremely happy but then their
25 happiness returned to the earlier level. Similarly, people with
spine injuries were miserable at first but then their
well-being came back to the same level as before
the accident.

Does this mean that Carter will remain unhappy all his life?
30 Not really. In another study psychologists checked the level
of happiness among identical twins. The results show that
50% of our happiness comes from our genes and we have
no control over it. Psychologists explain that another 10%
of our happiness results from good or bad things that
35 happen in our life such as winning the lottery or having
an accident. This means that 40% of our happiness depends
on us. Psychologists believe that the happiness set point is
important but everyone can also influence their own
well-being. So Carter *can* feel happier if he starts working on it.

VOCABULARY

FEELINGS

14 Choose the correct option.

0 We were (surprised) / relaxed when we saw Emily
   at the party. Nobody invited her.

1 I feel *afraid* / *excited* because it's the last day
   of school. I can't wait to get up late tomorrow.

2 Lisa fell off her chair in front of her classmates.
   She was really *surprised* / *embarrassed*.

3 We spent a great day at the beach. I feel so *relaxed* /
   angry now.

4 The trip to London took us eight hours. We were
   very *tired* / *scared* when we finally arrived.

5 I'm going to have my first job interview tomorrow.
   I feel *tired* / *stressed*.

6 I feel a bit *sad* / *excited* because Jack forgot about
   my birthday.

7 He couldn't calm down after the argument with his
   friend. He was very *happy* / *angry*.

8 Annie is *embarrassed* / *worried* that she will not
   have enough time to finish her project.

**15 Match people's messages with adjectives
that describe their moods. There is one
extra adjective.**

0 [g] I'm so worried. I don't think I can do it!

1 [ ] Thank you for all your help.

2 [ ] I'm sure I'll win the tennis tournament.

3 [ ] I don't want to get out of bed. I'm sad.

4 [ ] Yeah! I passed my driving test!

5 [ ] I've got no friends and no one to talk to.

6 [ ] This is terrible news but I just can't cry all day.
      I'll try to do better next time.

7 [ ] This article made me think about my life.
      I'll become a better person.

8 [ ] I listened to relaxing music and did yoga
      for one hour.

a	calm	**f**	lonely
b	close	**g**	nervous / anxious
c	depressed	**h**	proud
d	grateful	**i**	resilient
e	inspired	**j**	self-confident

GRAMMAR PRACTICE

less and the least

Choose the correct options.

We use *less* / *least* in the comparative form of all the adjectives and *the less* / *the least* in the superlative form. This creates a comparison with the meaning opposite to *more* and *the most*.

➡ See **GRAMMAR REFERENCE** page 123

16 **Complete the sentences using the adjectives in brackets and *less* or *(the) least*.**

0   I am **less patient** than my sister. (*patient*)

1   This is my .... song in this album. (*favourite*)

2   Strawberries are .... than bananas. (*sweet*)

3   During today's performance I was .... than during the one we did yesterday. (*nervous*)

4   This is .... maths exercise in the whole book. (*complicated*)

5   Jason and Tom are .... boys in our class. (*hard-working*)

6   My bedroom is .... room in our house. (*spacious*)

7   Ms Smith's lessons are usually .... than Mrs Benn's. (*interesting*)

8   According to a recent study South Africa is among .... countries in the world. (*happy*)

17 **Rewrite the sentences using *less* or *the least*.**

0   Indian restaurants are more popular than Korean restaurants. (*popular*)
    Korean restaurants are less popular than Indian restaurants.

1   Jeans are more comfortable than skirts. (*comfortable*)

2   This is the easiest crossword puzzle in this book. (*difficult*)

3   Joe is the most pessimistic person I know. (*optimistic*)

4   I am more self-confident than my friends. (*self-confident*)

5   Adam is a more experienced basketball player than Ed. (*experienced*)

6   My uncle Phil is the meanest person in the family. (*generous*)

(not) as ... as

Complete the rules.

We sometimes use *as* + ... + *as* to talk about two things that are the same.
We use *not as* + ... + *as* to talk about two things that are different.

➡ See **GRAMMAR REFERENCE** page 123

18 **Write the sentences using *as ... as* or *not as ... as*.**

0   pizza / not / healthy / salad
    Pizza isn't as healthy as a salad.

1   England / not / sunny / Turkey

2   Amy / resilient / her sister

3   Zebras / not / dangerous / lions

4   Izmir / not / crowded / Istanbul

5   My camera / expensive / yours

6   Tony / relaxed / Mark

19 **Complete the blog with the verb *be* and the adjectives in brackets using *as ... as* or *not as ... as*.**

15th October, Monday

These are my best friends Sarah, Megan and Ally. Megan [0] **isn't as tall as** (*not / tall*) Ally and Sarah. She's about 1.60 m. Sarah and Ally have got blonde hair but Sarah's hair [1] .... (*not / fair*) Ally's. Megan and Sarah make me laugh all the time but they [2] .... (*not / funny*) Ally. She jokes all the time. All my friends are good at sports. Ally and Megan win a lot of races, I think Megan [3] .... (*fast*) Ally but Ally always says that Megan runs faster. Sarah is also in the school tennis team. Ally, Megan and I also play tennis but we [4] .... (*not / good*) Sarah so we're not in the team. Although we [5] .... (*hard-working*) Sarah, we [6] .... (*not / talented*) she is. Sarah thinks of becoming a professional tennis player in the future. The rest of us have no idea what to do in the future.

SPEAKING SKILLS

MAKING COMPARISONS

20 Put the words in the correct order. Tick (✓) all the expressions of agreement.

0 it / forget / ! **Forget it!**

1 at / that / on / how / it / you / depends / look

2 know / oh / , / don't / I

3 be / you / serious / can't

4 sure / I'm / not

5 again / you / that / say / can / !

6 right / too / !

21 Choose the correct option. Then respond using one of the expressions of agreement (A) or disagreement (D).

0 It isn't healthy to sleep for (fewer) / more few than eight hours. (D)

   A You can say that again!

   B Too right!

   Ⓒ That depends on how you look at it.

1 Let's order *the most expensive* / *more expensive* ice-cream in the café. (A)

   A Oh, come on!

   B Absolutely!

   C That's not going to happen any time soon!

2 If you eat a lot before bedtime, you will have the *worst* / *baddest* nightmares. (A)

   A You can say that again.

   B That depends on how you look at it.

   C You can't be serious.

3 Arrogant people are the *happier* / *happiest* of all. (D)

   A Too right!

   B I'm not sure.

   C I agree.

4 People who have a lot of friends live *more long* / *longer*. (D)

   A You can say that again!

   B Absolutely!

   C That depends on how you look at it.

5 Jenny is more self-confident *than* / *that* her sister. (A)

   A Too right!

   B Forget it!

   C You can't be serious.

6 British comedies aren't as *funny* / *funnier* as the Turkish ones. (D)

   A You can say that again!

   B I agree.

   C You can't be serious.

LISTENING SKILLS

22 Look at the picture. How do the two girls feel?

1 angry   **3** relaxed

2 grateful   **4** tired

23 🔊 **[1.18] Listen to the conversation and complete the gaps with the missing information.**

Maya and Lucas are coming back from
[1]......................... . They are talking about a / an
[2]........................ which [3]........................ read last week.
It describes relations between [4]........................ and
[5]........................ . Maya's got a / an [6]........................
brother. His name is [7]........................ .

24 🔊 **[1.18] Listen again and choose the correct option.**

1 Where are Maya and Lucas going?

   A To school.

   B Home.

   C To the library.

2 Maya's parents think that Matthew is .... than Maya.

   A more hard-working

   B less intelligent

   C angrier

3 Why did Maya read the book?

   A To find ways to talk to her friends.

   B To understand that she and her brother are good students.

   C To get advice about how to make her parents understand her feelings.

4 Matthew thinks that Maya is .... than he is.

   A lonelier   **B** fitter   **C** funnier

5 What did Maya learn from the book?

   A That it's good to be someone else.

   B That you can't believe what other people say about you.

   C That everyone has different talents.

EXAM SKILLS

25 Why did the author write these sentences? Choose the correct option.

0 The job is easy and enjoyable.

   A describe

   B offer

   C agree

1 First you put on a helmet, then you get on a special kind of motorbike.

   A improve   **B** convince   **C** explain

2 Drive only when you have seat belts on.

   A agree   **B** advise   **C** realise

3 You can stay in a hotel at the top of the mountain.

   A discuss   **B** agree   **C** suggest

4 Try it on your next holiday. It's an amazing experience.

   A persuade   **B** show   **C** prefer

26 Read the text on page 75. Then choose the correct option to answer the questions.

1 What is Tamara Jones doing in the text?

   A Explaining why people need to protect sea life.

   B Giving advice on how to spend a holiday in Fuerteventura.

   C Giving her opinion of a submarine tour.

   D Persuading others to go on a submarine tour.

2 What is Tamara worried about at first?

   A The boats aren't comfortable for the passengers.

   B She won't see any fish.

   C The boat can be too loud.

   D The windows aren't big enough to see the fish.

3 What is the company's attitude towards fish and other sea life?

   A They're going to organise more environmentally-safe sea tours in the future.

   B They want to introduce battery-powered submarines in the next year.

   C They can't explain to people what they do to protect the environment.

   D They want to protect the sea life and not disturb the fish.

4 What does Tamara say about the inside of the submarine?

   A It didn't allow everyone to see the fish.

   B There were too many people.

   C There weren't enough seats for all the passengers.

   D It met the needs of the passengers.

5 What might Tamara write in an email to a friend about the trip?

   A The submarines are wonderful but I'm sure that they aren't safe for the sea life.

   B The tour was great. I saw a lot of fish swimming at the bottom of the ocean.

   C Taking a tour was great fun. I only wish the company offered more modern boats.

   D It was the best tour we did on our holiday. I know a lot about different fish now. The captain told us a lot about them.

Submarine trip

Sixteen-year-old Tamara Jones talks about her holiday adventure

In July my parents, my brother and I spent two weeks in Fuerteventura, one of Spain's largest Canary Islands. Fuerteventura is an amazing island with its beautiful white sandy beaches and the greatest weather possible – sunny
5 and warm but also pleasantly windy. On the third day of our stay Dad suggested we could go on a submarine trip.

My brother was really excited about the idea but I was really worried and didn't want to go at all. Why? Well, first of all, being inside a small submarine scared me a lot because
10 of the lack of space and fresh air. Also, I love nature and I thought that submarines disturbed sea creatures and polluted the water. I was definitely against it!

Instead of trying to convince me my dad took us to the company which organises these tours so I could ask
15 the questions that bothered me and find out everything about the trip. I was surprised to learn that the company cares about the environment as much as I do. Their submarines are battery-powered and don't cause any water pollution. They are also quiet and the captains know how to operate
20 them without disturbing the fish. What's more, last year the company built an artificial reef so that more fish and sea creatures could live safely in this area.

I felt I could give it a try and believe it or not – this was my favourite Fuerteventura experience. The boats were
25 passenger-friendly, quite spacious and ventilated with fresh air. Everyone got a seat in front of a large window so it wasn't too crowded. The tour took about 30 minutes but I will never forget the wonderful sea life we saw that day. It was an amazing experience to see all the fish in their
30 natural environment!

EXAM STRATEGY

Speaking – Interview

The interview is about 2–3 minutes long. During this part the examiner will ask you a few single questions about you, your daily routines, your hobbies and your school. Answer giving the relevant information. If you don't understand, ask for repetition. Remember that you don't have to give very long answers but it's important to say more than just a few words.

27 Read the questions and decide which category they belong to: personal information (PI), family (F), school (S), the place where you live (L), future projects (FP), hobbies and interests (H).

0 What's your name? PI
1 How old are you?
2 Where do you come from?
3 What's the most interesting part of your town?
4 What do you do?
5 Do you study English at school?
6 What's your favourite hobby? Why?
7 What kind of job would you like to do in the future?
8 Tell us about a city that you would like to visit.
9 What do you like doing in your free time?
10 Can you tell me about your family?
11 What is your favourite type of music?
12 Where do you live?

28 **Match the questions and answers.**

0 [b] Which sports do you enjoy? Why?
1 ☐ Tell us about your hometown.
2 ☐ How do you get to school?
3 ☐ Are you a student or do you work?
4 ☐ How long have you lived there?
5 ☐ Tell us about your friends.
6 ☐ What do you enjoy doing at the weekends?

a I've got two best friends – Emma and John. Emma is 16 years old and she lives in the same block of flats as I do. We go to the same school and like doing the same things. John is older than me. I met him last year at a photography course.

b I love basketball and tennis. I like them because I can play with my friends. I'm also very competitive. I like to win.

c Five years. I moved to Ankara when I was ten and my dad got a job here. Now we love this place.

d I love hanging out with my friends. We usually go to the cinema, bowling or to a café. I also like reading books and drawing.

e I live in Burford. It's a small historic town in Oxfordshire. It's 30 km northwest of Oxford.

f I usually walk to school but if it rains, I prefer to take the bus. It takes me about ten minutes to get to school.

g I'm a secondary school student. I go to Grovenor Secondary School in York, my hometown. I'm in my first year.

8 Home

GRAMMAR PRACTICE

must / have to for obligation

Choose the correct options.

We use *must* and *have to* to talk about *strong obligations / abilities.*

Sentences with *must* and *have to* talk about actions that are *optional / necessary.*

Sentences with *don't have to / mustn't* describe actions that aren't necessary.

Sentences with *don't have to / mustn't* describe actions that aren't allowed.

In questions we use *have to / must* because *have to / must* sounds very formal.

➡ See **GRAMMAR REFERENCE** page 124

1 **Write affirmative sentences using *must.***

0   They / study / tonight
     They must study tonight.
1   Amelia / help / her parents / today
2   All students / wear / a uniform
3   I / get rid of / my old clothes
4   You / listen / to the news
5   Patrick / finish / his essay
6   We / work harder / in the next semester
7   My brother / tidy up / the living room
8   Toby and I / come back home / at 7 o'clock

2 🔊 **Choose the correct option.**

0   I ⟨have⟩ / *has* to go now.
1   They *have to / have* take some time off.
2   My dad *has to have / have to has* lunch with his boss from time to time.
3   We *has / have* to bring a few holiday photos to school tomorrow.
4   Noah *has / have* to get up early on Tuesdays.
5   I *have to help / have to helping* my brother every day.
6   I *have to / have* do the laundry.
7   You *have to wear / have wearing* a hat and a scarf today.
8   My parents sometimes have *work / to work* overtime.

3 🔊 **Write what you and your family need to do each week. Use *must* and *have to.***

     I have to do the washing-up three times a week.

4 🔊 **Write sentences about the park rules using *mustn't.***

     You mustn't leave rubbish.

> ## PARK RULES
>
> * **No rubbish.**
> * **No dogs in the fountain.**
> * **No loud music.**
> * **No cars.**
> * **No skateboarding in the car park.**
> * **No fires.**
> * **No bicycles in the playground.**

5 🔊 **Rewrite the sentences using *don't have to* or *doesn't have to.***

0   We have to cook tonight.
     We don't have to cook tonight.
1   Sophie and Charlie have to stay at home on Sunday.
2   We have to leave now.
3   Amy has to check her emails.
4   My grandma has to work in the garden alone.
5   A present has to be expensive.
6   I have to buy a new pair of jeans.

6 🔊 **Tick (✓) the correct sentences. Correct the mistakes.**

0   You mustn't bring any books to school today.
     We're going on a trip to the museum. **don't have to**
     You mustn't open the windows in the cafeteria.
     It's not allowed. ✓
1   You mustn't bring any food to the party.
     My mum bought everything yesterday.
2   My sister doesn't have to eat any nuts.
     She's allergic to them.
3   You mustn't tell Julie about it. This is our secret.
4   Sam loves Sundays because he mustn't wake up early.

7 🔊 **Use the prompts to ask questions about housework and give short answers.**

Housework	Anita	Tim	Henry
• take out the rubbish	Mon		Fri
• unload the dishwasher	Wed, Thu	Mon, Tue	Fri, Sat, Sun
• tidy up the kitchen	Sat		Sat
• vacuum	Tue, Sat		
• lay the table		every day	
• wash the floors		Tue	Sat

0 Anita and Tim / take out rubbish / Fridays

'*Do Anita and Tim have to take out the rubbish on Fridays?*' '*No, they don't.*'

1 Anita / take out the rubbish / Mondays

2 Tim / unload the dishwasher / Mondays and Tuesdays

3 Anita and Henry / tidy up the kitchen / Sundays

4 Henry / vacuum / Saturdays

5 Tim / lay the table / Wednesdays

6 Anita / wash the floors / Tuesdays

7 Tim and Henry / wash the floors / Mondays

8 Henry / do any housework / at the weekend

8 🔊 **Choose the correct option.**

0 You .... bring pencils to school. They are in every classroom.

    A mustn't   Ⓑ don't have to   **C** don't have

1 You .... talk loudly in the library. It's a quiet study place.

    A don't have to   **B** mustn't   **C** must

2 I .... to make my bed every morning. My mum tells me to do it.

    A has   **B** have   **C** must

3 Linda .... practice piano today. She has a concert next week.

    A has to   **B** have to   **C** must to

4 My brother .... do any homework today. They are going on a school trip tomorrow.

    A doesn't have to **B** don't have to   **C** mustn't

5 You .... help me. I know how to do it.

    A have to   **B** don't have to   **C** mustn't

6 You .... leave dirty dishes on the table. Our rule is to put them in the dishwasher.

    A don't have to   **B** must   **C** mustn't

9 🔊 **Complete the online discussion forum with the correct form of *must* or *have to*. In some cases both forms are correct.**

@Toby17	My bedroom is always messy and I **0** ....**must learn**......... (*learn*) to keep it clean every day. I don't know how to start! Any advice?
@Max	Why **1** .... (*you / keep*) it clean every day? My mum says I **2** .... (*tidy up*) once a week 😊 .
@Toby17	I just hate the mess. My bedroom **3** .... (*not / look*) perfect but just a bit better than now. My friends visit me and I feel bad about what my room looks like.
@CathyT	Hi Toby! It's easy to keep your room tidy and you **4** .... (*not / spend*) a lot of time cleaning it. My advice? You **5** .... (*make*) your bed first thing in the morning.
@Ryan	I agree with @CathyT. Also, you **6** .... (*put*) things away when you don't use them. You **7** .... (*not / leave*) clothes on the floor or empty cups on your desk.
@Toby17	Thanks everyone! What about rubbish? **8** .... (*I / take*) it out every day?

10 🔊 **Correct the mistakes.**

0 We ~~don't have to~~ use phones at school. **mustn't**

1 Do you must take your dog for a walk every day?

2 I must to look after my little brother today.

3 Does Martin has to study so much?

4 You mustn't put the tomatoes in the fridge.

5 What do we have do after school today?

6 Amy mustn't to use her dad's laptop.

READING SKILLS

11 🔊 [1.19] **Read and listen to the text and match the headings to the paragraphs.**

1 ☐ A house specialist for all your needs
2 ☐ Smart homes
3 ☐ Bring spring to your home
4 ☐ The best price for your home
5 ☐ Everything in its place

12 **Read the text again and decide if the sentences are true (T) or false (F). Correct the false ones.**

1 A plumber repairs sinks in the bathroom. ☐T ☐F

2 Different specialists know how
to improve our homes. ☐T ☐F

3 Carla works only in spring
and at New Year. ☐T ☐F

4 Carla puts everything back
in the boxes in your garage. ☐T ☐F

5 Vicky knows how to store
and organise your things. ☐T ☐F

6 Vicky gives advice about
what to throw away. ☐T ☐F

7 Martin works for people who want
to buy a house. ☐T ☐F

8 Martin thinks people shouldn't hang
family photos on the walls
if they want to sell their house. ☐T ☐F

9 Caleb knows a lot about
new technologies. ☐T ☐F

HOW CAN WE HELP YOU AT HOME?

A We call a plumber when a sink is broken and a painter when we want new colours for the walls. There are many people who help us to make our house look and function well. Let's meet some of them
5 today.

B Carla Brown is a seasonal decorator. She specialises in seasonal and holiday decorations. Her favourite decorations are for spring and New Year but she works all year long. Why do you need Carla? She can make your
10 house look great at any time of the year. Better still, you don't have to worry about boxes with decorations in your cellar or garage. When the season is over, Carla takes down the decorations and keeps them at her office until the next year.

13 **Look at the photo and choose the correct options to complete the text.**

Last week we finished redecorating my room. It looks amazing now! I love my new white bed with all its purple cushions. There's also a rug ⁰............ the bed in the same colour as the cushions. There's a pink wardrobe ¹............ the wall and the desk. I keep all my clothes ²............ this wardrobe. There's a shelf ³............ the wardrobe. It's a perfect place for all my school books and notebooks. I try to keep my study place tidy so there's only a laptop and some pens ⁴............ my desk. I'm planning to buy a few posters to decorate my room. I want to hang some pictures on the wall ⁵............ the bed and maybe put an armchair ⁶............ the bed. How do you like my new room?

0	**A** between	**B** under	**C** near
1	**A** next	**B** behind	**C** between
2	**A** on	**B** in	**C** under
3	**A** next to	**B** in front of	**C** behind
4	**A** in	**B** near	**C** on
5	**A** behind	**B** between	**C** under
6	**A** in front	**B** opposite	**C** on

C Vicky Taylor loves organising things. In her little flat everything is neatly put away, usually in a nice box with a label. Vicky turned her talent into a job. She's a personal organiser. This means she organises people's homes or offices by, for example, sorting out clothes in a wardrobe or documents in a study. She also helps her clients to decide which things they can get rid of.

15

20

25

D Martin Adams is a home stager. Last year he helped 50 families sell their houses at an attractive price. He helps homeowners make their house look great for buyers. Of course, it always depends on the house or flat but his general rules are: 'I rearrange furniture or add new pieces, change decorations and reduce clutter at home. I tell my clients to remove family photos because buyers want to imagine that this can be their home.'

30

E Caleb Quinn is a smart home technician. He helps people choose and install smart devices for their homes. Caleb knows the market and offers the best products. His favourites? Smart shutters for windows which you can control through an app on your phone and a smart fridge camera. It tells you what's in your fridge, reminds you about the expiry dates of the products and even suggests recipes.

35

40

HOUSE AND FURNITURE

14 Complete each sentence with the missing word.

0 William opened his bag and took ....**out**......... the lunchbox.

1 I can't find anything in my room because I never put things ....

2 We got .... of our fridge because it stopped working.

3 Ann dropped her books so I helped her to pick them ....

4 Don't throw .... your old school notes. You can use them one day.

5 We have to sort .... photos for an album.

15 Correct the sentences. Replace the underlined text with these words. There are three extra words.

attic ▪ curtains ▪ dishwasher ▪ front door ▪ garage ▪ gate ▪ hall ▪ ~~outside~~ ▪ stairs ▪ study ▪ washing machine ▪ worktop

0 The fence is <u>inside</u> the house. **outside**

1 You keep a car in the <u>cellar</u>.

2 The <u>patio</u> is the top room in the house.

3 The <u>roof</u> is the main entrance to your house.

4 A <u>balcony</u> is a passage inside the house which leads to all the rooms.

5 You use the <u>shutters</u> to go to rooms on the first floor.

6 You can find a bookcase and a desk in the <u>sink</u>.

7 People decorate windows with <u>ceilings</u>.

8 You use the <u>storage unit</u> to do the laundry.

GRAMMAR PRACTICE

should for advice

Choose the correct options.

We use *should* to *talk about abilities / give advice*.
In affirmative sentences we use *should* and the *infinitive / -ing form* of the verb. In negative sentences we use *shouldn't / don't should* and the infinitive. In questions, we put *should before / after* the subject.

➡ See **GRAMMAR REFERENCE** page 124

16 **Cross out the extra word in each sentence.**

0 We d̶o̶ should mop the floor in the kitchen.
1 Katie should sort sorts out her school notes.
2 I should clean cleaning in the attic today.
3 They study should study more.
4 We should buy should a new mirror.
5 Karen and Olivia should be are at home now.
6 Matt shoulds should get rid of old magazines.

17 **Complete the questions and short answers with *should* or *shouldn't* and the verbs in brackets.**

0 'How often **should I exercise** (*I / exercise*)?'
   'Twice a week.'
1 'What .... (*we / tell*) the teacher?'
   'The truth!'
2 '............................... (*I / take*) a raincoat tomorrow?'
   'Yes, ...'
3 '............................... (*they / get off*) the bus now?'
   'No, they ....'
4 What time .... (*I / get up*) in the
   morning? At 7:00.
5 'What .... (*we / eat*) before school?'
   'Maybe some cereal.'
6 '............................... (*Nathan / talk*) to his sister first?'
   'No, ...'

18 **Complete the sentences with *should* or *shouldn't* and the verbs in brackets.**

0 Tim **shouldn't get rid of** (*get rid of*) his old
   English books.He can use them again in the future.
1 You .... (*turn up*) the heating.
   It's cold here.
2 Jamie .... (*climb*) up on the roof.
   It's too dangerous.

3 They .... (*paint*) the hall.
   The walls look dirty.
4 You .... (*run*) on the stairs.
   You can fall down.
5 I .... (*eat*) so many sweets.
   They're not healthy.

19 **Write the advice you would give in these situations. Use *should* or *shouldn't*.**

0 I am often sleepy at school.
   You shouldn't go to bed late.
   You should have a healthy breakfast
   in the morning.
1 I can't find time to do all my homework.
2 I always forget about everything!
3 I don't know how to use this app.
4 I want to get better at English.
5 My brother never lets me watch my favourite
   TV programmes.
6 I am often late.
7 I want to work in the summer.

20 **Choose the correct options.**

Damian You ⁰(*should*) / *don't have to* look
   in the mirror! Your hair looks weird today.

Josh Well, it's because I can't brush it
   in the morning.

Damian What? You can't …

Josh Shhh … You ¹*don't have to / must* shout!
   Do you think everyone in the cafeteria
   ²*mustn't / has to* know about my problem?

Damian But what is the problem?

Josh My sister! She spends hours in the bathroom.
   She leaves exactly when we ³*have to / must* go
   to the bus stop.

Damian You ⁴*don't have to / should* ask her to leave
   the bathroom sooner. She ⁵*mustn't / must*
   feel like she's the only person who wants
   to use the bathroom in the morning.
   Besides, she ⁶*doesn't have to / mustn't* look
   like a model every day.

Josh I tried but it didn't work.

Damian Maybe you ⁷*don't have to / should* get up
   early and get ready before she wakes up.

Josh Wake up at 6:00? You know, you ⁸*shouldn't /*
   should give such bad advice!

SPEAKING SKILLS

MAKING SUGGESTIONS

21 Reorder the words to make sentences. In each one there is an extra word. Then decide if the sentences express a suggestion (S) or a doubt (D).

0 ....**D**.... know / I / so / don't   **I don't know.**

1 .... don't / I / not / 'm / certain

....

2 .... probably / I / won't / likely / come

....

3 .... is / one / idea / to / sofa / will / the / replace

....

4 .... ask / why / how / you / don't / him / ?

....

5 .... about / how / of / why / a / tea / cup / ?

....

6 .... my / I / 've / sure / doubts / about / got / it

....

7 .... know / that / unlikely / 's

....

8 .... could / listening / about / to / how / music / ?

....

22 Give suggestions using the words in brackets. Then choose the correct option for each answer.

0 (new mirror)
  A How ....**about a new mirror**...........
  for the bathroom?
  B (*I'm not*) / *I don't* sure.

1 (wear a black jacket)
  A Why ....
  for the school photo?
  B I'm not *likely* / *sure*.

2 (put the armchair)
  A You ....
  next to the bookcase.
  B I don't *think* / *know* so. There isn't space.

3 (have a sleepover)
  A How about ....
  at my house this weekend?
  B That's not very *probably* / *likely*.

4 (ask)
  A One idea ....
  your brother for help.
  B I've got my doubts *about* / *with* it.

5 (have a party)
  A How about ....
  on Saturday?
  B *Certain* / *Perhaps*. I don't know.

LISTENING SKILLS

23 Look at the photo and complete the sentences.

1 The picture shows a *living room* / *kitchen* …
2 It looks *old* / *modern* …
3 I *don't like* / *like* the wooden furniture …

24 Look at the photo again and read the sentences in exercise 25. Try to guess the what the missing words are.

1 Who are the speakers?
2 What are they talking about?
3 What information is the girl looking for?
4 What plans has she got for Saturday?

25 🔊 [1.20] Listen to the conversation and write the missing words.

1 In the dialogue .... are talking.
2 The girl needs help with her .... homework.
3 She decides to write a review of an open-air ....
4 Juliana visited St Andrew's last ....
5 In St Andrew's there are more than .... old buildings.
6 The oldest buildings come from the time between the year 1300 and ....
7 Juliana remembers a house with a small ....
8 The museum is open every day from .... am to .... pm.
9 Juliana would like to go for a .... in St Andrew's next weekend.

ACADEMIC SKILLS

COMPLETING A FLOW CHART

SEVEN STEPS TO A SUCCESSFUL GARAGE SALE

A garage sale is a perfect way to get rid of unwanted clutter. These types of events are popular in the USA but people are starting to organise them in Europe, too. Here are a few steps for organising a garage sale.

1   Do you need a permit? Can you put up signs in the neighbourhood?
2   Next, look for the things you want to sell. These can be old books, clothes or furniture.
3   Have you got a list of things you want to sell? You might want to compare the prices of similar items at other garage sales.
4   Then choose the date and the time of your garage sale.
5   A few weeks before the day of the sale, start advertising. Put ads online or in local newspapers.
6   Before the sale starts, prepare your items. You have to clean everything and fix prices.
7   On the day of the sale set up tables and boxes and display your items. You want everything to look neat and well-organised.

GOOD LUCK WITH YOUR GARAGE SALE!

```
Check the rules
      ↓
Decide what to sell
      ↓
Compare the prices
      ↓
Choose the date
      ↓
Advertise
      ↓
Prepare the items
      ↓
Set up the sale
```

26 **Read the text again and decide if the sentences are true (T) or false (F). Correct the false ones.**

		T	F
0	Write each step of the process in a separate box.	✓	F
1	Steps in a flow chart must be in order.	T	F
2	Don't link the boxes with arrows.	T	F
3	Describe each step in three long sentences.	T	F
4	Flow charts describe a sequence of actions.	T	F
5	Use linkers such as *first, next, finally*.	T	F
6	Use imperatives: *Go …, Make …, Choose …*	T	F

27 **Read the text below and draw a flowchart to summarise it.**

Your guide to photo organisation

Do you want to organise your photos but you don't know how to start? Read our advice and just do it!

1   First, think about the best way for you to sort the photos. Some people choose to have albums with photos in chronological order, others sort by occasions such as holidays.
2   Next, plan where you want to store your photos. Do you prefer a photo book or a traditional album?
3   Now it's time to buy the albums. Once you have them at home you will feel motivated to start sorting.
4   Go through all your photos and choose the ones you like the most.
5   When you have finished selecting your favourite photos, print them.
6   It's time for some hard work. Get your albums and fill them up with your photos.
7   This is a great moment – the albums are ready! Show them to your family and friends. Enjoy!

EXAM STRATEGY

Speaking – Collaborative task

This speaking activity lasts about 2–3 minutes. The examiner will read the instructions and then you will work with the other candidate. You will receive pictures and will be asked to discuss a situation, using the pictures as prompts. It is important to work together with the other candidate when discussing the ideas. You should make and respond to suggestions, make recommendations and try to reach an agreement.

Dos and Don'ts in the exam:

- take turns, respond to the other candidate's ideas and ask for his / her opinion
- don't dominate the conversation
- don't reach a decision too quickly. Discuss all visual material

28 **Read the expressions and decide if they show agreement (A), disagreement (D), or an opinion (O).**

0	I'm not sure about that.	A	☑ D	O
1	You're right.	A	D	O
2	I'm sorry but I don't agree.	A	D	O
3	What do you think?	A	D	O
4	That's not a bad idea but …	A	D	O
5	Do you agree?	A	D	O
6	That sounds good.	A	D	O
7	I agree.	A	D	O
8	No, I don't think so because …	A	D	O

29 **Look at the picture and read the exam question. Then complete the conversation. The expressions from exercise 28 can help you.**

I'm going to describe a situation to you.
Here's a picture with some ideas to help you.

Exam situation

A group of exchange students from another country is going to visit your school. Talk together about the different places you could take them to on the first day and then decide which place would be the best.

Hannah So ⁰ ......**what**........ do you think? Where should we take the exchange students on the first day of their visit?

Connor We ¹ .... go to a shopping mall Everyone likes shopping

Hannah I'm not ² .... Those places are crowded and we won't have a chance to talk. How ³ .... a museum?

Connor I don't ⁴ .... so. I think we should get to know them first.

Hannah I ⁵ ....

Connor Why ⁶ .... we go to the beach or to the park? It's a good place to talk.

Hannah A park or a beach isn't a bad idea ⁷ .... we don't know what the weather is going to be like. Do ⁸ .... agree?

Connor Yes, you're ⁹ .... Let's go to the pizza place. We can talk and have something to eat.

Hannah That ¹⁰ .... good. Let's do it!

30 **Read the exam question and write a conversation using the expressions from exercises 28 and 29.**

I'm going to describe a situation to you.
Here's a picture with some ideas to help you.

Exam situation

Students at your school have collected £500 to buy new books for the library. Talk together about the different types of book the school could buy and then decide which two would be the best.

REVISE AND ROUND UP

1 🔊 **Complete the sentences with the comparative form of the adjectives in brackets.**

0   My flat is ......**bigger**...... than Jenny's. (*big*)

1   Your new sofa is definitely .... than the old armchairs. (*comfortable*)

2   Do you think that Anna is .... than other students in the class? (*smart*)

3   Let's go around the park. It's a .... route but I like it a lot. (*far*)

4   You have to go and wash your hands. They are .... than you think. (*dirty*)

5   Is anyone in your school a .... basketball player than Mike? (*good*)

6   In my opinion traffic on Friday evenings is .... than on Monday mornings. (*bad*)

2 🔊 **Choose the correct option.**

0   The kitchen is (*the sunniest*)/ *most sunnyest* room in my flat.

1   Monday is going to be the *hotest / hottest* day of the month.

2   Zurich is probably *the most expensive / the more expensive* city in Europe.

3   Is it true that on Tuesdays you can buy the *most cheap / cheapest* plane tickets?

4   This is *slowest / the slowest* train! It's got so many stops, we will never get there on time.

5   Tomorrow is *the most important / the more important* day in my life. I'm taking a driving test.

6   This is *the most narrow / the narrowest* street in Lisbon. We should take a picture here.

3 🔊 **Complete the sentences with the comparative or superlative forms of one of the adjectives in brackets.**

0   For me English is ....**easier than maths**.......... . (*easy / difficult*)

1   Going by bus is .... (*fast / comfortable*)

2   A holiday at the seaside .... (*boring / enjoyable*)

3   My best friend is .... (*funny / loyal*)

4   Today is .... (*cold / wet*)

5   Burgers are .... (*delicious / bad*)

4 🔊 **Cross out the extra word in each sentence.**

0   This café is usually ~~least~~ less crowded than the one on High Street.

1   When my mum cooks curry it's less spicy spicier than the one they serve in a restaurant.

2   Why are you watching this show? It's the less least interesting programme I know.

3   Don't worry! My brother says this film is less least frightening than the one we watched on Friday.

4   Start the test with the least more difficult exercise.

5   I always feel the less talented than Amelia.

6   My sister is the least active activest in our family. She doesn't do any sports.

7   Paul never says anything when more people are around. He turns into least the least talkative person in the world.

8   Mr White is a least less annoying neighbour than Mrs Cooper. She always asks me lots of questions.

5 🔊 **Make comparisons using (*not*) as ... as, these adjectives and your own ideas.**

> big · cold · difficult · enjoyable · fast · friendly · heavy · interesting · nice · noisy · slow · sunny · tasty · useful

0   elephant and monkey
    A monkey isn't as heavy as an elephant.

1   a fridge and a freezer

2   ice cream and pasta

3   dogs and cats

4   a house and a flat

5   a primary school and a secondary school

6   cars and buses

6 🔊 **Tick (✓) the correct sentences. Correct the mistakes.**

0   You mustn't run down the stairs. ✓
    They mustn't ~~jumping~~ on the beds. **jump**

1   I mustn't eating any nuts. I'm allergic.

2   We mustn't drink in the class.

3   You must stop when the traffic lights are red.

4   You musn't tell anyone your password.

5   Tim and Ed mustn't are late.

6   You mustn't be shout.

7   They don't must be rude.

8   On campsites you must being quiet after 10 pm.

7 📶 **Make sentences using the prompts and *don't have to* or *doesn't have to*.**

0 we / do our homework / today
We don't have to do our homework today.

1 I / close the windows / in the attic

2 Sophie / sort out all the things / in her chest of drawers / today

3 my parents / go to work / on Monday

4 our dog / go for a walk / five times a day

8 📶 **Choose the correct options to complete the text messages.**

Freya, you must **0**........................... me! I have **1**........................... a letter to our school headteacher and I don't know how to do it. **2**........................... start with Dear Mr Davis or Dear Headteacher?

Why **3**........................... write a letter to the headteacher?

Because I **4**........................... apologise to him for something.

Oh, I see. I can come later but I must **5**........................... my mum and I **6**........................... my homework first.

Thanks! You're awesome!

0	Ⓐ help	**B**	to help	**C**	helping
1	**A** write	**B**	to write	**C**	writing
2	**A** Must				
	B Do I have				
	C Does it have to				
3	**A** must you				
	B do you have to				
	C do you have				
4	**A** must	**B**	have	**C**	must to
5	**A** asks	**B**	to ask	**C**	ask
6	**A** must to finish				
	B must finishing				
	C have to finish				

9 📶 **Correct the mistakes.**

0 You shouldn't ~~to keep~~ tomatoes in the fridge. **keep**

1 You shouldn't worrying about the test.

2 What I should do now?

3 I should came back home at 10 o'clock.

4 We should to leave early tomorrow morning.

Read the sentences and answer the questions.

1 *Carla is the tallest girl in the class.*

(Answer Yes / No / Your own words)

0 Is anyone in the class taller than Carla? **No**

1 Is this a comparative or a superlative form of the adjective?

2 What is the comparative form of the adjective *tall*?

3 Can you replace *the tallest* with *the intelligentest*? If not, what is the correct form?

2 *Tom's room isn't as big as Sarah's.*

(Answer Yes / No / Your own words)

0 Are both rooms the same size? **No**

1 Whose room is bigger?

2 What is the form of the adjective between *as* and *as*?

3 How can you change the sentence to say that both rooms are the same size?

3 *I must call my mum.*

(Answer Yes / No / Your own words)

0 Is this an obligation or advice? **Obligation**

1 Can you replace *must* with *have to*?

2 How can you turn this sentence into a question?

3 Is this sentence correct in the negative form using *mustn't*?

4 *We don't have to book the restaurant in advance.*

(Answer Yes / No / Your own words)

0 What is the word that you put between *don't have* and the verb? **To**

1 Does this sentence describe an action that is unnecessary or not allowed?

2 How will this sentence change if we replace *we* with *she*?

3 How can you turn that sentence into a question?

5 *You should drink more water.*

(Answer Yes / No / Your own words)

0 Is this a strong obligation or advice? **Advice**

1 What is the verb form after *should*?

2 Do we use *do* to turn this sentence into a question?

3 What is the negative form of this sentence?

➤ See **GRAMMAR REFERENCE** pages 123-124

GRAMMAR PRACTICE

Present perfect with *ever* / *never*

Choose the correct options and complete the rules.

We use the present perfect to talk about actions that happened at *a definite* / *an indefinite* time in the past. We also use it when the time when the experience happened *is* / *isn't* important.

To make the present perfect we use ....

or .... and the past participle form of the verb.

We use *never* and *ever* with the present perfect. We use .... in questions. It means 'at any time in my life'. We use .... as a negative word with a positive verb. It means 'at no time in my life'.

➡ See **GRAMMAR REFERENCE** page 125

1 🔊 **Complete the sentences with *have* or *has*.**

0 I ....**have**........ met new friends.
1 Amy .... visited Asia.
2 We .... ridden a camel.
3 My friends .... forgotten their passports.
4 You .... made a delicious salad.
5 My neighbour .... swum in the Pacific Ocean.
6 Cameron .... sailed a boat on a lake.
7 I .... never eaten veggie burgers.
8 It .... been an amazing trip.

2 🔊 **Write the past participles.**

0	spend	.......**spent**.......
1	show	....
2	run	....
3	give	....
4	know	....
5	bring	....
6	go	....
7	lose	....
8	tell	....
9	take	....
10	come	....
11	travel	....

3 🔊 **Write sentences in the present perfect.**

0 Holly / sell / her old laptop
   Holly has sold her old laptop.
1 We / have / a great day
2 My brother / hurt / his leg
3 A lot of students / take part / in a photo competition
4 I / win / a trip to Barcelona
5 Lily and Chloe / drink / all the juice
6 You / give / me / the best present

4 🔊 **Complete the sentences with the negative form of the verbs in brackets in the present perfect.**

0 I ...**haven't stayed**... (*stay*) in a four-star hotel.
1 Tom .... (*read*) any books in Spanish.
2 We .... (*fly*) a plane.
3 Many students in our class .... (*see*) *The Hunger Games*.
4 Liam and Archie .... (*try*) bungee jumping.
5 My dad .... (*beat*) my uncle at tennis.
6 I .... (*be*) to Paris.

5 🔊 **Cross out the extra word in each question.**

0 ~~Has~~ have you taken any piano lessons?
1 Has she has written to you?
2 Do have we met?
3 Dave has Dave bought a new camera?
4 Has have Jenny and Abby passed their exam?
5 Have did they slept in a tent?
6 Have you drank drunk coconut water?

6 🔊 **Write questions about yourself, your friends or your family.**

0 '.............**Have you driven a car?**.............'
   'No, I haven't.'
1 '...'
   'Yes, they have.'
2 '...'
   'No, she hasn't.'
3 '...'
   'Yes, he has.'
4 '...'
   'Yes, we have.'

7 🔊 Tick (✓) the correct sentences.

0 ✓ I have never heard this song.
☐ I have ever heard this song.

1 ☐ Has he ever ridden a motorbike?
☐ Has ever he ridden a motorbike?

2 ☐ Have you never worked in a supermarket?
☐ Have you ever worked in a supermarket?

3 ☐ We haven't never seen the Eiffel Tower.
☐ We've never seen the Eiffel Tower.

4 ☐ Sarah never has played basketball.
☐ Sarah has never played basketball.

5 ☐ Has Jake broken his arm ever?
☐ Has Jake ever broken his arm?

6 ☐ This has never happened before.
☐ This have never happened before.

8 🔊 Complete each question or sentence with *ever* or *never*.

0 Have you ***ever*** played the guitar?
1 We have _____ swum in the ocean.
2 Finley has _____ learnt Japanese.
3 Have they _____ seen Big Ben?
4 Have you _____ cooked Indian food?
5 I have _____ left my hometown.

9 🔊 Choose the correct options to complete the conversation.

Molly ⁰(Have) / *Has* you ¹*ever* / *never* visited any other continents besides Europe?

Noah Yes, I ²*have* / *haven't*. I have ³*was* / *been* to Asia and Africa.

Molly Wow!

Noah How about you?

Molly I have ⁴*travelled* / *travelling* a lot around Europe but I have ⁵*ever* / *never* visited any other continents.

Noah Where would you like to go?

Molly I ⁶*'s* / *'ve* read a fascinating book about South America and I'd like to see Brazil, Argentina or Chile.

Noah My dad has ⁷*spent* / *spended* some time in Brazil.

Molly Oh, really? ⁸*Has he visited* / *He has visited* any other South American countries?

Noah No, he ⁹*hasn't* / *haven't*. But maybe one day we can go there.

Molly That would be great! I ¹⁰*haven't* / *have* never planned a trip like this. We can do it together.

10 🔊 Imagine that your PE teacher gave you this sports questionnaire asking about different activities you have tried. Complete it and then write a conversation between you and your teacher.

PE teacher: Have you ever played badminton?

SPORTS QUESTIONNAIRE

	YES	NO
play badminton	☐	☐
have swimming lessons	☐	☐
do karate	☐	☐
go rollerblading	☐	☐
try skateboarding	☐	☐

11 🔊 Correct the mistakes.

0 I haven't ~~call~~ my grandparents. ***called***
1 Have you studied French ever?
2 We've ever lived in a flat.
3 She haven't spoken to the teacher.
4 I have had a garden never.
5 Maria is been to the zoo.
6 They have lend me some books.
7 Has your mum ever get angry with you?

READING SKILLS

12 [1.21] Read and listen to the descriptions of the places and the profiles of the people. What information is given about the cities?

1 which hotels to stay at
2 how much the trips are going to cost
3 what places are worth seeing in each city
4 the names of the restaurants which people recommend

13 Read the descriptions of the places and match them to the people.

14 Read the text again and complete these sentences.

1 Daniel is from ....
2 Daniel likes eating ....
3 Laura's hobby is ....
4 .... likes running.
5 People who are interested in fashion should visit
....
6 In Rome you can learn about .... history.
7 La Grand Place is the .... square in Brussels.

A ▪ Paris

The capital of France is perfect for those who love art, fashion and history. In the Louvre
5 Museum you can see the picture of Mona Lisa. Walking around Paris gives you a chance to see the Eiffel Tower,
10 the Arc de Triomphe and many other famous buildings. Paris is a must for fashion lovers, with lots of amazing
15 second-hand shops, flea markets and boutiques.

If you like ancient history and amazing food, Rome is the place to go. Visit the Colosseum or the Roman Forum and find out how people lived
20 thousands of years ago. Relax in one of the thousands of amazing restaurants which serve the best pizza, pasta and ice-cream in the world.

B ▪ Rome

1 ◯ Daniel, USA

Daniel wants to visit a European city where he can see some old buildings. He also plans to try local food, especially their desserts. At school he learns French so he'd like to go to a country where he can practise this language.

2 ◯ Laura, Brazil

Laura is into photography. During her trip she wants to take photos of the most famous buildings in the world. She also hopes to do some clothes shopping and maybe visit a few art museums.

C ■ Berlin

25 Visit Berlin if you want to learn about recent world history. Thanks
30 to Berlin's museums and monuments you can find out a lot about World War II. It's a green city with many
35 parks and cycle routes. It also has a large system of lakes where you can try water sports such as sailing or canoeing. Berlin is a cool modern city with great vegetarian restaurants and fantastic flea markets.

40 Everyone who comes to Brussels falls in love with its beautiful architecture, especially La Grand Place, the main square with incredible seventeenth-century buildings. Don't worry about communication. In Brussels most people
45 speak French or know some English. You can't leave Brussels without trying some of the world's best chocolate and waffles.

D ■ Brussels

3 ◯ Tomoki, Japan

Tomoki is interested in twentieth-century history. He's vegetarian and doesn't eat meat and eggs. Tomoki likes to be active – he runs but wants to try other sports. He's planning to buy souvenirs for his friends. They love old gadgets so maybe he'll visit a flea market.

VOCABULARY

TRAVEL AND TRANSPORT

15 Circle the odd word out in each group.

0	*fly by*	plane	(bus)	helicopter
1	*sail by*	boat	ferry	coach
2	*take*	a bus	a helicopter	the underground
3	*ride*	the tube	a scooter	a motorbike
4	*catch*	a plane	a tram	a ship
5	*ride*	a taxi	a bike	a rickshaw
6	*miss*	a plane	a bike	a bus
7	*get off*	a car	a bus	a train
8	*get in*	a train	a car	a taxi

16 Complete the sentences with the missing words.

0 Don't forget to pay before you get ......*out of*...... the taxi.

1 If we set .... for Cambridge at 10 am, we will be there at lunchtime.

2 Come on, get .... the car. I'll give you a lift to school today.

3 I'm always nervous when the plane takes ....

4 This is our bus stop. We're getting .... here.

5 We got .... from Paris last Sunday. The trip was great but it's good to be home.

6 Look, your train is here. Be careful when you get ....

17 Compare the options and choose one.

What is:

0 faster – (a plane) or a bus?

1 more expensive to use – a helicopter or the underground?

2 more crowded – a tram or a taxi?

3 easier to find in London – a bus or a rickshaw?

4 more common in Rome – a taxi or a ferry?

5 slower – a scooter or the metro?

6 less crowded – a ship or a bike?

GRAMMAR PRACTICE

been / gone

Choose the correct options.

We use *been / gone* with the present perfect when we want to say that a person went somewhere and returned. We use *been / gone* with the present perfect when we want to say that a person went somewhere and is still there.

➡️ See **GRAMMAR REFERENCE** page 125

18 🔊 **Complete the sentences with *been* or *gone*.**

0 Have you ever ....**been**........ to Scotland? Does it rain there a lot?

1 Lily isn't at home. She's .... shopping.

2 'Where are your parents?' 'They have .... to work but they should be back soon.'

3 I have .... to Brighton six times. It's beautiful. We should go there together next time.

4 My neighbours have .... on holiday. They're coming back next week.

5 We have .... to the seaside. We came back last night.

6 Have you ever .... to Oak Park? It's nice there at this time of year.

19 🔊 **Complete the dialogue with *have / has gone* or *have / has been*.**

Alan ⁰........**Have**........ you ....**been**........ to the hairdresser? Your hair looks different.

Evie No, I haven't but I ¹..................... at the seaside. My parents and I were there for two weeks and the sun always makes my hair lighter.

Alan I see. Did your brother go with you?

Evie No, Tom ²..................... to York. He's visiting our grandparents but he's coming back tomorrow.

Alan Perfect! I've got two tickets for a basketball game on Sunday. I know he ³..................... never .... to a big sports event …

Evie He'll be so happy! What about your summer plans, Alan?

Alan I ⁴..................... to Oxford but now I have to stay at home. My parents ⁵..................... on a cruise and I'm looking after my little brother when they are away.

Evie OK, so where is your brother now? Did you leave him alone at home?

Alan No, he ⁶..................... to football practice. I need to pick him up in ten minutes. So I have to go!

Evie Bye.

Present perfect v past simple

Choose the correct options.

We use the *present perfect / past simple* to talk about a period of time that continues to the present. We use the *present perfect / past simple* to talk about a finished time.

➡️ See **GRAMMAR REFERENCE** page 125

20 🔊 **Choose the correct option.**

0 I *'ve never taken* / *never took* the ferry.

1 Last month Emma *has invited / invited* us to her house.

2 I *have had / had* a great day yesterday.

3 *Have you ever lost / Did you ever lose* your money?

4 Our English teacher *has never been / never was* late to class.

5 We *have bought / bought* a new laptop two weeks ago.

6 Tom isn't at school. He's *gone / went* to the doctor with his mum.

7 The show *has started / started* at 6 o'clock.

8 *Has Jane been / Was Jane* to London?

21 🔊 **Complete the sentences with the correct form of the verbs in brackets**

0 Amanda ......**called**...... (*call*) you two hours ago.

1 I .... (*never / drink*) pink lemonade.

2 Where .... (*you / go*) last week?

3 We .... (*do*) all our homework yesterday.

4 .... (*you / see*) *The Lord of the Rings*?

5 Our bus .... (*arrive*) at 4:55.

6 My mum .... (*travel*) to Japan three times.

7 Aiden .... (*finish*) tidying up his room a few minutes ago.

8 .... (*they / ever / try*) ice skating?

22 🔊 **Complete the text message with the correct form of the verbs in brackets.**

Hi Ryan! I heard you ¹..................... (come) back from Paris yesterday. How ²..................... (be) the trip? ³..................... (you / see) all the famous places when you ⁴..................... (be) there? I ⁵..................... (never go) been to France but I ⁶..................... (be) sure it's beautiful …

SPEAKING SKILLS

ASKING FOR AND GIVING DIRECTIONS

23 Choose the correct option.

0 (Where) / How is the cinema?
1 Go *along* / *at* Park Road.
2 *Take* / *Turn* right at the traffic lights.
3 What's the best way *in* / *to* the café?
4 *Take* / *Go* past the supermarket.
5 *Take* / *Turn* the second on the left.
6 How do I *get* / *make* to the airport?
7 It's *opposite* / *next* to the bus stop.
8 The school is *in* / *on* the left.

24 Complete the dialogues with these words.

> ~~can~~ ▪ got ▪ right ▪ straight ▪ way

1 **A** ....*Can*.......... you tell me the ....
   to the train station?
   B Go .... on. It's on the ....
   A I've .... that.

> isn't ▪ near ▪ see ▪ street ▪ take ▪ turn

2 **A** Is the supermarket .... here?
   B Yes, it is. Go along this .... for about 20
      metres. .... right at the roundabout.
      Then .... the second left.
   A I .... First right, then left. It's next
      to the post office, ... it?

> clear ▪ don't ▪ past ▪ third ▪ to ▪
> understood ▪ opposite

3 **A** You remember how to get ....
      Amelia's house, ... you?
   B Not really.
   A Go .... the school.
   B ....
   A Then, take the .... on the left.
   B That's ....
   A Amelia's house is .... the park.

> between ▪ go ▪ got ▪ right ▪ with

4 **A** Where's the football field?
   B .... to the Town Park first.
   A .... it!
   B It's .... this park and the Chinese
      restaurant.
   A I'm .... you. It's between the park and
      the restaurant.
   B .... !

LISTENING SKILLS

25 Tick (✓) the things you always bring on a trip.

- ☐ a mobile phone
- ☐ a camera
- ☐ a guidebook
- ☐ a map
- ☐ a hat or a cap
- ☐ a raincoat
- ☐ a passport
- ☐ books and magazines

26 🔊 **[1.22] Listen to the radio programme and match the type of holiday to the things you should bring with you.**

1 ☐ a camping trip   **a** a travel journal
2 ☐ a beach holiday   **b** hand sanitiser
3 ☐ a hiking trip   **c** jewellery
4 ☐ a skiing holiday   **d** lip balm
5 ☐ a cruise   **e** first aid kit
6 ☐ a sightseeing tour   **f** sunscreen

27 🔊 **[1.22] Cross out and correct the mistakes.**

0 This is Radio ~~WMM~~. **WFM**
1 Jessica Davies is the creator of the website *Tourist Tips*.
2 Jim's website gives advice about travelling.
3 Men should take a hat when they go on a cruise.
4 Skiers often complain that they have a leg injury.
5 Campers and sightseeing tourists shouldn't take too many things.
6 Jessica says that when you you're hiking a mosquito can bite you.
7 Jim is travelling to Ireland next week.
8 Write your memories in the travel journal once a week.

EXAM SKILLS

EXAM STRATEGY

Listening – Multiple choice (gist)

You will hear six short conversations and you have to choose the correct multiple-choice answer. You have to listen for general understanding, not specific facts and focus on the speakers' attitudes and opinions. Before you start listening, read the questions and answers and make sure you understand them.

28 [1.23] **Listen and choose the correct option.**

You will hear two friends talking about a film they've seen. What did the girl like best about it?

A the story

B the music

C the actors

29 Read the audio script and underline the part that contains the correct answer. Then read it again and explain why the other two answers are wrong.

Boy

That was great! I really enjoyed it. What did you think?

Girl

It was quite good, I thought, but I've seen better films. I mean, the story wasn't very exciting, was it?

Boy

No, you're right but that didn't matter for me. It was really funny and a good way to spend an afternoon.

Girl

There were some of my favourite actors in it, too. I love Damon Matthews! But what I enjoyed most was the music. There were some of my favourite songs in it.

---

30 [1.24] **Listen again and choose the correct options.**

1

You will hear two friends talking about a music magazine. The girl advises the boy to:

A buy the magazine.

B read the magazine.

C lend her the magazine.

2

You will hear two friends talking about a holiday course. They agree that:

A it's too expensive.

B it's interesting.

C it's in a nice place.

3

You will hear two friends talking about a train journey. How did the boy feel at the end of the journey?

A tired

B excited

C annoyed

4

You will hear two friends talking about going out. The girl suggests going to:

A a new place.

B the usual club.

C a friend's house.

EXAM STRATEGY

Writing – An email

You will see an email from a friend and some notes that you've made. You have to write a reply to your friend. You must include all the information in the four notes and your email should be about 100 words long. Remember to use an informal style and to begin and end the email appropriately.

31 Choose the correct way to start and finish an informal letter.

0 (Hi Sue,) / hi Sue
1 Deer Tom / Dear Tom,
2 Thank you for your letter. / Thanks you for your letter.
3 I like hear from you. / It was great to hear from you.
4 How are you? / I ask how you are.
5 I'm sorry I don't write for so long. I'll be busy. /
  I'm sorry I haven't written for so long. I've been busy.
6 I look forward to hear from you. / I look forward
  to hearing from you.
7 Write back soon. / Let's write back soon.
8 Love, Emily / Yours faithful Emily

32 Complete Emily's email to Charlotte with phrases a–g.

a Best wishes
b Thanks for your email.
c I'm interested in playing chess.
d Hi Charlotte,
e We enjoy checking out different local events
  such as concerts or festivals.
f I look forward to hearing from you.
g This is always a lot of fun!

33 Read Harry's email and write notes for your reply to it.

To: ....
From: Harry

We're going on a trip on Saturday.   — *Great idea!*

Do you want to come with us?   — *Yes!*

We can go to the seaside or the new water park. Which would you prefer?   — *tell Harry*

What shall we do in the evening?

Let me know as soon as possible.

Harry   — *suggest …*

34 Now write your reply to Harry using your notes. Write about 100 words.

0 ___d___
1 .... It was great to hear from you.
In your letter you ask me about my free time.
2 .... I go to a chess club twice a week. It's a fantastic way of improving logical thinking and problem-solving. My friends aren't into chess but we do other fun things together. 3 ....
Sometimes, we go roller-skating by the lake.
4 .... Do you roller skate?
5 ....
6 ....
Emily

10 Free time

GRAMMAR PRACTICE

Present perfect with *just*, *already* and *yet*

Choose the correct options and complete the rules.

We use the present perfect with *just* / *yet* to talk about an action that happened very recently.

We use *already* / *yet* in negative sentences to say an action hasn't happened and in questions to ask if it has happened.

We use *already* / *yet* in positive sentences to say that something has happened before the moment of speaking or sooner than expected.

.... and .... go between *have* or *has* and the past participle, but .... goes at the end of the sentences or questions.

➡ See **GRAMMAR REFERENCE** page 126

1 🔊 **Use the prompts to write sentences with the present perfect and *just*.**

0   I / speak / to him
    I have just spoken to him.

1   Amy / tidy up / her room
    ....

2   They / come back / from school
    ....

3   I / have / a shower
    ....

4   You / drink / a glass of juice
    ....

5   My brother / go out
    ....

6   The cat / jump / on the sofa
    ....

2 🔊 **Read the situations and for each one write a sentence with *just*. Imagine that you have just done something.**

0   I'm angry.
    I've just had a fight with my best friend.

1   I'm disappointed.

2   I'm happy.

3   I'm cold.

4   I'm laughing.

5   I'm tired.

6   I'm thirsty.

3 🔊 **Complete the sentences with *already* and the present perfect of the verbs in brackets.**

0   They __have already done__. (*already* / *do*) their homework.

1   We .... (*already* / *buy*) a present.

2   I .... (*already* / *see*) this film.

3   My friends .... (*already* / *be*) to France.

4   Max .... (*already* / *leave*).

5   Our teacher .... (*already* / *tell*) us about the final exams.

6   My parents .... (*already* / *park*) the car in the garage.

4 🔊 **Complete the questions with the correct form of the verbs in brackets and *yet*.**

0   Have you ............ ?
    (*reply to Sarah's email*)

1   Have they .... ?
    (*wash the dishes*)

2   Has Jack .... ?
    (*have a shower*)

3   Have you .... ?
    (*write your essay*)

4   Has the postman .... ?
    (*bring the mail*)

5   Have they .... ?
    (*order their food*)

6   Have you .... ?
    (*make any new friends*)

5 🔊 **Write answers to the questions using *yet*.**

0   'Have you invited Josh to the party?'
    'No! **I haven't invited Josh to the party yet**.'

1   'Has Daniel taken his English test?'
    'No! ....'

2   'Have you been to the art gallery on High Street?'
    'No! ....'

3   'Have your parents talked to you about the party?'
    'No! ....'

4   'Have Sam and Ethan ordered their school photos?'
    'No! ....'

5   'Have you been to the hairdresser?'
    'No! ....'

6   'Has Lucy gone to Ankara?'
    'No! ....'

6 🔊 Rewrite the sentences using the words in brackets.

0 Have you paid for our ice-cream? (*yet*)
...........**Have you paid for our ice-cream yet?**...........

1 We haven't listened to the news. (*yet*)
....

2 Tom has called me. (*just*)
....

3 Have Amelia and Ruby got dressed? (*yet*)
....

4 I've spent all my pocket money. (*already*)
....

5 My sister has found a new job. (*just*)
....

6 The baby has woken up. (*just*)
....

7 I have brushed my teeth. (*already*)
....

8 We have travelled by ferry. (*already*)
....

7 🔊 Choose the correct option.

0 The football match hasn't begun ....
   A just   **B** already   Ⓒ yet

1 Take off your shoes! I've .... cleaned the floor.
   A just   **B** already   **C** yet

2 Emma hasn't done her homework ....
   A just
   B already
   C yet

3 'Where's your old bike?'
   'Paul has .... sold it. Somebody came to buy it last week.'
   A just   **B** already   **C** yet

4 'Have you taken the dog for a walk .... ?'
   'No, but I'll do it now.'
   A just
   B already
   C yet

5 'Do you want to watch *Batman*?'
   'No, thanks. I've .... seen it.'
   A just   **B** already   **C** yet

6 We're not hungry. We've .... eaten some sandwiches.
   A just
   B already
   C yet

8 🔊 Cross out the incorrect word in each sentence.

0 We haven't ~~just~~ played football yet.
1 They have yet already bought cinema tickets.
2 Have you yet painted the walls in your room yet?
3 I haven't just been to the bowling alley yet.
4 What a lovely smell! I think Megan has already just baked a cake.
5 This app on my phone says we have yet already walked 5 km.
6 They just have just opened a new skatepark in our town.
7 Don't bring any snacks. I've just already bought some crisps and biscuits.
8 Oliver hasn't already got on the bus yet.

9 🔊 Choose the correct option.

Connor Are you going to the concert?
Lola I can't! I haven't finished my homework **0**(yet)/ *already*.
Connor How long will it take you?
Lola Let me think. I've **1***yet / already* done my maths exercises but I haven't written the essay **2***yet / just*.
Connor Can't you do it tomorrow? We have to give it in on Friday.
Lola That's good news! But I have to ask my mum first. I haven't told her about the concert **3***already / yet*.
Connor Don't worry! I've **4***yet / already* spoken to my mum. My mum and your mum are at a school meeting together. They both know we're planning to go to a concert.

10 🔊 Complete the text messages using the correct form of the verbs in brackets.

Jamie! Do you remember that we've got guests tonight? **1**.................. .... (you / tidy) up your room yet?

Yes! And Molly **2**.............. .... (already / clean) the kitchen.

Perfect! Dad and I **3**.............. .... (just / do) the shopping. I think we're ready.

Almost. I **4**.............. .... (not / vacuum) the living room yet but I can do it now.

READING SKILLS

11 🔊 [1.25] **Read and listen to the text. Where do you think it is from?**

1 a coursebook for psychology students
2 a magazine for runners
3 a lifestyle magazine for teenagers
4 a leaflet for karate classes

12 **Read the text again and tick (✓) the advantages of having a hobby.**

1 you have a better memory
2 you meet new people
3 you learn more about the world around you
4 you are able to focus more
5 you work more quickly
6 you aren't so stressed
7 you solve problems without asking others for help
8 you have a lot of ideas
9 you are stronger and look better
10 you learn better and faster
11 you've got more energy to work
12 you don't get sick so often

13 **Read the text again and answer the questions.**

1 What, according to research, do successful people have in common?
2 What are three benefits of reading?
3 Why can people who read do some tasks faster?
4 What happens in our mind when we do sports such as running or cycling?
5 What quality do people who do sports regularly have?
6 Where, according to the article, can you take classes?
7 What can happen to people who only focus on work?
8 How, according to one study, do people's lives change when they spend time with their family and friends?
9 Why are people who spend time with friends and family healthier?

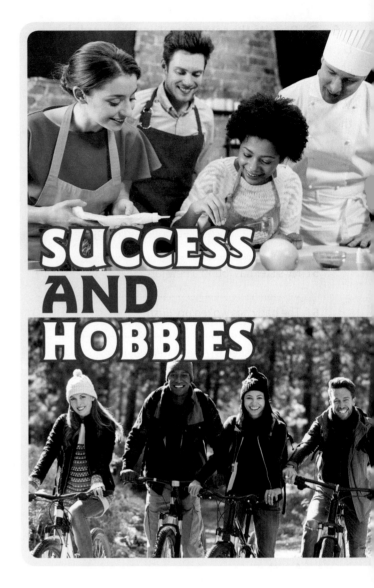

SUCCESS AND HOBBIES

14 🔊 **Choose the correct options to complete the expressions with *get*.**

1 I got .... from my cousin yesterday.
   A an email   **B** off   **C** cold
2 When I run fast I get .... very quickly.
   A ready   **B** tired   **C** up
3 In winter the days are shorter and it gets .... early.
   A hot   **B** jeans   **C** dark
4 It's such a sunny day! Let's get .... and have a picnic in the park.
   A outside   **B** off   **C** in
5 For my birthday I got a ....
   A shoes   **B** better   **C** laptop
6 My mum gets .... at 6:30 am. She doesn't even need an alarm clock.
   A up   **B** off   **C** into
7 What time did you get .... yesterday evening?
   A house   **B** at home   **C** home

Did you know that there is a link between free-time activities and success in life? Research shows that successful people spend their time in a similar way. What are the most popular leisure activities that they do? 5

1 **Reading** improves our concentration and memory. People who read can focus on their tasks better and complete them in a shorter time. What's more, books teach us new words and when we have broader vocabulary our speaking 10 and writing skills improve too. Reading also helps us to get our energy back after a long day and get ready for the next event.

2 **Doing sports** such as running or cycling clears our mind and allows us to get new ideas. It also 15 reduces stress and makes us more confident about our abilities. Regular exercise requires self-discipline which can be extremely useful when following dreams or different career paths.

3 **Taking classes** is a great free-time activity for 20 anyone at any age. It doesn't matter whether you choose dance lessons, a cake decorating course or karate. You can learn anywhere. It might be in a local leisure centre, at a university or online in your own home. Developing new skills will give 25 you energy to work harder and improve your ability to think and learn.

4 **Having a hobby** is not only enjoyable but essential if you want to be successful. People who focus only on work experience a lot of stress 30 and might suffer from a burn-out. Taking up a hobby relaxes you and allows you to enjoy both your career and your leisure time.

5 **Spending time with family and friends** brings a lot of benefits. According to one study 35 people who find time for friends and family live longer. They are also healthier because social life boosts the immune system and protects from illnesses.

It's good to have big dreams for your future. 40 Focusing all your efforts on one goal is helpful but to succeed you must be confident, creative and healthy. Having a balanced life with passions and friends by your side increases your chances of making your dreams come true. 45

VOCABULARY

LEISURE TIME

15 Answer the questions using these words.

art gallery ▪ bowling alley ▪ ice rink ▪ leisure centre ▪ multiplex cinema ▪ museum ▪ skatepark ▪ theatre ▪ water park

In which place/s can you …?

0 go swimming:
.. **water park** ., **leisure centre**

1 look at paintings:
………………………., ……………………….

2 see a film:
……………………….

3 see a play:
……………………….

4 do sports:
………………………., ………………………., ……………………….,
……………………….

5 meet friends and play a game by rolling a heavy ball:
……………………….

16 Circle the odd word out in each group and explain why.

0	actors	(photography)	stage
1	photography	painting	fitness
2	museum	drama group	dance class
3	actors	ice rink	play
4	audience	leisure centre	arts centre
5	stage	exercise	trainer
6	bowling alley	skatepark	swimming costume

17 Choose the correct option.

0 We went to the (art gallery) / theatre to see some paintings.

1 Jake wants to be an actor / a trainer.
Last year he took part in a few school plays.

2 Don't forget to take your swimming costume when we go to the ice rink / water park on Sunday.

3 We went to see our favourite singer at a music festival but she appeared on stage / audience for 30 minutes only.

4 Jessica doesn't go to dance classes, she prefers to do some leisure / exercises like yoga.

5 It's safer to wear a helmet when you go skateboarding in a bowling alley / skatepark.

6 Amy wants to study photography / fitness.
Her pictures are amazing.

GRAMMAR PRACTICE

Present perfect with *for* / *since*

Choose the correct options and complete the rule.

We use *for* and *since* to talk about a situation that started in the *present* / *past* and continues in the *present* / *future*. We use .... with a point in time and we use .... with a period of time.

➡ See **GRAMMAR REFERENCE** page 126

18 **Choose the correct option.**

0 (*for*) / *since* a week
1 *for* / *since* two hours
2 *for* / *since* last Tuesday
3 *for* / *since* 7 o'clock
4 *for* / *since* a year
5 *for* / *since* 2015
6 *for* / *since* I was ten
7 *for* / *since* a long time

19 **Complete the sentences using *for* or *since*.**

0 We have had this car ......*since*........ 2016.
1 This town has changed .... I last visited it.
2 I've been at home .... 40 minutes.
3 Caleb hasn't eaten .... this morning.
4 This shop has been closed .... December.
5 They haven't visited us .... three months.
6 It has been cold and snowy .... over a week.

20 **Answer the questions using *for* or *since* and the words in brackets.**

0 'How long have you been here?' (*ten minutes*)
   '............**I've been here for ten minutes.**............'
1 'How long has your sister worn glasses?' (*she was 7*)
   '..'
2 'How long have you known Jesse?' (*ages*)
   '..'
3 'How long have you and your brother studied French?' (*primary school*)
   '..'
4 'How long has Mrs Russell been in hospital?' (*four days*)
   '..'
5 'How long have you played football?' (*a year*)
   '..'
6 'How long have they lived in this flat?' (*they got married*)
   '..'

21 **Write sentences about yourself or your family using the prompts and *for* or *since*.**

0 have your laptop / computer
   I've had my laptop for six months.
1 be awake
2 study in this school
3 have the same haircut
4 your parents know each other
5 be interested in your hobby
6 use your bike / skateboard / Rollerblades

22 **Choose the correct options.**

Hi George,
How are you? I haven't heard from you ⁰............ ages!
Have you taken all your final exams ¹............?
I've ²............ finished mine and officially I have been on holiday ³............ yesterday evening! Yay!
I wanted to let you know that Mark and I started karate training in the leisure centre. I have wanted to do it ⁴............ months. We've ⁵............ had two classes but we haven't learnt much ⁶............ . It's difficult but fun!
Do you want to join us? Let me know!
Take care,
Brian

0	**A** since	(B) for	**C** in
1	**A** yet	**B** already	**C** just
2	**A** since	**B** yet	**C** just
3	**A** for	**B** yet	**C** since
4	**A** since	**B** for	**C** yet
5	**A** already	**B** yet	**C** just
6	**A** already	**B** just	**C** yet

SPEAKING SKILLS

MAKING ARRANGEMENTS

23 **Match the sentence halves.**

0 [f] What are you …
1 [ ] What …
2 [ ] Is that all right …
3 [ ] Perhaps another …
4 [ ] Do you …
5 [ ] Is that …
6 [ ] Can …
7 [ ] Are you …
8 [ ] How about …

a convenient for you?
b time?
c free on Tuesday?
d for you?
e about going to the ice rink?
f doing on Wednesday?
g prefer that?
h another time?
i you make it?

24 **Complete the conversations with these words.**

about ▪ asking ▪ ~~busy~~ ▪ can ▪ idea ▪ I'll ▪ I'm ▪
it ▪ like ▪ ~~on~~ ▪ rather ▪ thanks ▪ want ▪ would

0 **A** What are you doing ....**on**.......... Sunday?
   Do you want to go to the cinema?
   B I think I'm ....**busy**........ then.
1 **A** How .... having a party
   at the weekend?
   B .... think about ....
2 **A** Would you .... to play tennis with me
   on Saturday?
   B That's a nice .... but I don't think
   I ....
3 **A** Do you .... more juice?
   B No, ...
4 **A** .... you like to go shopping today?
   B No, I'd .... not.
5 **A** What about going to a concert on Friday?
   B Thanks for ...., but I don't think so.
6 **A** Can we meet on Tuesday?
   B I think .... busy then.

LISTENING SKILLS

25 **Choose the words that you think best describe the activity in the photo.**

[ ] dangerous
[ ] easy
[ ] frightening
[ ] exciting
[ ] fun
[ ] incredible
[ ] safe
[ ] difficult

26 ◣ [1.26] **Listen to Maya and Oliver and answer the questions.**

1 Who are Maya and Oliver?
2 What does Maya suggest doing on Saturday?
3 What do you do in this place?
4 Does Oliver want to join Maya?

27 ◣ [1.26] **Listen again and decide if the sentences are true (T) or false (F). Correct the false ones.**

1 Maya is asking Oliver about
  his Sunday plans. [T] [F]
2 Maya, Caroline and Jake are planning
  to go to the Treetop Walk. [T] [F]
3 Oliver has already been
  to the Treetop Walk. [T] [F]
4 In the Greenside Forest there is a river
  and hills. [T] [F]
5 The paths in the Treetop Walk
  are eight metres above the ground. [T] [F]
6 There are 19 tasks
  in the extreme part of the Treetop Walk. [T] [F]
7 When you buy tickets online
  they cost £30. [T] [F]

ACADEMIC SKILLS

LABELLING A DIAGRAM

28 Match the phrases to the symbols.

0 $\boxed{E}$ on the left
1 $\square$ on the right
2 $\square$ in the centre
3 $\square$ in the east
4 $\square$ in the south
5 $\square$ in the west
6 $\square$ in the north

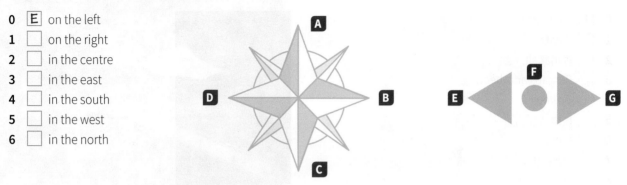

29 Read the text about Riverside Park and label the map with these words.

a basketball court ▪ a café ▪ a car park ▪
a football field ▪ an ice-cream shop ▪
a lake ▪ a playground ▪ toilets

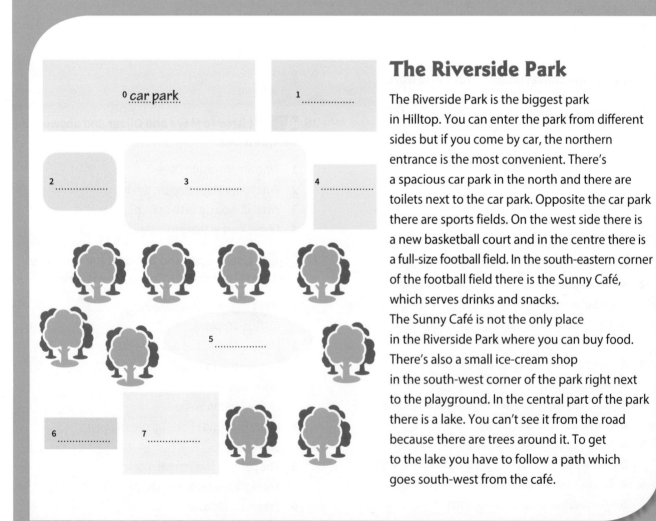

0 car park

1 ....

2 ....

3 ....

4 ....

5 ....

6 ....

7 ....

The Riverside Park

The Riverside Park is the biggest park
in Hilltop. You can enter the park from different
sides but if you come by car, the northern
entrance is the most convenient. There's
a spacious car park in the north and there are
toilets next to the car park. Opposite the car park
there are sports fields. On the west side there is
a new basketball court and in the centre there is
a full-size football field. In the south-eastern corner
of the football field there is the Sunny Café,
which serves drinks and snacks.

The Sunny Café is not the only place
in the Riverside Park where you can buy food.
There's also a small ice-cream shop
in the south-west corner of the park right next
to the playground. In the central part of the park
there is a lake. You can't see it from the road
because there are trees around it. To get
to the lake you have to follow a path which
goes south-west from the café.

30 Draw a map of a park in your city or an imaginary one.
Describe the services and facilities in the park and say where they are.

EXAM STRATEGY

Speaking – Describing a photo

In this speaking activity the examiner gives each candidate one minute to describe a photograph. When you talk about your photo be precise. Imagine you are describing it to someone who can't see it. Give a general description of what you can see in the photo. Then focus on the details: say what the people look like and what they are doing. Talk about the weather and time of day or year. Try to guess how the people feel. If you don't remember the words for the things you see in the picture, paraphrase or describe them using words you do know.

31 Look at the photo and read how it was described during the examination. Tick (✓) the topics mentioned.

1   who is in the picture
2   the place where they are
3   what they are doing
4   their clothes
5   the reason why they are doing this activity
6   how they feel
7   the background of the picture
8   the weather
9   the season
10   the time of the day

This picture shows four teenagers having fun on the beach. I think it's a beach because there is a lot of sand and some dry grass and a surfboard in the background. There are two girls and two boys. A boy and a girl are sitting on beach chairs, the other boy and girl are sitting on a blanket. They are all smiling. The girl sitting on the blanket is playing the guitar. They all look very happy. They're probably having a picnic because in the foreground there's a picnic bag.
It's a cloudy day but I think it's summer because I can see that they're wearing T-shirts, shorts and sunglasses. They are all having a great time.

32 Look at the photo and write what you see.

EXAM STRATEGY

Speaking – Discussion

You and your partner will have a short discussion about topics related to the task.
The examiner won't ask direct questions to each candidate, but will read out questions for you both to discuss together. You will be asked to talk about your preferences, habits, opinions and whether you agree or disagree.

33 Look again at exercise 29 on page 100.
Read the following questions and make notes for your answers.

- Which places in your town would be interesting for a group of exchange students from another country?
- Do you think exchange visits for students are a good idea? Why?
- Have you ever been on an exchange visit? What was it like?
- Would you like to go on an exchange visit? Where?
- What can students learn from visiting other countries?

REVISE AND ROUND UP

1 📶 Complete the table with the infinitive without *to*, the past simple or the past participle.

infinitive without *to*	past simple	past participle
..........be..........	was / were	....
catch	....	....
....	....	worn
....	came	....
....	took	....
buy	....	....
write	....	....
....	got	....
....	....	seen
think	....	....
fly	....	....
....	heard	....

2 📶 Write sentences or questions using the present perfect.

0 we / take pictures / of the Eiffel Tower
   We have taken pictures of the Eiffel Tower.

1 you / be / to the London Zoo?
   ....

2 I / not / fly / a plane
   ....

3 Mark / give / me / the best present
   ....

4 they / win / the lottery?
   ....

5 my mum / run / a marathon
   ....

6 your grandma / meet / the queen?
   ....

3 📶 Add *ever* or *never* to these sentences.

0 I have **never** eaten pizza with broccoli.
1 Have you seen a falling star?
2 Has your sister got a bad mark on a test?
3 I have worn a straw hat.
4 My friends have played bingo.
5 Have you driven a car?
6 They have heard this band.

4 📶 Choose the correct option.

0 My parents have just left. They've *been* / (*gone*) to the supermarket.

1 I've *been* / *gone* to this new gym a few times. Do you want to go there with me tomorrow?

2 Our teacher has *been* / *gone* to the headteacher's office. He'll be back in ten minutes.

3 'You're back!' 'Yes! My parents and I have *been* / *gone* camping. It was a great trip.'

4 Have you ever *been* / *gone* to this Japanese restaurant? They serve great food.

5 'Is your brother at home?' 'No, he's *been* / *gone* to a piano lesson.'

6 They've *been* / *gone* to London twice this month. They always go there by train.

5 📶 Use the time expressions and the past simple or present perfect to write sentences about you.

0 yesterday
   I had fish for lunch yesterday.

1 ever
   ....

2 last month
   ....

3 on Wednesday
   ....

4 never
   ....

5 two hours ago
   ....

6 📶 Rewrite the sentences using one of the words in brackets.

0 Max hasn't read this book about coding. (*just* / *yet*)
   Max hasn't read this book about coding yet.

1 Don't water the plants. Mum has done it. (*already* / *yet*)
   ....

2 Have you called your parents? (*just* / *yet*)
   ....

3 Good news! I've found a new job! (*yet* / *just*)
   ....

4 She hasn't replied to my email. (*just* / *yet*)
   ....

5 Look! I've saved £30. (*yet* / *already*)
   ....

6 Josh has made some tea. It's still hot. (*just* / *yet*)
   ....

7 🔊 Write sentences using *for* or *since*.

0 my friends / be / in a café / an hour
   My friends have been in a café for an hour.

1 I / not drink / water / 6 o'clock
   ....

2 it / be / sunny / two days
   ....

3 we / be / friends / we started primary school
   ....

4 Amelia / not / change / at all / she was a girl
   ....

5 they / have / two dogs / October
   ....

6 we / not speak / weeks
   ....

8 🔊 Choose the correct options.

Chloe   ⁰(*Have you seen*) / *Did you see* this new
   science-fiction film ¹*yet* / *just*?

Jordan   Yes, I ²*have* / *did*. I ³*have gone* / *went*
   to the cinema ⁴*for last week* / *last week*.

Chloe   Do you think it's better than the book?

Jordan   I ⁵*haven't read* / *didn't read* the book ⁶*already*
   / *yet*. I've ⁷*just* / *yet* borrowed it from
   the library. Look! I've got it in my bag.

Chloe   Really? This ⁸*has been* / *was* my favourite book
   ⁹*for* / *since* I ¹⁰*was* / *have been* eight years old. I
   think I've read it more than 20 times.

Jordan   I've ¹¹*ever* / *never* read any book twice! ¹²*Have* /
   Did you read it again last week before seeing
   the film?

9 🔊 Complete the message with the correct form
   of the verbs in brackets.

Hi Mum,
I ¹............... (go) to the basketball court to
play with Andrew. We ²............... (not
practise) for months. Our last basketball
match ³............... (be) in October. Don't
worry! I ⁴............... (already do) my
homework but I ⁵............... (not eat)
anything yet. Can we have dinner when
I ⁶............... (get) back?
Love,
Jack

CONCEPT CHECK

**Read the sentences and answer
the questions.**

1 *I have ridden a motorcycle.*

0 Does this sentence refer to the present, future
   or past? **Past**

1 Do we know when this activity happened?

2 What is more important in this sentence: the time
   when it happened or the fact that it happened?

3 What is the form of the verb in this sentence?

4 Can you add *not* to this sentence? If so, where?

2 *I rode a motorcycle last week.*

0 Does this sentence refer to the present, future
   or past? **Past**

1 Do we know when this activity happened?

2 What other time expressions can we use in this
   sentence?

3 What is more important in this sentence: the time
   when it happened or the fact that it happened?

4 What is the form of the verb in this sentence?

3 *I've just talked to Martha.*

0 What is the meaning of *just* in this sentence?
   Very recently

1 Can we rewrite this sentence with *yet*? Where will
   it go? How will the meaning change?

2 Can we replace *just* with *already*? Where will it go?

4 *We have had this sofa for five years.*

0 Is this a finished activity or does it continue from
   past till present? **It continues from past till
   present**

1 Do you use *for* with a point or period in time?

2 What other time expressions can follow *for* in this
   sentence?

3 If we replace *five years* with *2012*, what word will
   we use instead of *for*?

➡ See **GRAMMAR REFERENCE**
pages 125-126

WORDLIST

STARTER A

American (adj) /əˈmer.ɪ.kən/
British (adj) /ˈbrɪt.ɪʃ/
Chilean (adj) /ˈtʃɪl.i.ən/
Chinese (adj) /tʃaɪˈniːz/
French (adj) /frentʃ/
German (adj) /ˈdʒɜː.mən/
Greek (adj) /griːk/
Indian (adj) /ˈɪn.di.ən/
Italian (adj) /ɪˈtæliən/
Japanese (adj) /ˌdzæp.əˈniːz/
Mexican (adj) /ˈmek.sɪ.kən/
Nigerian (adj) /naɪˈdʒɪə.ri.ən/
Polish (adj) /ˈpəʊ·lɪʃ/
Spanish (adj) /ˈspæn.ɪʃ/
Turkish (adj) /ˈtɜːkɪʃ/

STARTER B

brother (n) /ˈbrʌð.ər/
cousin (n) /ˈkʌz.ən/
daughter (n) /ˈdɔː.tər/
granddaughter (n) /ˈgræn.dɔː.tər/
grandfather (n) /ˈgræn.fɑː.ðər/
husband (n) /ˈhʌz.bənd/
nephew (n) /ˈnef.juː/
niece (n) /niːs/
only child (n) /ˈəʊn.li tʃaɪld/
sister (n) /ˈsɪs.tər/
son (n) /sʌn/
uncle (n) /ˈʌŋ.kl̩/

STARTER C

April (n) /ˈeɪ.prəl/
art (n) /ɑːt/
at (prep) /ət/
August (n) /ɔːˈgʌst/
biology (n) /baɪˈɒl.ə.dʒi/
December (n) /dɪˈsem.bə/
English (n) /ˈɪŋ.glɪʃ/
February (n) /ˈfeb.ru.ər.i/
Friday (n) /ˈfraɪ.deɪ/
geography (n) /dʒiˈɒg.rə.fi/
history (n) /ˈhɪs.tər.i/
ICT (n) /ˌaɪ.siːˈtiː/
in (prep) /ɪn/
January (n) /ˈdʒæn.jʊ.ri/
July (n) /dʒʊˈlaɪ/
June (n) /dʒuːn/
March (n) /mɑːtʃ/
maths (n) /mæθs/
May (n) /meɪ/

Monday (n) /ˈmʌn.deɪ/
November (n) /nəʊˈvem.bə/
October (n) /ɒkˈtəʊ.bə/
on (prep) /ɒn/
PE (n) /ˌpiːˈiː/
Saturday (n) /ˈsæt.ə.deɪ/
science (n) /ˈsaɪəns/
September (n) /sepˈtem.bə/
Spanish (n) /ˈspæn.ɪʃ/
Sunday (n) /ˈsʌn.deɪ/
Thursday (n) /ˈθɜːz.deɪ/
Tuesday (n) /ˈtjuːz.deɪ/
Wednesday (n) /ˈwenz.deɪ/

STARTER D

beef (n) /biːf/
biscuit (n) /ˈbɪs.kɪt/
box (n) /bɒks/
bread (n) /bred/
butter (n) /ˈbʌt.ər/
cheese (n) /tʃiːz/
cookery (n) /ˈkʊk.ər.i/
egg (n) /eg/
eighth (n) /eɪtθ/
fifth (n) /fɪfθ/
first (n) /ˈfɜːst/
fish (n) /fɪʃ/
fourth (n) /fɔːθ/
fruit juice (n) /fruːt dʒuːs/
grape (n) /greɪp/
milk (n) /mɪlk/
muffin (n) /ˈmʌf.ɪn/
nectarine (n) /ˈnek.tər.iːn/
ninth (n) /naɪnθ/
olive (n) /ˈɒl.ɪv/
onion (n) /ˈʌn.jən/
packet (n) /ˈpæk.ɪt/
pea (n) /piː/
peach (n) /piːtʃ/
pear (n) /peər/
potato (n) /pəˈteɪ.təʊ/
rice (n) /raɪs/
second (n) /ˈsek.ənd/
seventh (n) /ˈsev.ənθ/
sixth (n) /sɪksθ/
special offer (n) /ˈspeʃ.əl ˈɒf.ər/
spinach (n) /ˈspɪn.ɪtʃ/
strawberry (n) /ˈstrɔː.bər.i/
tea (n) /tiː/
tenth (n) /tenθ/
third (n) /θɜːd/

tomato (n) /təˈmɑː.təʊ/
yogurt (n) /ˈjɒg.ət/

STARTER E

bike ride (n) /baɪk raɪd/
book (n) /bʊk/
film (n) /fɪlm/
football (n) /ˈfʊt.bɔːl/
friend's house (n) /frendz haʊs/
go (v) /gəʊ/
guitar (n) /gɪˈtɑːr/
gym (n) /dʒɪm/
have (v) /hæv/
magazine (n) /ˌmæg.əˈziːn/
meet (v) /miːt/
piano (n) /piˈæn.əʊ/
play (v) /pleɪ/
read (v) /riːd/
shopping (n) /ˈʃɒp.ɪŋ/
swimming pool (n) /ˈswɪm.ɪŋˌpuːl/
television (n) /ˈtel.ɪ.vɪʒ.ən/
video game (n) /ˈvɪd.i.əʊ geɪm/
volleyball (n) /ˈvɒl.i.bɔːl/
walk (n) /wɔːk/
watch (v) /wɒtʃ/

UNIT 1

always (adv) /ˈɔːl.weɪz/
be into (phr v) /biː ˈɪn.tuː/
brush your teeth (phr v) /brʌʃ jɔːr tiːθ/
busy (adj) /ˈbɪz.i/
can't stand (v) /kænt stænd/
check your phone (phr v) /tʃek jɔːr fəʊn/
don't like (v) /dəʊnt laɪk/
don't mind (v) /dəʊnt maɪnd/
each other (pron) /ˌiːtʃ ˈʌðər/
early bird (n) /ˈɜː.li bɜːd/
enjoy (v) /ɪnˈdʒɔɪ/
finish (v) /ˈfɪn.ɪʃ/
get dressed (phr v) /get drest/
get home (phr v) /get həʊm/
get up (phr v) /ˈget.ʌp/
hardly ever (adv) /ˈhɑːd.li ˈev.ər/
hate (v) /heɪt/
have a shower (phr v) /hæv ə ʃaʊər/
have breakfast (phr v) /hæv ˈbrek.fəst/
have dinner (phr v) /hæv ˈdɪn.ər/
have lunch (phr v) /hæv lʌntʃ/
height (n) /haɪt/
homework (n) /ˈhəʊm.wɜːk/

leave (v) /liːv /
like (v) /laɪk/
love (v) /lʌv/
night owl (n) /naɪt aʊl/
often (adv) /ˈɒf.ən/
online (adv) /ˈɒn.laɪn/
quiet (adj) /kwaɪət/
skin (n) /skɪn/
sometimes (adv) /ˈsʌm.taɪmz/
start (v) /stɑːt /
together (adj) /təˈɡeð.ər/
wake up (phr v) /weɪk ʌp/
weight (n) /weɪt/
work (n) /wɜːk/

UNIT 2

access (v) /ˈæk.ses/
acquire (v) /əˈkwaɪər/
average (n) /ˈæv.ər.ɪdʒ/
badly (adv) /ˈbæd.li/
carefully (adv) /ˈkeə.fəl.i/
challenge (n) /ˈtʃæl.ɪndʒ/
developed world (n) /dɪˈvel.əpt wɜːld/
developing country (n) /dɪˈvel.ə.pɪŋ ˈkʌn.tri/
early (adv) /ˈɜː.li/
easily (adv) /ˈiː.zɪ.li/
exam (n) /ɪɡˈzæm/
facilities (n) /fəˈsɪlətiz/
fast (adv) /fɑːst/
foreign (adj) /ˈfɒr.ən/
fully (adv) /ˈfʊl.i/
hard (adv) /hɑːd/
knowledge (n) /ˈnɒl.ɪdʒ/
late (adv) /leɪt/
learn (v) /lɜːn/
mark (n) /mɑːk/
praise (n) /preɪz/
properly (adv) /ˈprɒp.əl.i/
rather than (phr) /ˈrɑː.ðər ðæn/
receive (v) /rɪˈsiːv/
report (n) /rɪˈpɔːt/
test (n) /test/
well (adv) /wel/
work (v) /wɜːk/

UNIT 3

app (n) /æp/
attach (v) /əˈtætʃ/
attachment (n) /əˈtætʃ.mənt/
cable (n) /ˈkeɪ.bl̩/

charger (n) /ˈtʃɑː.dʒər/
click (v) /klɪk/
close (v) /kləʊz/
code (n) /kəʊd/
console (n) /kənˈsəʊl/
copy (v) /ˈkɒp.i/
cut (v) /kʌt/
delete (v) /dɪˈliːt/
desktop computer (n) /ˈdesk.tɒp kəmˈpjuː.tər/
download (v) /ˌdaʊnˈləʊd/
drag (v) /dræɡ/
e-reader (n) /ˈiː.riː.dər/
earphones (n) /ˈɪə.fəʊnz/
external hard drive (n) /ɪkˈstɜː.nəl hɑːd draɪv/
file (n) /faɪl/
function (n) /ˈfʌŋk.ʃən/
game controller (n) /ɡeɪm kənˈtrəʊ.lər/
hard disk (n) /hɑːd dɪsk/
icon (n) /ˈaɪ.kɒn/
install (v) /ɪnˈstɔːl/
laptop (n) /ˈlæp.tɒp/
link (n) /lɪŋk/
log in (phr v) /ˈlɒɡ.ɪn/
log out (phr v) /lɒɡ aʊt/
memory stick (n) /ˈmeməri ˌstɪk/
mouse (n) /maʊs/
open (v) /ˈəʊ.pən/
overload (adj) /ˌəʊ.vəˈləʊd/
paste (v) /peɪst/
post (v) /pəʊst/
postal service (n) /ˈpəʊ.stəl ˈsɜː.vɪs/
press (v) /pres/
printer (n) /ˈprɪn.tər/
privacy settings (n) /ˈprɪv.ə.si ˈset.ɪŋz/
save (v) /seɪv/
scanner (n) /ˈskæn.ər/
screen (n) /skriːn/
search (v) /sɜːtʃ/
select (v) /sɪˈlekt/
social media (n) /ˈsəʊ.ʃəl ˈmiː.di.ə/
software (n) /ˈsɒft.weər/
speakers (n) /ˈspiː.kəz/
steam train (n) /stiːm treɪn/
stone (n) /stəʊn/
swipe (v) /swaɪp/
tablet (n) /ˈtæb.lət/
telegram (n) /ˈtel.ɪ.ɡræm/
unknown (adj) /ʌnˈnəʊn/
upload (v) /ʌpˈləʊd/

website (n) /ˈweb.saɪt/
wheel (n) /wiːl/

UNIT 4

addict (n) /ˈædɪkt/
afford (v) /əˈfɔːd/
affordable (adj) /əˈfɔːdəbəl/
belt (n) /belt/
biodegrade (v) /baɪəʊdɪˈɡreɪd/
blame (v) /bleɪm/
boots (n) /buːts/
brand (n) /brænd/
buttons (n) /ˈbʌt.ənz/
cap (n) /kæp/
cardigan (n) /ˈkɑː.dɪ.ɡən/
chain (n) /tʃeɪn/
checked (adj) /tʃekt/
coat (n) /kəʊt/
collar (n) /ˈkɒl.ər/
combats (n) /ˈkɒm.bæts/
consumer (n) /kənˈsuːmər/
dress (n) /dres/
fashion (n) /ˈfæʃən/
gloves (n) /ɡlʌvz/
handbag (n) /ˈhænd.bæɡ/
heel (n) /hiːl/
high street (n) /haɪ striːt/
hoodie (n) /ˈhʊd.i/
jeans (n) /dʒiːnz/
jewellery (n) /ˈdʒuː.əl.ri/
joggers (n) /dʒɒɡəz/
jumper (n) /ˈdʒʌm.pər/
lace-up shoes (n) /leɪs ʌp ʃuːz/
laces (n) /leɪsɪz/
leggings (n) /ˈleɡ.ɪŋz/
luxury (n) /ˈlʌk.ʃəri/
outfit (n) /ˈaʊtfɪt/
patterned (adj) /ˈpæt.ənd/
plain (adj) /pleɪn/
pocket (adj) /ˈpɒk.ɪt/
recession (n) /rɪˈseʃən/
retailer (n) /ˈriːteɪlər/
trend (n) /trend/
sandals (n) /ˈsæn.dəlz/
scarf (n) /skɑːf/
shirt (n) /ʃɜːt/
shoes (n) /ʃuːz/
shorts (n) /ʃɔːts/
show off (phr v) /ʃəʊ ɒf/
striped (adj) /straɪpt/
sunglasses (n) /ˈsʌŋˌɡlɑː.sɪz/

WORDLIST

sustainable (adj) /sə'steɪnəbəl/
sweatshirt (n) /'swet.ʃɜːt/
T-shirt (n) /'tiː.ʃɜːt/
tie (n) /taɪ/
tights (n) /taɪts/
trainers (n) /'treɪnəz/
vicious circle (n) /'vɪʃəs 'sɜːkəl/

UNIT 5

accountant (n) /ə'kaʊn.tənt/
administration (n) /əd,mɪn.ɪ'streɪ.ʃən/
agriculture (n) /'æg.rɪ.kʌl.tʃər /
badly paid (adj) /'bæd.li peɪd/
builder (n) /'bɪl.dər/
construction (n) /kən'strʌk.ʃən/
cook (n) /kʊk/
creative (n) /kri'eɪ.tɪv/
dangerous (adj) /'deɪn.dʒər.əs/
debt (n) /det/
degree (n) /dɪ'griː/
downside (n) /'daʊn.saɪd/
earn (v) /ɜːn/
engineer (n) /,en.dʒɪ'nɪər/
environment (n) /ɪn'vaɪ.rən.mənt/
farmer (n) /'fɑː.mər/
fashion designer (n)
   /'fæʃ.ən dɪ'zaɪ.nər/
finance (n) /'faɪ.næns/
freelance (adj) /'friː.lɑːns/
full-time (adj) /,fʊl'taɪm/
get the sack (phr v) /get ðiː sæk/
give up (phr v) /gɪv ʌp/
graduate (n) /'grædʒ.u.ət/
hairdresser (n) /'heə,dres.ər/
healthcare (n) /'helθ.keər/
IT (n) /,aɪ'tiː/
job (n) /dʒɒb/
law (n) /lɔː/
lawyer (n) /'lɔɪ.ər/
loan (n) /ləʊn/
mechanic (n) /mə'kæn.ɪk/
media (n) /'miː.di.ə /
money (n) /'mʌn.i/
nurse (n) /nɜːs/
overtime (n) /'əʊ.və.taɪm/
part-time (adj) /,pɑːt'taɪm/
pay rise (n) /peɪ raɪz/
plumber (n) /'plʌm.ər/
police officer (n) /pə'liːs,ɒf.ɪ.sər/
promotion (n) /prə'məʊ.ʃən/
retail (n) /'riː.teɪl/

salary (n) /'sæl.ər.i/
secretary (n) /'sek.rə.tər.i/
services (n) /'sɜːvɪsɪz/
shift (n) /ʃɪft/
shop assistant (n) /'ʃɒp.ə,sɪs.tənt/
sick pay (n) /sɪk peɪ/
software developer (n) /'sɒft.weər
   dɪ'vel.ə.pər/
supply teacher (n) /sə'plaɪ 'tiː.tʃər/
top up (v) /'tɒp.ʌp/
training (n) /'treɪ.nɪŋ/
wage (n) /weɪdʒ/
waiter/waitress (n) /'weɪ.tər 'weɪ.trəs/
well-paid (adj) /,wel'peɪd/
work (v) /wɜːk/

UNIT 6

advice (n) /əd'vaɪs/
arm (n) /ɑːm/
back (n) /bæk/
bacteria (n) /bæk'tɪəriə/
bone (n) /bəʊn/
brain (n) /breɪn/
chest (n) /tʃest/
elbow (n) /'el.bəʊ/
finger (n) /'fɪŋ.gər/
foot (n) /fʊt/
hand (n) /hænd/
head (n) /hed/
heart (n) /hɑːt/
hip (n) /hɪp/
immune system (n) /ɪ'mjuːn,sɪs.təm/
knee (n) /niː/
leg (n) /leg/
muscle (n) /'mʌs.əl/
neck (n) /nek/
samples (n) /'sɑːm.pəlz/
shoulder (n) /'ʃəʊl.dər/
skin (n) /skɪn/
sore throat (n) /sɔːr θrəʊt/
stomach (n) /'stʌm.ək/
tooth (n) /tuːθ/

UNIT 7

afraid (adj) /ə'freɪd/
angry (adj) /'æŋ.gri/
anxious (adj) /'æŋk.ʃəs/
arrogant (adj) /'ær.ə.gənt/
better (adj) /'bet.ər/
big (adj) /bɪg/
calm (adj) /kɑːm/

cheerful (adj) /'tʃɪə.fəl/
close (adj) /kləʊz/
confident (adj) /'kɒn.fɪ.dənt/
cool (adj) /kuːl/
depressed (adj) /dɪ'prest/
easy (adj) /'iː.zi/
easy-going (adj) /,iː.zi'gəʊ.ɪŋ/
embarrassed (adj) /ɪm'bær.əst/
excited (adj) /ɪk'saɪ.tɪd/
expensive (adj) /ɪk'spen.sɪv/
friendly (adj) /'frend.li/
funny (adj) /'fʌn.i/
further/farther (adj) /'fɜː.ðər 'fɑː.ðər/
happy (adj) /'hæp.i/
hard-working (adj) /,hɑːd'wɜː.kɪŋ/
hit (v) /hɪt/
inequality (n) /,ɪn.ɪ'kwɒl.ə.ti/
inspired (adj) /ɪn'spaɪəd/
intelligent (adj) /ɪn'tel.ɪ.dʒənt/
intense (adj) /ɪn'tens/
kind (adj) /kaɪnd/
laugh (v) /læf/
lonely (adj) /'ləʊn.li/
make fun of (phr v) /meɪk fʌn əv/
nervous (adj) /'nɜː.vəs/
noisy (adj) /'nɔɪ.zi/
normal (adj) /'nɔː.məl/
organised (adj) /'ɔː.gən.aɪzd/
policy (n) /'pɒl.ə.siz/
popular (adj) /'pɒp.jʊ.lər/
quiet (adj) /kwaɪət/
rank (v) /ræŋk/
relaxed (adj) /rɪ'lækst/
reserved (adj) /rɪ'zɜːvd/
resilient (adj) /rɪ'zɪl.i.ənt/
rude (adj) /ruːd/
sad (adj) /sæd/
satisfied (adj) /'sæt.ɪs.faɪd/
scared (adj) /skeəd/
self-confident (adj) /,self'kɒn.fɪ.dənt/
serious (adj) /'sɪə.ri.əs/
small (adj) /smɔːl/
standard of living (n) /'stæn.dəd
   əv 'lɪv.ɪŋ/
stressed (adj) /strest/
surprised (adj) /sə'praɪzd/
tired (adj) /taɪəd/
trust (n) /trʌst/
worried (adj) /'wʌr.id/
worse (adj) /wɜːs/

UNIT 8

air conditioning (n) /ˈeə.kənˌdɪʃ.ən.ɪŋ/
armchair (n) /ˈɑːm.tʃeər/
arrange (v) /əˈreɪndʒ/
balcony (n) /ˈbæl.kə.ni/
bath (n) /bɑːθ/
bathroom (n) /ˈbɑːθ.rʊm/
bed (n) /bed/
bedroom (n) /ˈbed.rʊm/
behind (prep) /bɪˈhaɪnd/
between (prep) /bɪˈtwiːn/
bookcase (n) /ˈbʊk.keɪs/
chair (n) /tʃeər/
chest of drawers (n) /ˌtʃest.əvˈdrɔːz/
cluttered (adj) /ˈklʌt.əd/
cooker (n) /ˈkʊk.ər/
cupboard (n) /ˈkʌb.əd/
curtains (n) /ˈkɜː.tənz/
desk (n) /desk/
dishwasher (n) /ˈdɪʃ.wɒʃ.ər/
domestic appliance (n)
   /dəˈmes.tɪk əˈplaɪ.ənts/
empty (v) /ˈemp.ti/
fence (n) /fens/
floor (n) /flɔːr/
freezer (n) /ˈfriː.zər/
fridge (n) /frɪdʒ/
front door (n) /frʌnt dɔːr/
garden (n) /ˈgɑː.dən/
gate (n) /geɪt/
get rid of (phr v) /get rɪd əv/
heating (n) /ˈhiː.tɪŋ/
in (prep) /ɪn/
in front of (prep) /ɪn frʌnt əv/
kitchen (n) /ˈkɪtʃ.ən/
lights (n) /laɪts/
living room (n) /ˈlɪv.ɪŋ.rʊm/
maximise (v) /ˈmæk.sɪ.maɪz/
media unit (n) /ˈmiː.di.ə ˈjuː.nɪt/
mirror (n) /ˈmɪr.ər/
move (v) /muːv/
near (prep) /nɪər/
next to (prep) /nekst tuː/
on (prep) /ɒn/
opposite (prep) /ˈɒp.ə.zɪt/
pack (v) /pæk/
patio (n) /ˈpæt.i.əʊ/
pick up (phr v) /ˈpɪk.ʌp/
put back (phr v) /pʊt bæk/
roof (n) /ruːf/
set (n) /set/

shower (n) /ʃaʊər/
shutters (n) /ˈʃʌtəz/
sink (n) /sɪŋk/
sofa (n) /ˈsəʊ.fə/
sort out (phr v) /ˈsɔːt.aʊt/
stairs (n) /steəz/
storage unit (n) /ˈstɔː.rɪdʒ ˈjuː.nɪt/
study (n) /ˈstʌd.i/
stuff (n) /stʌf/
take out (phr v) /ˈteɪk.aʊt/
throw away (phr v) /ˈθrəʊ.ə.weɪ/
toilet (n) /ˈtɔɪ.lət/
toy building brick (n) /tɔɪ ˈbɪl.dɪŋ brɪk/
under (prep) /ˈʌn.dər/
wall (n) /wɔːl/
wardrobe (n) /ˈwɔː.drəʊb/
washbasin (n) /ˈwɒʃ.beɪ.sən/
washing machine (n) /ˈwɒʃ.ɪŋ.məˌʃiːn/
worktop (n) /ˈwɜːk.tɒp/
wrap (v) /ræp/

UNIT 9

bike (n) /baɪk/
boat (n) /bəʊt/
bus (n) /bʌs/
cable car (n) /ˈkeɪ.bl̩ kɑːr/
catch (v) /kætʃ/
coach (n) /kəʊtʃ/
cycle rickshaw (n) /ˈsaɪ.kl̩ ˈrɪk.ʃɔː/
drive (v) /draɪv/
ferry (n) /ˈfer.i/
fly (v) /flaɪ/
get back (phr v) /get bæk/
get in (phr v) /get ɪn/
get off (phr v) /get ɒf/
get on (phr v) /get ɒn/
get out of (phr v) /get aʊt əv/
helicopter (n) /ˈhel.ɪˌkɒp.tər/
horse (n) /hɔːs/
inline skates (n) /ˈɪn.laɪn skeɪts/
jump (v) /dʒʌmp/
kayak (n) /ˈkaɪ.æk/
motorbike (n) /ˈməʊ.tə.baɪk/
pedal boat (n) /ˈped.əl bəʊt/
plane (n) /pleɪn/
ride (v) /raɪd/
river bus (n) /ˈrɪv.ər bʌs/
sail (v) /seɪl/
sailing (v) /ˈseɪ.lɪŋ/
scooter (n) /ˈskuː.tər/
set off (phr v) /ˈset.ɒf/

shelter (n) /ˈʃel.tər/
ship (n) /ʃɪp/
survive (v) /səˈvaɪv/
take (v) /teɪk/
take off (phr v) /ˈteɪk.ɒf/
taxi/taxicab (n) /ˈtæk.si /ˈtæk.si.kæb/
train (n) /treɪn/
tram (n) /træm/
(the) Tube (n) /tjuːb/
underground (n) /ˌʌn.dəˈgraʊnd/

UNIT 10

5-a-side football (n) /faɪv ə saɪd ˈfʊt.bɔːl/
actors (n) /ˈæk.təz/
art gallery (n) /ɑːt ˈgæl.ər.i/
audience (n) /ˈɔː.di.əns/
bowling alley (n) /ˈbəʊ.lɪŋ ˈæl.i/
changing rooms (n) /ˈtʃeɪn.dʒɪŋ ruːmz/
dance class (n) /dɑːns klɑːs/
drama group (n) /ˈdrɑː.mə gruːp/
exercise (n) /ˈek.sə.saɪz/
expectation (n) /ˌek.spekˈteɪ.ʃən/
fitness (n) /ˈfɪt.nəs/
fitness studio (n) /ˈfɪt.nəs ˈstjuː.di.əʊ/
gym (n) /dʒɪm/
ice rink (n) /aɪs rɪŋk/
leisure centre (n) /ˈleʒ.ər ˈsen.tər/
multiplex cinema (n)
   /ˈmʌl.tɪ.pleks ˈsɪn.ə.mə/
museum (n) /mjuːˈziː.əm/
painting (n) /ˈpeɪn.tɪŋ/
photography (n) /fəˈtɒg.rə.fi/
play (n) /pleɪ/
prevent (v) /prɪˈvent/
prisoner (n) /ˈprɪz.ən.ər/
proud (adj) /praʊd/
recharge (v) /ˌriːˈtʃɑːdʒ/
self-esteem (n) /ˌself.ɪˈstiːm/
skate park (n) /ˈskeɪt.pɑːk/
sports hall (n) /spɔːts hɔːl/
stage (n) /steɪdʒ/
swimming costume (n)
   /ˈswɪm.ɪŋˌkɒs.tjuːm/
swimming pool (n) /ˈswɪm.ɪŋ.puːl/
theatre (n) /ˈθɪə.tər/
trainer (n) /ˈtreɪ.nər/
unwind (v) /ʌnˈwaɪnd/
water park (n) /ˈwɔː.tər pɑːk/

WORDLIST

LITERATURE SKILLS 1

fir tree (n) /'fɜːr triː/
hard set (adj) /hɑːd set/
prod (v) /prɒd/
row (n) /raʊ/
sleeve (n) /sliːv/

LITERATURE SKILLS 2

disagreeable (adj) /ˌdɪs.ə'griː.ə.bḷ/
draw attention (v) /drɔː ə'ten.ʃən/
handsome features (phr)
  /'hæn.səm 'fiː.tʃəz/
proud (adj) /praʊd/
waste (v) /weɪst/

LITERATURE SKILLS 3

achieve (v) /ə'tʃiːv/
blouse (n) /blaʊz/
even though (phr) /'iː.vən ðəʊ/
pane of glass (n) /peɪn əv glɑːs/
stone-dust (n) /stəʊn dʌst/
stonemason (n) /'stəʊnˌmeɪ.sən/
wise (adj) /waɪz/

LITERATURE SKILLS 4

bee (n) /biː/
faded (adj) /'feɪ.dɪd/
frost (n) /frɒst/
hum (v) /hʌm/
prithee (phr) /'prɪð.i/
unfading (adj) /ʌn'feɪ.dɪŋ/

LITERATURE SKILLS 5

barley (n) /'bɑː.li/
cornfield (n) /'kɔːn.fiəld/
fathom (n) /'fæð.əm/
fern (n) /fɜːn/
freeze over (v) /friːziz 'əʊ.vər/
goats-flesh (n) /gəʊts fleʃ/
kettle (n) /'ket.ḷ/
loch (n) /lɒk/
mount (v) /'maʊn.tɪd/
naked (adj) /'neɪ.kɪd/
oatmeal (n) /'əʊt.miːl/
shilling (n) /'ʃɪl.ɪŋ/
steep (adj) /stiːp/
thatch (n) /θætʃ/

CLIL A

beekeeper (n) /'biːˌkiː.pər/
buzz (n) /bʌz/

[CLIL A continued]

crops (n) /krɒps/
hind leg (n) /haɪnd leg/
pollinate (v) /'pɒl.ə.neɪt/
swarm (v) /swɔːm/

CLIL B

fallow (v) /'fæl.əʊ/
grain (n) /graɪn/
graze (v) /graɪz/
pest (n) /pest/
well-being (n) /ˌwel'biː.ɪŋ/

CLIL C

amount (n) /ə'maʊnt/
felt (n) /felt/
patented (adj) /'peɪtəntɪd/
therefore (adv) /'ðeə.fɔːr/

CLIL D

deception (n) /dɪ'sepʃən/
femininity (n) /ˌfemɪ'nɪnəti/
fidelity (n) /fɪ'deləti/
grace (n) /greɪs/
laziness (adv) /'leɪzi'nəs /
meanness (n) /'miːn.nəs/
nobility (n) /nəʊ'bɪləti/
survival (n) /sə'vaɪvəl/
warmth (n) /wɔːmθ/

CLIL E

borough (n) /'bʌr.ə/
building (n) /'bɪl.dɪŋ/
corner (n) /'kɔː.nər/
crowded (adj) /'kraʊ.dɪd/
household (n) /'haʊs.həʊld/
per square kilometre (phr) /pɜːr
  skweər kɪ'lɒmɪtər/
size (n) /saɪz/

WRITING EXPANSION 1

bye (excl) /baɪ/
hello (excl) /hel'əʊ/
hi (excl) /haɪ/
see you later (phr) /siː juː 'leɪ.tər/
see you soon (phr) /siː juː suːn/
take care (phr) /teɪk keər/
talk soon (phr) /tɔːk suːn/
thanks (n) /θæŋks/

WRITING EXPANSION 4

finally (adv) /'faɪ.nə.li/
first (adv) /'fɜːst/
first of all (idiom) /'fɜːst əv ɔːl/
in the end (expr) /ɪn ðiː end/
joke (n) /dʒəʊk/
next (adv) /nekst/
then (adv) /ðen/

WRITING EXPANSION 6

dry (v) /draɪ/
rinse (v) /rɪns/
rub (v) /rʌb/
soap (n) /səʊp/
towel (n) /taʊəl/
wet (v) /wet/

WRITING EXPANSION 7

appreciation (n) /əˌpriː.ʃi'eɪ.ʃən/
bad mood (n) /bæd muːd/
give up (v) /gɪv ʌp/
round the corner (phr) /raʊnd ðiː
  'kɔː.nər/
the end of the world (phr) /ðiː end
  əv ðiː wɜːld/

WRITING EXPANSION 8

asap (as soon as possible) (abbr)
  /ˌeɪ.es.eɪ'piː/
btw (by the way) (abbr) /-/
compass (n) /'kʌm.pəs/
route (n) /ruːt/
work out (v) /wɜːk aʊt/

WRITING EXPANSION 10

accompanied (adj) /ə'kʌm.pə.nid/
afford (v) /ə'fɔːd/
brainwave (n) /'breɪn.weɪv/
unfair (adj) /ʌn'feər/

VOCABULARY EXTENSION 1

break (n) /breɪk/
fun (n) /fʌn/
have a wash (phr v) /hæv ə wɒʃ/

picnic (n) /ˈpɪk.nɪk/

rest (n) /rest/

snack (n) /snæk/

VOCABULARY EXTENSION 2

(not) at all (adv) /ˈæt.ɔːl/

extremely (adv) /ɪkˈstriːm.li/

quite (adv) /kwaɪt/

really (adv) /ˈrɪə.li/

very (adv) /ˈver.i/

VOCABULARY EXTENSION 3

desktop (n) /ˈdesk.tɒp/

network (n) /ˈnet.wɜːk/

password (n) /ˈpɑːs.wɜːd/

screensaver (n) /ˈskriːn.seɪ.vər/

search engine (n) /sɜːtʃ ˈen.dʒɪn/

spyware (n) /ˈspaɪ.weər/

VOCABULARY EXTENSION 4

do up (phr v) /də ʌp/

dress (v) /dres/

fit (v) /fɪt/

have got something on(v) /hæv gɒt ˈsʌm.θɪŋ ɒn/

put on (phr v) /ˈpʊt.ɒn/

suit (v) /suːt/

take off (phr v) /ˈteɪk.ɒf/

try on (phr v) /traɪ.ən/

wear (v) /weər/

VOCABULARY EXTENSION 5

excited (adj) /ɪkˈsaɪ.tɪd/

exciting (adj) /ɪkˈsaɪ.tɪŋ/

interested (adj) /ˈɪn.trəs.tɪd/

interesting (adj) /ˈɪn.trəs.tɪŋ/

relaxed (adj) /rɪˈlækst/

relaxing (adj) /rɪˈlæk.sɪŋ/

surprised (adj) /səˈpraɪzd/

surprising (adj) /səˈpraɪ.zɪŋ/

tired (adj) /taɪəd/

tiring (adj) /ˈtaɪə.rɪŋ/

worried (adj) /ˈwʌr.id/

worrying (adj) /ˈwʌr.i.ɪŋ/

VOCABULARY EXTENSION 6

bite (v) /baɪt/

blink (v) /blɪŋk/

blow (v) /bləʊ/

clap (v) /klæp/

eye (n) /aɪ/

foot (n) /fʊt/

head (v) /hed/

hug (v) /hʌg/

kick (v) /kɪk/

kneel (v) /niːl/

lick (v) /lɪk/

mouth (n) /maʊθ/

nose (n) /nəʊz/

point (v) /pɔɪnt/

sneeze (v) /sniːz/

tongue (n) /tʌŋ/

wave (v) /weɪv/

VOCABULARY EXTENSION 7

allergic (adj) /əˈlɜː.dʒɪk/

angry (adj) /ˈæŋ.gri/

bored (adj) /bɔːd/

boring (adj) /ˈbɔː.rɪŋ/

careful (adj) /ˈkeə.fəl/

confident (adj) /ˈkɒn.fɪ.dənt/

delicious (adj) /dɪˈlɪʃ.əs/

different (adj) /ˈdɪf.ər.ənt/

dirty (adj) /ˈdɜː.ti/

easy (adj) /ˈiː.zi/

energetic (adj) /ˌen.əˈdʒet.ɪk/

enormous (adj) /ɪˈnɔː.məs/

famous (adj) /ˈfeɪ.məs/

fantastic (adj) /fænˈtæs.tɪk/

heavy (adj) /ˈhev.i/

independent (adj) /ˌɪn.dɪˈpen.dənt/

joyful (adj) /ˈdʒɔɪ.fəl/

nervous (adj) /ˈnɜː.vəs/

pessimistic (adj) /ˌpes.ɪˈmɪs.tɪk/

urgent (adj) /ˈɜː.dʒənt/

useful (adj) /ˈjuːs.fəl/

wonderful (adj) /ˈwʌn.də.fəl/

VOCABULARY EXTENSION 8

(do the) cleaning (n) /ˈkliː.nɪŋ/

(do the) cooking (n) /ˈkʊk.ɪŋ/

(do the) ironing (n) /ˈaɪə.nɪŋ/

(do the) shopping (n) /ˈʃɒp.ɪŋ/

(do the) washing (n) /ˈwɒʃ.ɪŋ/

clean (v) /kliːn/

housework (n) /ˈhaʊs.wɜːk/

load/unload (v) /ləʊd ʌnˈləʊd/

take out (phr v) /ˈteɪk.aʊt/

tidy (v) /ˈtaɪ.di/

vacuum (v) /ˈvæk.ju:m/

VOCABULARY EXTENSION 9

bus stop (n) /ˈbʌs.stɒp/

car park (n) /ˈkɑːˌpɑːk/

crossroads (n) /ˈkrɒs.rəʊdz/

footpath (n) /ˈfʊt.pɑːθ/

lamppost (n) /ˈlæmp.pəʊst/

one-way street (n) /wʌn ˈweɪ striːt/

pedestrian crossing (n) /pəˌdest-riən ˈkrɒsɪŋ/

petrol station (n) /ˈpet.rəlˌsteɪ.ʃən/

road sign (n) /rəʊd saɪn/

speed bump (n) /spiːd bʌmp/

speed camera (n) /spiːd ˈkæm.rə/

streetlight (n) /ˈstriːt.laɪt/

traffic jam (n) /ˈtræf.ɪkˌdʒæm/

traffic light (n) /ˈtræf.ɪkˌlaɪt/

VOCABULARY EXTENSION 10

athletics (n) /æθˈlet.ɪks/

basketball (n) /ˈbɑː.skɪt.bɔːl/

boxing (n) /ˈbɒk.sɪŋ/

cycling (n) /ˈsaɪ.klɪŋ/

do (v) /də/

go (v) /gəʊ/

gymnastics (n) /dʒɪmˈnæs.tɪks/

hockey (n) /ˈhɒk.i/

karate (n) /kəˈrɑː.ti/

Pilates (n) /ˌpəˈlɑː.tiːz/

play (v) /pleɪ/

rugby (n) /ˈrʌg.bi/

running (n) /ˈrʌn.ɪŋ/

skating (n) /ˈskeɪ.tɪŋ/

skiing (n) /ˈskiː.ɪŋ/

snowboarding (n) /ˈsnəʊ.bɔː.dɪŋ/

swimming (n) /ˈswɪm.ɪŋ/

volleyball (n) /ˈvɒl.i.bɔːl/

water polo (n) /ˈwɔː.təˌpəʊ.ləʊ/

VERB TABLES

be

affirmative		negative		questions	short answers	
full	contracted	full	contracted		affirmative	negative
I am	I'm	I am not	I'm not	Am I?	Yes, I am.	No, I'm not.
you are	you're	you are not	you aren't	Are you?	Yes, you are.	No, you're not.
she/he/it is	she/he/it's	she/he/it is not	she/he/it isn't	Is she/he/it?	Yes, she/he/it is.	No, she/he/it isn't.
we are	we're	we are not	we aren't	Are we?	Yes, we are.	No, we aren't.
you are	you're	you are not	you aren't	Are you?	Yes, you are.	No, you aren't.
they are	they're	they are not	they aren't	Are they?	Yes, they are.	No, they aren't.

Present simple

affirmative	negative		questions	short answers	
full	full	contracted		affirmative	negative
I read	I do not read	I don't read	Do I read?	Yes, I do.	No, I don't.
you read	you do not read	you don't read	Do you read?	Yes, you do.	No, you don't.
she/he/it reads	she/he/it does not read	she/he/it doesn't read	Does she/he/it read?	Yes, she/he/it does.	No, she/he/it doesn't.
we read	we do not read	we don't read	Do we read?	Yes, we do.	No, we don't.
you read	you do not read	you don't read	Do you read?	Yes, you do.	No, you don't.
they read	they do not read	they don't read	Do they read?	Yes, they do.	No, they don't.

Present continuous

affirmative		negative	
full	contracted	full	contracted
I am talking	I'm talking	I am not talking	I'm not talking
you are talking	you're talking	you are not talking	you aren't talking
she/he/it is talking	she/he/it's talking	she/he/it is not talking	she/he/it isn't talking
we are talking	we're talking	we are not talking	we aren't talking
you are talking	you're talking	you are not talking	you aren't talking
they are talking	they're talking	they are not talking	they aren't talking

questions	short answers	
	affirmative	negative
Am I talking?	Yes, I am.	No, I'm not.
Are you talking?	Yes, you are.	No, you're not.
Is she/he/it talking?	Yes, she/he/it is.	No, she/he/it isn't.
Are we talking?	Yes, we are.	No, we aren't.
Are you talking?	Yes, you are.	No, you aren't.
Are they talking?	Yes, they are.	No, they aren't.

Past simple: *be*

affirmative	negative		questions	short answers	
full	full	contracted		affirmative	negative
I was	I was not	I wasn't	Was I?	Yes, I was.	No, I wasn't.
you were	you were not	you weren't	Were you?	Yes, you were.	No, you weren't.
she/he/it was	she/he/it was not	she/he/it wasn't	Was she/he/it?	Yes, she/he/it was.	No, she/he/it wasn't.
we were	we were not	we weren't	Were we?	Yes, we were.	No, we weren't.
you were	you were not	you weren't	Were you?	Yes, you were.	No, you weren't.
they were	they were not	they weren't	Were they?	Yes, they were.	No, they weren't.

Past simple

affirmative	negative		questions	short answers	
full	full	contracted		affirmative	negative
I played	I did not play	I didn't play	Did I play?	Yes, I did.	No, I didn't.
you played	you did not play	you didn't play	Did you play?	Yes, you did.	No, you didn't.
she/he/it played	she/he/it not play	she/he/it didn't play	Did she/he/it play?	Yes, she/he/it did.	No, she/he/it didn't.
we played	we did not play	we didn't play	Did we play?	Yes, we did.	No, we didn't.
you played	you did not play	you didn't play	Did you play?	Yes, you did.	No, you didn't.
they played	they did not play	they didn't play	Did they play?	Yes, they did.	No, they didn't.

be going to

affirmative		negative	
full	contracted	full	contracted
I am going to eat	I'm going to eat	I am not going to eat	I'm not going to eat
you are going to eat	you're going to eat	you are not going to eat	you aren't going to eat
she/he/it is going to eat	she/he/it's going to eat	she/he/it is not going to eat	she/he/it isn't going to eat
we are going to eat	we're going to eat	we are not going to eat	we aren't going to eat
you are going to eat	you're going to eat	you are not going to eat	you aren't going to eat
they are going to eat	they're going to eat	they are not going to eat	they aren't going to eat

questions	short answers	
	affirmative	negative
Am I going to eat?	Yes, I am.	No, I'm not.
Are you going to eat?	Yes, you are.	No, you aren't.
Is she/he/it going to eat?	Yes, she/he/it is.	No, she/he/it isn't.
Are we going to eat?	Yes, we are.	No, we aren't.
Are you going to eat?	Yes, you are.	No, you aren't.
Are they going to eat?	Yes, they are.	No, they aren't.

VERB TABLES

will

affirmative		negative		questions	short answers	
full	contracted	full	contracted		affirmative	negative
I will	I'll	I will not	I won't	Will I?	Yes, I will.	No, I won't.
you will	you'll	you will not	you won't	Will you?	Yes, you will.	No, you won't.
she/he/it will	she/he/it'll	she/he/it will not	she/he/it won't	Will she/he/it?	Yes she/he/it will.	No, she/he/it won't.
we will	we'll	we will not	we won't	Will we?	Yes, we will.	No, we won't.
you will	you'll	you will not	you won't	Will you?	Yes, you will.	No, you won't.
they will	they'll	they will not	they won't	Will they?	Yes, they will.	No, they won't.

Present perfect

affirmative		negative	
full	contracted	full	contracted
I have seen	I've seen	I have not seen	I haven't seen
you have seen	you've seen	you have not seen	you haven't seen
she/he/it has seen	she/he/it's seen	she/he/it has not seen	she/he/it hasn't seen
we have seen	we've seen	we have not seen	we haven't seen
you have seen	you've seen	you have not seen	you haven't seen
they have seen	they've seen	they have not seen	they haven't seen

questions	short answers	
	affirmative	negative
Have I seen?	Yes, I have.	No, I haven't.
Have you seen?	Yes, you have.	No, you haven't.
Has she/he/it seen?	Yes, she/he/it has.	No, she/he/it hasn't.
Have we seen?	Yes, we have.	No, we haven't.
Have you seen?	Yes, you have.	No, you haven't.
Have they seen?	Yes, they have.	No, they haven't.

forma base	past simple	past participle
be	was / were	been
beat	beat	beaten
become	became	become
begin	began	begun
bend	bent	bent
bet	bet	bet
bite	bit	bitten
bleed	bled	bled
blow	blew	blown
break	broke	broken
bring	brought	brought
build	built	built
burn	burned / burnt	burned / burnt
burst	burst	burst
buy	bought	bought
catch	caught	caught
choose	chose	chosen
come	came	come
cost	cost	cost
cut	cut	cut
deal	dealt	dealt
dig	dug	dug
do	did	done
draw	drew	drawn
dream	dreamed / dreamt	dreamed / dreamt
drink	drank	drunk
drive	drove	driven
eat	ate	eaten
fall	fell	fallen
feed	fed	fed
feel	felt	felt
fight	fought	fought
find	found	found
fly	flew	flown
forbid	forbade	forbidden
forget	forgot	forgotten
forgive	forgave	forgiven
freeze	froze	frozen
get	got	got
give	gave	given
go	went	gone
grow	grew	grown
hang	hung	hung
have	had	had
hear	heard	heard
hide	hid	hidden
hit	hit	hit
hold	held	held
hurt	hurt	hurt
keep	kept	kept
know	knew	known
lay	laid	laid
lead	led	led
learn	learned / learnt	learned / learnt
leave	left	left
lend	lent	lent
let	let	let
lie	lay	lain

forma base	past simple	past participle
lie	lied	lied
light	lit	lit
lose	lost	lost
make	made	made
mean	meant	meant
meet	met	met
pay	paid	paid
put	put	put
read /riːd/	read /red/	read /red/
ride	rode	ridden
ring	rang	rung
rise	rose	risen
run	ran	run
say	said	said
see	saw	seen
seek	sought	sought
sell	sold	sold
send	sent	sent
set	set	set
sew	sewed	sewn / sewed
shake	shook	shaken
shine	shone	shone
shoot	shot	shot
show	showed	shown
shrink	shrank	shrunk
shut	shut	shut
sing	sang	sung
sink	sank	sunk
sit	sat	sat
sleep	slept	slept
smell	smelled / smelt	smelled / smelt
speak	spoke	spoken
spell	spelled / spelt	spelled / spelt
spend	spent	spent
split	split	split
spread	spread	spread
spring	sprang	sprung
stand	stood	stood
steal	stole	stolen
stick	stuck	stuck
sting	stung	stung
stink	stank	stunk
strike	struck	struck
swear	swore	sworn
sweep	swept	swept
swim	swam	swum
swing	swung	swung
take	took	taken
teach	taught	taught
tear	tore	torn
tell	told	told
think	thought	thought
throw	threw	thrown
understand	understood	understood
wake	woke	woken
wear	wore	worn
win	won	won
write	wrote	written

Grammar Reference

STARTER A

be (all forms)

affirmative	
I	**am / 'm**
you	**are / 're**
he / she / it	**is / 's**
we / you / they	**are / 're**
negative	
I	**am not / 'm not**
you	**are not / aren't**
he / she / it	**is not / isn't**
we / you / they	**are not / aren't**
interrogative	
Am	I?
Are	you?
Is	he / she / it?
Are	we / you / they?
short answers	
Yes, I **am**. Yes, he / she / it **is**. Yes, you / we / they **are**. No, I**'m not**. No, he / she / it **isn't**. No, you / we / they **aren't**.	

Form

We always use the subject.
> ✔ *I am British.*
> ✗ *A̶m̶ British.*

We use contracted forms with all subjects including proper nouns. We use *'re* only with subject pronouns (*you, we, they*) and not after nouns.
> ✔ *We're British.*
> ✗ *The g̶i̶r̶l̶s̶'̶r̶e̶ British.*

In the interrogative, *wh-* words (*what, which, who,* etc.) go before the verb be.
> *Where are you?*

We only use the contracted form in short answers if the answer is negative.
> ✔ *Yes, I am.*
> ✗ *Yes, I̶'m̶.*

Use

We use the verb *be* to give personal information (nationality, age, job).
- *She is British.*
- *I am 16.*
- *He's a teacher.*

Subject pronouns and possessive adjectives

subject pronouns	possessive adjectives
I	my
you	your
he	his
she	her
it	its
we	our
you	your
they	their

Form and use of subject pronouns

We never omit subject pronouns in English. *I* is always a capital letter. We use *you* for formal and informal situations and its form is the same in the singular and plural. We use *he* for the third person masculine singular, *she* for the third person feminine singular and *it* for the third person singular (for objects and countries).

They is the third person plural and we also use it for expressions when we don't know whether a man or a woman is talking.

Form and use of possessive adjectives

Possessive adjectives do not change gender or number:
my dog, my mum, my sisters / brothers.
The article never comes before possessive adjectives:
> ✔ *my dog*
> ✗ *t̶h̶e̶ my dog*

Possessive adjectives agree with the owner in gender and number:
- in the third person:
  *Jack is British, but **his** (not her) mum is Peruvian.*
- and in the plural:
  Jack is British and his (not their) brothers are British too.

Possessive 's

Form and use

The possessive **'s** indicates the owner of something. Note the differences:
- *Jack**'s** bag* (singular)
- *the boys' bags* (regular plural: add ' after the name)
- *Jack and Sam**'s** house* (when there is more than one owner **'s** is added to the last one.
- *the children**'s** dog* (in irregular plurals, e.g. men, women, people add **'s**)
- *James' dog (*when the owner's name finishes in *-s* add either ' or **'s**

Possessive pronouns

subject pronouns	possessive adjectives	possessive pronouns
I	my	mine
you	your	yours
he	his	his
she	her	hers
it	its	-
we	our	ours
you	your	yours
they	their	theirs

Form

We add -s to the possessive adjective to form the possessive pronoun:

- *her* → *hers*

The exceptions are *mine* and *his*.

There is no possessive pronoun for the third person singular *it*.

Use

We use possessive pronouns to avoid repetition and we omit the noun they refer to:

- *'Whose bag is that?' 'It's mine.'* (= it's my bag.)

We generally use possessive pronouns to answer questions beginning with *whose*.

STARTER B

have got (all forms)

affirmative	
I / you / we / you / they	**have got / 've got**
he / she / it	**has got / 's got**
negative	
I / you / we / you / they	**have not got / haven't got**
he / she / it	**has not got / hasn't got**

interrogative		
Have	I / you / we / you / they	**got?**
Has	he / she / it	

short answers
Yes, I / you / we / they **have**. Yes, he / she / it **has**.
No, I / you / we / they **haven't**. No, he / she / it **hasn't**.

Form

In general, we use the contracted form, especially in spoken language. In the interrogative the *wh-* words (*who, why, which, what* etc.) go before *have*:

- *What have you got?*

In short answers, *got* is omitted:

- *'Have you got a sister?' 'Yes, I have.'*

Use

Have got is used for:

- possession: *We've got a small house.*
- relationships: *I've got three brothers.*
- physical descriptions: *Jane's got blond hair.*

Indefinite article: *a / an*

Use

The indefinite articles in English are *a / an*. We use *a* before singular nouns beginning with a consonant (*a dog, a bag*) and *an* before singular nouns beginning with a vowel (*an elephant*). We use *a* for singular nouns beginning with *u* when the *u* is pronounced /juː/ (*a university campus*) and *an* when the *u* is pronounced /ʌ/ (*an uninterested child*).

We use *an* when the noun begins with a vowel sound: (*an MP3 player*).

Plural nouns

Form

We add -s to form regular plural nouns:

- *bag* → *bag**s***; *sister* → *sister**s***

Exceptions:

- nouns ending in: -x, -s, -ch, -o add -es:
  box → *box**es***
  bus → *bus**es***
  watch → *watch**es***
  tomato → *tomato**es***
- nouns ending in -y, drop the -y, add -ies:
  city → *cit**ies***
- irregular plurals:
  man → **men**
  woman → **women**
  person → **people**
  child → **children**
  foot → **feet**
- nouns ending in -f: -f changes to -ves:
  shelf → *shel**ves***

this / that / these / those

	near	far
singular	this	that
plural	these	those

Form and use

This / that / these / those do not change according to gender.

This / these indicate things near the speaker; *that / those* indicate things far away from the speaker.

We can only use the contracted form with *that* (not with *this, these* or *those*):

- *That's my dog.*

We can use *this / that, these / those* as adjectives and also as pronouns:

- *This bag is mine.* (adjective)
- *This is my sister.* (pronoun)

GRAMMAR REFERENCE

Question words

Form

We use *Wh-* words to ask questions. The most common are: *what, when, where, who, which, why, whose.* These words always go before the verb.

How combines with other words:

- *how often* – to ask about frequency;
- *how old* – to ask about age;
- *how much* – to ask the price or quantity of something;
- *how long* – to ask about duration;
- *how big / small / wide / tall / high* for size and dimensions.

STARTER C

there is / there are

	singular	plural
+	there **is** / **'s**	there **are**
–	there **is not** / **isn't**	there **are not** / **aren't**
?	**Is** there …?	**Are** there …?

Form and use

We use *there is / are* with the verb *be* to talk about where buildings, people and things are. In the negative and interrogative forms no auxiliary verbs are necessary.

a / some / any

	singular	plural
+	There is **a** campus.	There are **some** labs.
–	There isn't **a** campus.	There aren't **any** labs.
?	Is there **a** campus?	Are there **any** labs?

Form and use

We use *a* to talk about a singular object. We use *some* and *any* to talk about undefined quantities. *Some* is used in the affirmative and *any* in the negative and interrogative. In requests, *some* can be used in the interrogative:

- *Can I have some biscuits, please?*

STARTER D

Countable and uncountable nouns

Form

Nouns in English are countable and uncountable (referring to things, objects that we cannot count).

Countable nouns have a singular and plural form: *a dog, two dogs.* We use singular countable nouns with the indefinite article *a* and plurals with a number or with *some*: *a dog, two dogs, some dogs.*

Uncountable nouns have no singular and plural and we do not put the indefinite article *a* in front of them: *cheese, pasta, bread.*

To indicate quantity we use *some* and *any*:

- *I like cheese but I don't like pasta.*

Uncountable nouns always use the verb in the singular:

- *That pasta comes from Italy.*

Some nouns can be both countable and uncountable according to the context. For example:

- *I like chocolate.* (uncountable, referring to chocolate in general)
- *Please, have a few chocolates.* (countable, referring to a number of chocolates)

a / some / any / with countable and uncountable nouns

	countable		uncountable
	singular		plural
+	There is **an** egg.	There are **some** eggs.	There is **some** bread.
–	There isn't **an** egg.	There aren't **any** eggs.	There isn't **any** bread.
?	Is there **an** egg?	Are there **any** eggs?	Is there **any** bread?

Use

We cannot use uncountable nouns with *a / an*. To indicate an undefined quantity we use *some* and *any*.

We use *some* with plural countable nouns and uncountable nouns in the affirmative form.

We use *any* with plural countable nouns and uncountable nouns in the negative and interrogative forms.

much / many / lots of / a lot of

	countable	uncountable
Interrogative	**How many** eggs are there?	**How much** bread is there?
Small quantities	There **aren't many** eggs.	There **isn't much** bread.
Large quantities	There are **lots of** / **a lot of** eggs.	There is **lots of** / **a lot of** bread.

Use

We use *much* and *many* to indicate quantity. We use *many* with countable plural nouns and *much* with uncountable nouns.

We use *how many* with countable nouns and *how much* with uncountable nouns to ask questions about quantity.

We use *not many* with countable nouns and *not much* with uncountable nouns to talk about small quantities.

We use *lots of* / *a lot of* with both countable and uncountable nouns to indicate large quantities.

STARTER E

can for ability, requests, permission and possibility

affirmative		
I / You / He / She / It / We / They	**can**	play tennis.
negative		
I / You / He / She / It / We / They	**can't**	speak English.
interrogative		
Can	I / you / he / she / it / we / they	run fast?
short answers		
Yes, I / you / he / she / it / we / they **can**.		
No, I / you / he / she / it / we / they **can't**.		

Form and use

Can is a modal verb, which means:
- it does not change its form;
- it does not need an auxiliary verb for the negative and interrogative forms;
- the base form of the verb without *to* comes after it.

We use *can*:
- to express ability:
  'Can you swim?' 'Yes, I can.'
- to make requests:
  Can you come to the cinema with me?
- to ask permission:
  Can I open the window?
- to express possibility:
  We can go to the shops after school.

The imperative

+	Start! Go!
–	Don't start! Don't go!

Form and use

We form the imperative with the base form of the verb without *to*. In affirmative sentences, we use the base form of the verb. In negative sentences *don't* goes in front of the verb. We use the imperative to give orders or commands.

Its form does not change and is the same for formal and informal situations in the singular and plural.
- *Come here!*
- *Don't forget to buy some bread when you go out.*

Object Pronouns

subject pronoun	object pronoun
I	me
you	you
he	him
she	her
it	it
we	us
you	you
they	them

Form and use

We use object pronouns to substitute nouns:
- *She loves swimming.* → *She loves it.*
- *Jack hates vegetables.* → *Jack hates them.*

Object pronouns always come after the verb:
  ✓ *Jonathan loves her.*
  ✗ *Jonathan her loves.*

UNIT 1

Present simple

affirmative		
I / You		sing.
He / She / It		sing**s**.
We / You / They		sing.
negative		
I / You	**don't**	
He / She / It	**doesn't**	sing.
We / You / They	**don't**	
interrogative		
Do	I / you	
Does	he / she / it	sing?
Do	we / you / they	
short answers		
Yes, I / you / we / they **do**. Yes, he / she / it **does**.		
No, I / you / we / they **don't**. No, he / she / it **doesn't**.		

Form

In the affirmative the present simple uses the same base form of the verb for the subjects (*I, you, we, they*). For the third person singular (*he, she, it*), we add *-s* to the base form of the verb.

In the negative and interrogative short answer forms, we use the auxiliary verbs *do* and *does*.

GRAMMAR REFERENCE

Wh- words (*what, who, when, where, why, how often, which* etc.) go before the interrogative form:
- *Where do you come from?*

Use

We use the *present simple*:
- to talk about habitual or repeated actions:
  I get up at 6:30 on weekdays.
- to give facts:
  That family are vegetarians. They don't eat meat.
- to talk about things that are always true:
  Water boils at 100 °C.

Present simple: Third person singular spelling

In most cases the third person singular is formed by adding *-s* to the base form of the verb. However, the following spelling rules apply:

• Regular verbs:	walk → walk**s**; live → live**s**
• Verbs ending in a consonant + *-y*:	reply → repl**ies**
• Verbs ending in a vowel + *-y*:	play → play**s**; say → say**s**
• Verbs ending in *-sh*:	push → push**es**
• Verbs ending in *-ch*:	watch → watch**es**
• Verbs ending in *-ss*:	pass → pass**es**
• Verbs ending in *-o*:	go → go**es**; do → do**es**
• Verbs ending in *-x*:	relax → relax**es**

Adverbs of frequency

The present simple often uses adverbs of frequency, for example *always, usually, often, sometimes, hardly ever* and *never*.

Form and Use

Adverbs of frequency indicate how often an action happens. We use *never* in the affirmative even if it has a negative meaning.
- *He <u>always</u> listens to music.*
- *She <u>never</u> eats meat.*

Adverbs always follow the verb *be*.
- *He is <u>often</u> late.*

We use *How often* to ask questions about the frequency of an action.
- *'How often do you get up early?' 'I <u>always</u> get up early.'*

Adverbs of frequency generally go before the main verb but after auxiliary verbs in negative sentences.
- *He doesn't <u>always</u> play football.*

Adverbs of frequency always go after the verb *be* in negative sentences.
- *He isn't <u>usually</u> late.*

Adverbs of frequency go after the subject in the interrogative.
- *Does Kelly <u>often</u> play football on Saturdays?*

Expressions of frequency

We use the following expressions when we talk about frequency:
- *once / twice / three times a week / a month / a year*
- *every day*
- *two times a week*
- *on Saturdays / Tuesdays*
- *in the morning / afternoon / evening*
- *at weekends.*

Form

Expressions of frequency generally come at the end of the sentence
- *I go to the gym every day.*
- *I play football once a week.*

We usually use these expressions in response to the question *How often*.
- *'How often do you listen to music?'*
  'I listen to music every hour.'
  'I listen to music three times a day.'

Verbs of preference + *-ing*

The base form of the verb + *-ing* generally follows verbs that express a preference or liking, for example, *like, love, enjoy, be into, don't mind, don't like, can't stand* and *hate*:
- *I like playing football.*
- *I can't stand eating vegetables.*

Use

We often use modifiers to change the meaning of an expression, for example, *really, quite, (not) … at all*:
- *I really like playing football.*
- *I don't like playing football at all.*

Nouns can follow verbs of preference:
- *I don't like football.*
- *I can't stand Beyoncé.*

We add *-ing* to the base form of the verb to create the *-ing* form of the verb, but observe the following spelling rules:

• Regular verbs:	wait → wait**ing**; stand → stand**ing**
• Verbs ending in *-e*:	live → liv**ing**; take → tak**ing**
• Verbs ending in *-y*:	reply → reply**ing**; play → play**ing**; study → study**ing**
• Verbs with the emphasis on the final syllable and ending in a consonant:	begin → begin**ning**; stop → stop**ping**; travel → travel**ling**
• Verbs ending in *-ie*:	die → d**ying**; lie → l**ying**

UNIT 2

Present continuous

Affirmative

I	am / 'm	
You	are / 're	learn**ing**.
He / She / It	is / 's	
We / You / They	are / 're	

Negative

I	am not / 'm not	
You	are not / aren't	learn**ing**.
He / She / It	is not / isn't	
We / You / They	are not / aren't	

Interrogative

Am	I	
Are	you	learn**ing**?
Is	he / she / it	
Are	we / you / they	

Short answers

Yes, I **am**.
Yes, he / she / it **is**.
Yes, you / we / they **are**.

No, I'**m not**.
No, he / she / it **isn't**.
No, you / we / you / they **aren't**.

Form

We form the present continuous with the verb *be* + verb + *-ing*. In the interrogative, the verb *be* comes before the subject. In the negative, we add *not* to *be*. We do not use other auxiliary verbs. In short answers we can contract in the negative form but not in the affirmative:

✓ *Yes, you are.*
✗ *Yes, you're.*

In questions, *wh-* words come before the verb:

- *What are you doing?*

Use

We use the present continuous:

- to talk about something happening at the moment of speaking:
  - *Daniel's not here right now – he's travelling around Europe.*
  - *Mum's not working at the moment – she's sitting on the sofa.*
  - *Why are you packing your suitcase?*
- to talk about temporary situations:
  - *They're showing a great travel programme on TV this week.*
  - *Our internet isn't working this week.*
  - *How's your sister getting on in New York?*

- to talk about situations that are changing or developing:
  - *The weather is getting warmer. The Arctic ice cap is shrinking.*
- to describe actions in photos:
  - *In this picture, three girls are swimming in the sea.*

-*ing* form spelling

We add *-ing* to the base form of the verb to make the *-ing* form of the verb, but observe the following spelling rules:

- Regular verbs:	wait → wait**ing**; stand → stand**ing**
- Verbs ending in *-e*:	live → liv**ing**; take → tak**ing**
- Verbs ending in *-y*:	reply → reply**ing**; play → play**ing**; study → study**ing**
- Verbs with the emphasis on the final syllable and ending with a consonant:	begin → begi**nning**; stop → stop**ping**; travel → travel**ling**
- Verbs ending in *-ie*:	die → d**ying**; lie → l**ying**

Adverbs of manner

Form

We form adverbs of manner by adding *-ly* to the adjective.

- *quick → quick**ly**; slow → slow**ly**; bad → bad**ly***

For adjectives ending in *-y*, the *-y* becomes *-i* and then we add *-ly*.

- *easy → eas**ily**; happy → happ**ily**; angry → angr**ily***

In some cases, the adjectives and the adverb are identical.

- *early, fast, hard, late, loud* (or, sometimes *loudly*)

The adjective *good* is irregular. The corresponding adverb is *well*.

- *Jim is a good ballet dancer. → Jim dances well.*

In general, *adverbs of manner* come at the end of a sentence. However, if the adverb refers to the entire sentence, we can put it at the beginning.

- *Unfortunately, Jim broke his toe.*

Use

We use adverbs of manner to describe how an action happens.

Present simple v present continuous

Use

We use the present simple for habitual actions, and we use the present continuous for actions that are happening at the moment of speaking:

- *He often gets up late. / He is getting up at the moment.*

The present simple refers to permanent states, while the present continuous refers to temporary actions.

- *Jane lives in Bangkok. / Jane is living in London at the moment.*

GRAMMAR REFERENCE

The following time expressions can help identify which verb form to use.

present simple	present continuous
▪ *always*	▪ *at the moment*
▪ *usually*	▪ *now*
▪ *often*	▪ *this evening*
▪ *sometimes*	▪ *this weekend*
▪ *hardly ever*	▪ *today*
▪ *never*	▪ *tonight*
▪ *every day*	
▪ *once / twice a week*	
▪ *on Saturdays*	
▪ *at the weekend*	

VERBS OF STATE AND VERBS OF PERCEPTION

In general, we don't use the present continuous with verbs that indicate a state, for example, *be, believe, hate, know, like, love, understand, think, want, remember*.

- *I believe in God.*
- *I don't understand the question.*

On other occasions, we can use the present continuous with these verbs if we are talking about an action that is in progress:

- *What do you think of this programme?* (opinion)
- *What are you thinking of?* (action now)

Generally, we don't use the present continuous with verbs of perception, for example, *taste, sound, smell, look*.

- *That coat looks good on you.*
- *The lasagne tastes wonderful.*

UNIT 3

Past simple: *be*

affirmative		
I	**was**	late.
You	**were**	
He / She / It	**was**	
We / You / They	**were**	
negative		
I	**was not / wasn't**	late.
You	**were not / weren't**	
He / She / It	**was not / wasn't**	
We / You / They	**were not / weren't**	
interrogative		
Was	I	late?
Were	you	
Was	he / she / it	
Were	we / you / they	

short answers
Yes, I / he /she / it **was**.
Yes, you / we / they **were**.
No, I / he / she / it **wasn't**.
No, you / we / they **weren't**.

Form and use

The past simple of the verb *be* is *was* in the first person singular and the third person singular (*I, he / she / it*) and *were* for all of the other subjects.

In the interrogative, we invert the subject and verb:

- *David was 23 yesterday.*
- *Was David 23 yesterday?*

The negative is formed by adding *not* to the verb *be*.

- *He wasn't at school today.*

We use the past simple for actions that have started and finished in the past.

Past simple affirmative: Irregular verbs

I / You / He / She / It / We / You / They	**found** it.

Form and use

The past simple of irregular verbs can be quite different from the base form of the verb:

- *have → had*; *swim → swam*

We use the past simple for actions finished in the past. The form is the same for all subjects.

For a list of irregular verbs see page 113

Past simple affirmative: Regular verbs

I / You / He / She / It / We / You / They	**delivered** it.

Form and use

We form the past simple of regular verbs by adding *-ed* to the base form of the verb.

- *play → play**ed**; visit → visit**ed***

The form is the same for all subjects but remember these spelling rules:

▪ Verbs ending in *-e*:	live → live**d**; arrive → arrive**d**
▪ Verbs ending in a consonant plus *-y*:	marry → marr**ied**; try → tr**ied**
▪ Verbs ending in a vowel plus consonant:	stop → stop**ped**; travel → travel**led**; regret → regre**tted**

We use the past simple for actions that finished in the past:

- *We studied together yesterday.*
- *He played football for six months.*

We use the past simple for in narrative tenses:

- *He checked his email, then contacted his boss.*

UNIT 4

Past simple negative and questions

affirmative		
I / You / He / She / It / We / You / They	**liked** it.	
negative		
I / You / He / She / It / We / You / They	**did not / didn't**	**like** it.
interrogative		
Did	I / you / he / she / it / we / you / they	**like** it?
short answers		
Yes, I / you / he / she / it / we / they **did**.		
No, I / you / he / she / it / we / they **didn't**.		

Use

We form both the negative and interrogative forms of the past simple using the auxiliary verb *did* and *did not*. The form is the same for all subjects. *Did* and *did not* follow the base form of the verb without *to*.

We form short answers in the past simple with the auxiliary *did / didn't*: *Yes, I did. / No, I didn't*. Note that only the negative form contracts.

Why...? / Because....

We use *Why* in the interrogative to ask the reason for something. We use *Because* in the answer to explain the reason for something We never use *Because* in the interrogative.

- *'Why is Jane unhappy?' 'Because John didn't come to the party.'*

Expressions of past time

Use

We often use time expressions with the past simple to indicate exactly when something happened. The most common time expressions are:

- **last** week / month / year
- **at** ten / twelve o'clock
- **in** 1492 / 2012
- last night
- ten minutes / two hours / six weeks **ago**
- **on** Sunday / Monday (morning, afternoon, evening)
- yesterday
- **last** March / summer

The time expressions go at the beginning or the end of the sentence.

- *My uncle and aunt emigrated to Australia last year.*
- *Last year, my uncle and aunt emigrated to Australia.*

Note that we never use the definite article with time expressions:

- ✗ *He came home from hospital the last week.*

UNIT 5

be going to for predictions and intentions

affirmative		
I	**am / 'm**	
You	**are / 're**	
He / She / It	**is / 's**	**going to** leave.
We / You / They	**are / 're**	
negative		
I	**am not**	
You	**are / aren't**	
He / She / It	**is not / isn't**	**going to** leave.
We / You / They	**are not / aren't**	
interrogative		
Am	I	
Are	you	
Is	he / she / it	**going to** leave?
Are	we / you / they	
short answers		
Yes, I **am**.		
Yes, you / we / they **are**.		
Yes, he / she / it **is**.		
No, I**'m not**.		
No, you / we / they **aren't**.		
No, he / she / it **isn't**.		

Form and use

We form *be going to* with *be* + *going to* + the base form of the verb without *to*.

We use *be going to* when we talk about future plans and intentions.

Intentions are actions that are planned but are not yet definite.

- *I'm going to study hard for my exams. I really want to pass.*
- *Are you going to make a cake for my birthday?*

We use *be going to* when we make predictions, when it is evident that certain situations are going to happen. This form is also called the *evident future*.

- *The temperature is already 20 °C and it's only 8 am. It's going to be really hot today.*
- *Mum's going to be angry because I haven't tidied my room.*
- *There are clouds in the sky. It's going to rain.*

Expressions of future time

Future time expressions are generally used with *be going to* and other verb forms that refer to the future.

The most common future time expressions are:

- **next** Monday / week / month / year
- **tomorrow** morning / afternoon / evening
- the day after tomorrow
- **this** evening / week / month / year
- later (on)

GRAMMAR REFERENCE

- **on** *Tuesday / Wednesday / June 5th*
- **in** *May /* **in** *a month's time /* **in** *the future /* **in** *an hour /* **in** *a week /* **in** *a year*
- **in the next few** *days / weeks / months / years*

Present tenses for the future

We can use various verb forms to indicate the future.
We use the present continuous to talk about future events/arrangements that we have already planned and programmed. So the present continuous talks about definite plans and are different from those referred to using *be going to*.

- *I'm doing a presentation next week. It's on Thursday morning.* (It's a definite arrangement.)
- *Jane's having a party on Saturday. It starts at 8 pm. Are you going to go?* (The party is definite, but the intention to go is not.)

We use the present continuous more often with time expressions than *be going to* because it refers to definite arrangements. However, when we talk about future events, we can also use the present simple when we are referring to precise time or timetables.

- *The train leaves at 8:50. Don't be late.*

Note that often there is very little difference between *be going to* and the present continuous when we are talking about the future. Native English speakers tend to use both forms interchangeably and both are acceptable:

- *We are visiting my granny this Sunday. / We are going to visit my granny this Sunday.*

UNIT 6

will / won't

affirmative		
I / You / He / She / It / We / You / They	**will / 'll**	go.
negative		
I / You / He / She / It / We / You / They	**will not / won't**	go.
interrogative		
Will	I / you / he / she / it / we / you / they	go?
short answers		
Yes, I / you / he / she / it / we / they **will**.		
No, I / you / he / she / it / we / they **won't**.		

Form

We form the simple future with *will* + the base form of the verb without to.
Will does not change according to number or gender and has the same form for all subjects.
The affirmative form is *will* and the negative is formed by adding *not*: *will not* (or *won't* for the contracted form).
In the interrogative *will* comes before the subject and the main verb. We don't use auxiliary verbs.

Use

We use *will*:

- for making predictions based on opinions:
  - *Come and listen to this song. You'll love it.*
  - *I don't think you'll like that cake. It's got sultanas in it and you hate them!*
- for making spontaneous decisions:
  - *'I've got to go out to get some eggs.' 'I'll come with you.'*
- for offering to do something:
  - *Finish your work. I'll cook lunch.*
  - *Don't worry about the tickets. I'll go and pick them up.*
- for making a promise:
  - *I won't tell anyone. I promise.*
- for talking about events that will happen:
  - *I'll be 18 next week! It's my birthday on Tuesday.*

will / be going to for predictions

The main difference between *will* and *be going to* when making predictions is that we use *be going to* when there is proof that something is going to happen, while we use *will* for making predictions that we are not certain about and that we are basing on personal opinion.

- *Those stairs are wet! You're going to fall down.*
- *She loves him so much. She'll definitely marry him!*

In general, we use words and expressions like *be sure, expect, probably, think*.

- *I'm sure the teacher will understand your explanation.*
- *She doesn't think her parents will mind.*

With *will*, verbs like *definitely* are used.

- *John's worked really hard for his exams. He'll definitely pass.*

Infinitive of purpose

Form and use

The infinitive of purpose is used to explain why something is done.

- *He went to the shops to buy bread.*
- *They went on the expedition to get some outdoor experience.*

The infinitive of purpose is an abbreviated form of the expression in order to.

- *He goes to school in order to learn.*

The infinitive of purpose generally answers the question Why?

- *'Why are you going to the shops?' 'I'm going to the shops to buy some bread.'*

First conditional

We use the first conditional to talk about future events that can happen based on certain conditions. The second future event will certainly occur if the first event happens

Form

condition	consequence
If + present simple,	future simple
consequence	**condition**
future simple	*if* + present simple

- *If John comes to the party, Jane will be happy.*

We can invert the order of the clauses. In this case, we don't use a comma:

- *Jane will be happy if John comes to the party.*

We cannot put *will* or any other form of the future (conditional) after *if*. We can only use the future form to express the consequence:

> ✓ *If it rains, we won't go to the seaside.*
> ✗ *If it will rain …*

We can only use the interrogative form in the consequence clause and not in the *if* clause:

- *If John comes to the party, will Jane be happy?*
- *Will Jane be happy if John comes to the party?*

We can use the negative in both the condition and consequence clauses:

- *If John doesn't come to the party, Jane will be sad.*
- *If John doesn't come to the party, Jane won't be happy.*
- *Jane will be happy if Simon doesn't come to the party.*

UNIT 7

Comparative and superlative adjectives

Form and use

We form comparative adjectives by adding *-er* at the end of short adjectives of one syllable and we use *more* before longer multi-syllable adjectives:

- *cheap → cheaper (than)*
- *quiet → quieter (than)*
- *expensive → more expensive (than)*

We use the comparative form to compare two things or two groups of things. In general, we use *than to* introduce the terms of comparison.

We form superlative adjectives by adding *-est* at the end of short adjectives of one syllable and we use *most* before longer multi-syllable adjectives:

- *cheap → (the) cheapest*
- *quiet → (the) quietest*
- *expensive → (the) most expensive*

We usually place *the* before a superlative adjective. We use the superlative form when we are comparing three or more things. There are spelling rules for forming comparatives and superlatives. Some irregular adjectives completely change form:

Spelling rules

▪ Regular adjectives:	+ *-er* / *-est*
▪ Adjectives ending in *-y*:	drop *-y* + *-ier* / *-iest*
▪ Adjectives ending in *-e*:	+ *-r* / *-st*
▪ Adjectives ending in vowel + consonant:	double the final consonant
▪ Two or more syllables (+):	***more*** / ***most***
▪ Some two-syllable adjectives:	have two forms, *-er* / *-est* and ***more*** / ***most***

regular adjectives	comparatives	superlative
small	small**er than**	**the** small**est**
happy	happ**ier**	**the** happ**iest**
nice	nice**r**	**the** nice**st**
big	big**ger**	**the** big**gest**
expensive	**more** expensive **than**	**the most** expensive
clever	clever**er than** / **more** clever **than**	**the** clever**est** / **the most** clever

irregular adjectives	comparatives	superlative
good	**better than**	**the best**
bad	**worse than**	**the worst**
far	**further** / **farther than**	**the furthest** / **farthest**

LESS THAN AND *THE LEAST*

The comparative and superlative of *little* are *less* (*than*) and the *least*.

We use these forms in the same way as the other comparative and superlative adjectives.

- *That house is less expensive than the one we saw yesterday. It's the least expensive house in the street.*

(NOT) AS … AS

We use (*not*) *as … as* to compare the same characteristics in two different things.

- *The apple is as heavy as the banana.*
- *The boy is not as tall his brother.*

We can also use *not so … as* in the negative. However, we cannot use it in the affirmative and negative forms.

GRAMMAR REFERENCE

UNIT 8

must and *have to* for obligation

affirmative		
I / You / He / She / It / We / You / They	**must**	go.
negative		
I / You / He / She / It / We / You / They	**must not / mustn't**	go.
interrogative		

Do	I / you		
Does	he / she / it	**have to**	go?
Do	we / you / they		

short answers
Yes, he / she / it **does**.
Yes, I / you / we / they **do**.
No, he / she / it **doesn't**.
No, I / you / we / they **don't**.

affirmative		
I / You	**have to**	
He / She / It	**has to**	go.
We / You / They	**have to**	
negative		
I / You	**do not / don't**	
He / She / It	**does not / doesn't**	**have to** go.
We / You / They	**do not / don't**	
interrogative		
Do	I / you	
Does	he / she / it	**have to** go?
Do	we / you / they	

short answers
Yes, I / you / we / they **have**.
No, he / she / it **haven't**.

Form (*must*)

Must is a modal verb and is the same for all subjects. The base form of the verb without *to* always follows *must*. We add *not* to *must* in the negative and do not use an auxiliary verb:

- *I must not / mustn't eat peanuts.*

In general, we don't use *must* in the interrogative form. We substitute it with *have to*:

- *'Do you have to go to school tomorrow?' 'No, I don't.'*

Form (*have to*)

Have to is a normal verb which changes depending on the subject:

We use *have to* with *I, you, we, they* and *has to* with *he, she, it*. In the interrogative and the negative we use the auxiliaries *do* and *does*. To indicate the past tense, *have to* is irregular and becomes *had*

to. As with other past simple forms, the interrogative and negative use *did* and *didn't*:

- *I had to go to school yesterday.*
- *I didn't have to do my homework last week.*
- *Did you have to tidy your room on Saturday?*

Use (*must* and *have to*)

Must and *have to* both express an obligation or a suggestion, but there are some differences. *Must* expresses an obligation that we impose on ourselves (internal obligation):

- *I really must buy my mum a birthday card.*
- *I mustn't get home too late, my parents will worry.*

We use *must* to give an order:

- *You must finish your homework now.*

We use *must* can to express a suggestion or recommendation:

- *You must see that film, it's brilliant.*

We use *must* in formal written warnings:

- *You mustn't swim in the sea before 10 am.*

We also use *have to* to express an obligation but it is more official and stronger, imposed from outside, for example, a rule or a law:

- *You have to stop at the red light.* (It's the law.)
- *I have to do my homework.* (My teacher told me.)
- *He had to speak English to his exchange partner's parents because they couldn't understand Turkish.*

We also use *have to* to ask whether there is an obligation to do something:

- *'Do I have to drive on the left in the UK?' 'Yes, you do.'*

MUSTN'T AND DON'T / DOESN'T HAVE TO

Mustn't and *don't / doesn't have to* are completely different in meaning.

Mustn't expresses prohibition.

- *You mustn't talk during the exam.*
- *You mustn't leave the room before 10 am.*

Don't / doesn't have to express no obligation and indicates that it is not necessary to do something.

- *You don't have to write out the answer. You can use a computer.*
- *He doesn't have to get up early on Saturday. There's no school.*

Should for advice

Affirmative		
I / You / He / She / It / We / You / They	**should**	go.
Negative		
I / You / He / She / It / We / You / They	**should not / shouldn't**	go.
Interrogative		
Should	I / you / he / she / it / we / you / they	go?

Short answers
Yes, I / you / he / she / it / we / they **should**.
No, I / you / he / she / it / we / they **shouldn't**.

Form and use

Should is a modal verb. It has the same form for all subjects and does not need an auxiliary verb. We form the negative by adding *not* and the interrogative by inverting *should* and the subject of the phrase:

- *I should see the doctor tomorrow.*
- *'Should Jack come to the party?' 'Yes, he should.'*
- *Jane shouldn't tell her friend about Rob.*

We use *should* to give advice and to make suggestions:

- *You're not well, you should see the doctor.*
- *You should give the lost purse to the police.*

We also use *should* to ask for / to express opinions:

- *'What should do the government do about homeless people?' 'They should help them more.'*

UNIT 9

Present perfect

Affirmative		
I / You	**have / 've**	**left.**
He / She / It	**has / 's**	
We / You / They	**have / 've**	
Negative		
I / You	**have not / haven't**	**left.**
He / She / It	**has not / hasn't**	
We / You / They	**have not / haven't**	
Interrogative		
Have	I / you	**left?**
Has	he / she / it	
Have	we / you / they	
Short answers		
Yes, I / you / we / they **have.** Yes, he / she / it **has.**		
No, I / you / we / they **haven't.** No, he / she / it **hasn't.**		

Form

We form the present perfect with *have / has* + the past participle of the main verb. In general, the past participle of regular verbs is formed by adding *-d, -ed* or *-ied*: *arrived, finished, studied*. However, most of the most frequently used verbs are irregular (see list on page 113):

- *do → done; lose → lost; write → written*

We form the interrogative by inverting *have / has* and the subject. We form short answers using *have / has*:

- *'Have they finished their homework?' 'Yes, they have.'*

We form the negative by adding *not* to *have / has*:

- *They haven't seen John for a while.*

Use

We use the present perfect to connect the past and the present

- *Matt's lost his glasses.* (He hasn't got them now.)

We use the present perfect to talk about events that have happened in a time not specified in the past:

- *Have you ever visited France?*

PRESENT PERFECT WITH EVER AND NEVER

The present perfect uses the adverbs *ever* and *never*. The adverbs go before the main verb. We generally use *ever* in the interrogative, to ask for information relating to past events It goes before the past participle:

- *Have you ever seen Rihanna?*
  (We are asking about an event in a time not specified in someone's life.)

We use *never* in the affirmative to express negation:

- *He has never held a baby before.*
- *I've never seen Rihanna.*

BEEN / GONE

Been and *gone* are the past participles of the verbs *be* and *go* respectively. Even if the meaning of the two seem similar in meaning, they are different.

- *I've been to the shops. Here's the milk.*
  (this means that the person went to the shop but has now returned home, and that he/she is at home with the milk.)
- *'Where is Joan?' 'She's gone to the shops.'*
  (Here Joan is not at home because she is still at the shop.)

Present perfect v past simple

We use both the present perfect and the past simple to describe events and actions that have happened in the past. The main differences between the two forms are the following:

The past simple is used to describe events and actions that finished at a precise moment in the past:

- *He went to school yesterday.*
- *He moved to Mexico in 2015.*

The present perfect is used to describe events and actions that have finished at an undefined moment in the past:

- *He has lost his phone.* (We don't know when, but he hasn't got it now.)
- *'What's wrong with Jack?' 'He's broken his ankle.'*
  (We don't know when.)

In these examples, the action is more important than the moment when it happened.

We use the present perfect when we can still see the effects of a specific action at the moment of speaking.

- *Oh, look at Phil. He's cut his hair.* (We can see the effects now, even though we don't know when it happened.)

We use the present perfect when the action began in the past but continues to the present

- *He has lived in London for five years.* (He still lives in London now.)

GRAMMAR REFERENCE

The difference between the two tenses can be seen in the following dialogue:

Lily *Have you ever lived in a different country?*
Linda *Yes, I have. I lived in Berlin.*
Lily *When did you live there?*
Linda *I lived there in 2005. It was great.*

In this dialogue, the first question is in the present perfect because the speaker is asking Linda about a time not specified in her past. Linda replies using the past simple because she lived in Berlin at a point in the past but is now back in England. The period of time she lived in Berlin finished in a precise moment in the past.

Past time expressions can help identify the two tenses:

past simple	**present perfect**
(precise time)	(time period not specified)
- *yesterday*	- *already*
- **last** *week / month / year*	- *yet*
- *at Easter*	- *just*
- *on my birthday*	- *never*
- *one day / two weeks /*	- *ever*
three months **ago**	- **this** *week / month / year*
	- *for / since*
	- *today*

UNIT 10

Present perfect with *just*, *already* and *yet*

Affirmative (+ *just*, *already*)		
I / You	have / 've	
He / She / It	has / 's	just / already left.
We / You / They	have / 've	
Negative (+ *yet*)		
I / You	have not / haven't	
He / She / It	has not / hasn't	left yet.
We / You / They	have not / haven't	
Interrogative (+ *yet*)		
Have	I / you	
Has	he / she / it	left yet?
Have	we / you / they	
Short answers		
Yes, I / you / we / they **have**. Yes, he / she / it **has**.		
No, I / you / we / they **haven't**. No, he / she / it **hasn't**.		

We use the adverbs *just, already* and *yet* with the present perfect. The adverbs *just, already* and *yet* go before the main verb (between have / has and the past participle).

- *Olive has just had a baby girl.* (It happened very recently.)
- *Dani has already posted the news online.* (He has done this faster or before was originally expected.)

We generally use *just* and *already* in the affirmative.
We use *yet* only in the present perfect in the interrogative or in the negative. *Yet* always goes at the end of the phrase.
Yet expresses an expectation.

- *Has your sister moved house yet?* (We thought she was moving soon.)
- *I haven't done my homework yet.* (But I will do it soon.)

Present perfect with *for / since*

We use the present perfect with *for* and *since* to describe the duration of an action. We use *for* to indicate a period of time (*an hour, two weeks, three months, ten years* etc.) and *since* to indicate a precise moment or the beginning of a period of time (*two o'clock, yesterday morning, Thursday, November, 1995,* etc.).

- *Jane has been at the library since two o'clock today.*
- *My mother and my stepfather have been husband and wife for five years.*

The list below indicates the time expressions used with both words:

for	**since**
- *a long time*	- *yesterday*
- *a week / a month / a year*	- *I was born*
- *three / four days*	- **last** *week / month / year*
- *a few months*	- *last summer*
- *five minutes*	- *2016*
- *the past year*	- *Monday, June 16th*
- **the last few** *days / weeks /*	- *5:30 pm*
months	- *then*

THANKS AND ACKNOWLEDGEMENTS

The authors and publishers acknowledge the following sources of copyright material and are grateful for the permissions granted. While every effort has been made, it has not always been possible to identify the sources of all the material used, or to trace all copyright holders. If any omissions are brought to our notice, we will be happy to include the appropriate acknowledgements on reprinting and in the next update to the digital edition, as applicable.

The publishers are grateful to the following for permission to reproduce copyright photographs and material:

Key: T = Top, TL = Top Left, TR = Top Right, CL = Centre Left, CR = Centre Right, C = Centre, B = Below, BL = Below Left, BR = Below Right, L = Left, R = Right, Ex = Exercise, B/G = Background, U = Unit.

Photo
Cover Title: Lostanastacia

Cover Image: PetlinDmitry

p. 61 (Sensor): Dpa Picture Alliance/Alamy Stock Photo; p. 61 (Tooth): Reuters/Alamy Stock Photo;

All the below photos are sourced from Getty Images.

p. 5: Yinyang/IStock; p. 9 (digital clock): Hanibaram/IStock; p. 9 (analog clock): Kchungtw/IStock; p. 11: Klenger/IStock; p. 12: Pixitive/Digitalvision Vectors; p. 15: Purestock; p. 16 (TL): Pixinoo/IStock; p. 16 (BL): Compassionate Eye Foundation/Chris Ryan/Taxi; p. 16 (CL): Leezsnow/E+; p. 18: Yellow Dog Productions/The Image Bank; p. 19: Brauns/IStock; p. 20: Logorilla/Digitalvision Vectors; p. 21: 4X6/Digitalvision Vectors; p. 22: Thinkstock/Stockbyte; p. 23: RoyFWylam/iStock; pp. 24-25: Hero Images; p. 27 (TL): Monkeybusinessimages/IStock; p. 27 (TR): Westend61; p. 27 (BR): Foodcollection Rf; p. 29 (Ex 30.0A): Harmpeti/IStock; p. 29 (Ex 30.0B): Juefraphoto/IStock; p. 29 (Ex 30.0C): Dougal Waters/Digitalvision; p. 29 (Ex 30.1A): Lisa Quarfoth/Hemera; p. 29 (Ex 30.1B): Lisa Quarfoth/Hemera; p. 29 (Ex 30.1C): Lisa Quarfoth/Hemera; p. 29 (Ex 31.0A): Valentynvolkov/IStock; p. 29 (Ex 31.0B): Brian Macdonald/Digitalvision; p. 29 (Ex 31.0C): Love_Life/E+; p. 29 (Ex 31.1A): Arhiady/IStock; p. 29 (Ex 31.1B): Arhiady/IStock; p. 29 (Ex 31.1C): Arhiady/IStock; p. 29 (Ex 31.2A): James Emmerson/ Robertharding; p. 29 (Ex 31.2B): Peopleimages/Digitalvision; p. 29 (Ex 31.2C): Bernhard Lang/Photolibrary; p. 29 (Ex 31.3A): Ziviani/IStock; p. 29 (Ex 31.3B): Martin Leigh/Visitbritain; p. 29 (Ex 31.3C): Ishootphotosllc/E+; p. 29 (Ex 31.4A): Georgijevic/E+; p. 29 (Ex 31.4B): Jgi/Tom Grill/Blend Images; p. 29 (Ex 31.4c): Henry Arden/Cultura; p. 29 (Ex 31.5A): Pagadesign/E+; p. 29 (Ex 31.5B): Beylaballa/IStock; p. 29 (Ex 31.5C): T3 Magazine/Future; p. 31: Photodisc; p. 34: Demaerre/IStock; p. 37 (TR): Ken Lubas/Los Angeles Times; p. 37 (BL): Francois Xavier Marit/Afp; p. 37 (BR): Goir/IStock; p. 37 (BC): Anatolytiplyashin/IStock; p. 38 (Ex 28.0): Flashpop/Iconica; p. 38 (Ex 28.1): Sielemann/IStock; p. 38 (Ex 28.2): Ranplett/E+; p. 38 (Ex 28.3): Peopleimages/IStock; p. 38 (Ex 28.4): Neustockimages/E+; p. 39 (TR): Frankcangelosi/Digitalvision Vectors; p. 39 (B): A-Digit/Digitalvision Vectors; pp. 42-43: Terrababy/E+; p. 45 (Ex 25.1A, B, C): Mhatzapa/IStock; p. 45 (Ex 25.2A): Edward James/Filmmagic; p. 45 (Ex 25.2B): Tarzhanova/IStock; p. 45 (Ex 25.2C): Gsermek/IStock; p. 45 (Ex 25.3A): Andrew Watson/Lonely Planet Images; p. 45 (Ex 25.3B): Bloomberg; p. 45 (Ex 25.3C): Thorney Lieberman/ Photographer'S Choice; p. 45 (Ex 25.4A): Colin Anderson/Photographer'S Choice Rf; p. 45 (Ex 25.4B): Ron Levine/The Image Bank; p. 45 (Ex 25.4C): Bsip/Universal Images Group; p. 45 (Ex 25.5A: Pants): Tatniz/IStock; p. 45 (Ex 25.5A: White t-shirts): Flamingpumpkin/IStock; p. 45 (Ex 25.5B: Cargo): Bonetta/IStock; p. 45 (Ex 25.5B: Yellow Sweat-shirt): Clu/E+; p. 45 (Ex 25.5C: Red Shirt): Rolleiflextlr/IStock; p. 45 (Ex 25.5C: Blue Jeans): Suradech14/IStock; p. 47: Ulrike Hammerich/Eyeem; pp. 52-53: Image Source; p. 55 (CR): Kaczka/IStock; p. 55 (BL): Tomml/E+; pp. 56-57: Aurelien Meunier; p. 61 (Doctor): Reza Estakhrian/Stone; p. 61 (Arm): Valentynvolkov/IStock; p. 61 (Leg): Viktor_Gladkov/IStock; p. 61 (Pills): Jenifoto/IStock; p. 61 (Heart): Hudiemm/Digitalvision Vectors; p. 62: Maica/E+; p. 63 (Shoe): Zhaubasar/IStock; p. 63 (Cycle): Reinhold Foeger/Hemera; p. 63 (Goggles): Future Publishing; p. 67: Jutta Klee/Canopy; p. 69: Dmitry_Tsvetkov/IStock; p. 69: Popovaphoto/IStock; p. 69: Grassetto/IStock; p. 70: Bji/Blue Jean Images; p. 72: Omgimages/IStock; p. 73: Marijaradovic/IStock; p. 74 (BL): Antonio Camacho/Moment Open; p. 74 (T): Underwater Photography By Jordi Benitez/Moment; p. 74 (BR): Paul Kay/Oxford Scientific; p. 78 (TR): Comstock Images/Stockbyte; p. 78 (BR): Omegafotos/IStock; p. 79 (TL): Fancy/Veer/Corbis; p. 79 (CL): Cecilie_Arcurs/E+; p. 79 (BL): Wavebreakmedia/IStock; p. 79 (BR): Andrea Rugg/Corbis Documentary; p. 81: Dea/C. Sappa/De Agostini; p. 82: Weekend Images Inc./E+; p. 87: Gurpal Singh Dutta/Indiapicture; p. 88 (BL): Tony Anderson/Taxi; p. 88 (BR): Thais Lima De Sousa /Eyeem; p. 88 (CR): Monkeybusinessimages/IStock; p. 89 (TL): Wolfgang Kaehler/ Lightrocket; p. 89 (CL): Bornamir/IStock Editorial; p. 89 (BR): Javenlin/IStock Editorial; p. 89 (BL): Aid/Amana Images; p. 91: N·Ria Talavera/Moment Mobile; p. 92: Martinns/IStock; p. 93: Vasjakoman/Digitalvision Vectors; p. 96 (TR): Dolgachov/IStock; p. 96 (CR): Monkeybusinessimages/IStock; p. 96 (BL): Caiaimage/Paul Bradbury/Riser; p. 98: Garsya/IStock; p. 99: John Borthwick/Lonely Planet Images; p. 101 (TR): Fstop123/IStock; p. 101 (BL): Sturti/IStock.

Video
All video content is sourced from GettyImages.
Please follow the link below for full details of all clips.
http://www.cambridgelms.org/talent

Illustrations by Damiano Groppi.

Music
All music is sourced from GettyImages.
Please follow the link below for full details of all clips.
http://www.cambridgelms.org/talent

Video stills by Lada films.

Video produced by Lada films.

The publishers would like to extend a special thank you to all the teachers who helped shape the content of this book.